Contents

Acknowledgments	vii
Introduction: Stories of Queer Latinx Intimacies and Spatial Experiences	xi

I: Close to Home: Rescripting Domestic Spaces — 1

1. Reimagining the Family Home: The Queering of Domesticity in Puerto Rican Storytelling — 3
2. Enhancing Schools: Creating Social Alliances and Queer Spaces in the Young Adult Fiction of González and Sánchez — 35

II: Far from Home: Alternative and Imaginary Spaces — 67

3. Connecting and Performing Online: Interactive Experiences in Two Multimedia Texts by Queer Puerto Rican Artists — 69
4. Mapping Poetic Spaces: Subversive Intimacies of Humans and Nonhumans in the Scenes of Anzaldúa and Arroyo — 97
5. Navigating Spectacular Spaces: Regarding Bodies and Chilean American Lives in Reyes's *Madre and I: A Memoir of Our Immigrant Lives* — 123

Afterword: Looking to the Future: Remembering Spatial Creativities and Confronting Violence across Latinx Queer Contexts — 145

Appendix: Three Brief Resource Lists for Latinx and LGBTQ+ Communities — 159

Bibliography — 163

Index — 175

About the Author — 181

Imagining LatinX Intimacies

Imagining LatinX Intimacies

Connecting Queer Stories, Spaces, and Sexualities

Edward A. Chamberlain

ROWMAN & LITTLEFIELD
INTERNATIONAL

London • New York

Published by Rowman & Littlefield International, Ltd.
6 Tinworth Street, London SE11 5AL, United Kingdom
www.rowmaninternational.com

Rowman & Littlefield International, Ltd. is an affiliate of
Rowman & Littlefield
4501 Forbes Boulevard, Suite 200, Lanham, Maryland 20706, USA
With additional offices in Boulder, New York, Toronto (Canada), and London (UK)
www.rowman.com

Copyright © 2020 by Edward A. Chamberlain

All rights reserved. No part of this book may be reproduced in any form or by any electronic or mechanical means, including information storage and retrieval systems, without written permission from the publisher, except by a reviewer who may quote passages in a review.

British Library Cataloguing in Publication Information
A catalogue record for this book is available from the British Library

ISBN: HB 978-1-78661-432-2 | PBK 978-1-5381-4824-2

Library of Congress Cataloging-in-Publication Data Is Available

ISBN: 978-1-78661-432-2 (cloth)
ISBN: 978-1-5381-4824-2 (pbk)
ISBN: 978-1-78661-433-9 (electronic)

Acknowledgments

Storytelling expands our understanding of the world. Through stories, we weave together the experiences, ideas, and language that unite us as human beings. The storytellers among my family taught me how to observe an experience, explore the tension, and remember my roots. As a child of the 1980s, I came to love the stories that family members would share at our small house, a place where people gathered to tell tales about faraway lands, including Australia, Germany, and South Korea. During winter months, we kept the cold winds at bay by sharing tales in the warmth of our little kitchen. Then a family of crickets would find their way into the house, surprising us as we shared stories. An eclectic mix of stories and people shaped my early years and this book's development. They showed me how kinship and community can take many forms beyond the ones we are first taught. Hence, I wish to acknowledge how my family members and friends have fueled my love of stories, community, and places around the world.

My parents and siblings taught me to have humility and patience, which has enabled me to persist and refine my ability to tell a story in writing. We now live far from one another so we make do by sharing stories digitally. My grandmothers, aunts, and cousins also have taught me to remember the past, including the loved ones far from home. A good number of friends also have played key roles in keeping me levelheaded during challenging times. I am very grateful for the company of my friends as I made several moves and journeys. Erwin, John, and Chelis kept me focused during my visits to various parts of the world. I am also thankful for the sage advice of Kristen Yourno, who read portions of the manuscript at a key stage in the process. Her insights and questions led me to make the manuscript more accessible. Andrea Gutierrez, likewise, offered a great number of suggestions, which improved the writing. Additionally, I am lucky to have met several thoughtful people, including Alexandra, Dave, Derek, Jason, and Virginia. These lovely folks have kept me in good spirits as I adapted to new challenges in recent years. I also must recognize a kind group of friends in Bloomington, Indiana, who lent meaningful support.

Mentors and researchers at Indiana University opened my eyes to new approaches, concepts, and methods of research. Throughout the process, I benefited from dialogues with marvelous interdisciplinary scholars, including Angela Pao, Barbara Klinger, Colin Johnson, Deborah Cohen, Emily Maguire, Fedwa Malti-Douglas, Jeff Johnson, Melissa Dinverno, Micol Seigel, Patrick Dove, Shane Vogel, and Vivian Nun Halloran. Their ideas and questions have proven useful in a variety of contexts. My work also was shaped by a generous fellowship from the Center for Latin American and Caribbean Studies at Indiana University, which helped me to focus my efforts more effectively. An early research experience at the Kinsey Institute Library at Indiana University similarly opened my eyes to the cultural contexts and histories of gender and ethnicity. Later on, the Helen R. Whiteley Center and the Pack Forest Conference Center at the University of Washington provided supportive spaces for doing research in a peaceful manner. Outside of these spaces, I was fortunate to connect with excellent scholars such as Larry La Fountain and Martha Nell Smith, who inspired my research again and again. Their innovative studies of diverse cultural contexts have brought new life to my intellectual endeavors.

Further, I received some generous funding on two occasions from the Scholarship and Teaching Fund Committee in my present post at the University of Washington (UW) Tacoma. These funds helped me to expand my thinking and test ideas at conferences, which also helped me to connect with scholars and reimagine portions of the project. Colleagues, staff, and students at UW Tacoma also inspired new kinds of thinking during key moments in the research process. The expertise of the librarians at the University of Washington came in handy in multiple ways over the years. The UW Libraries repeatedly have made a space for people and projects that often are seen as different or seem like outsiders. In light of that backing, I honor the librarians' excellent work here by commending them on their dedication, open-mindedness, and warmth. In a comparable fashion, the Campus Writing Groups at UW Tacoma allowed me to focus, discuss new ideas, and connect with thinkers outside of my job in the Division of Culture, Arts, and Communication. I am thankful for the thoughts from colleagues who do wonderful work in the School of Interdisciplinary Arts and Sciences and across the UW Tacoma campus. Moreover, there have been many people at conferences that shaped this research. Early versions of my writing were presented at conferences, including the American Studies Association, the American Men's Studies Association, the Cultural Studies Association, the Latin American Studies Association, and the Modern Language Association. In these sessions, several attendees shared generative comments and queries that were very beneficial to the latter part of my revisions.

Beyond academia, the friendship and mentorship of multiple people also offered me encouragement, support, and new perspectives. Support from Jörg, Michael, and Tehanee helped me to understand the bigger picture and be a better mentor to young folks. People living in the cities of Tacoma and Seattle, likewise, helped me to make progress in several ways. In a similar, albeit unique way, several visual artists contributed their work to this production. The artists Tino Rodríguez and J. D. Casto kindly have allowed me to reprint their work here. Christopher Velasco and the Laura Aguilar Trust have permitted to reprint one of Laura Aguilar's powerful photographs. At the same time, I have been fortunate to connect with a myriad of communities along the way. I greatly appreciated opportunities to volunteer with nonprofits, which taught me new perspectives, including new ways of connecting with underrepresented populations. Another sort of community helped to make this book's production possible: my thanks go to the multiple reviewers, editors, journals, and staff members, who often remain behind the scenes. Their keen critiques and contributions opened my eyes to other possible ways of thinking and existing in the larger world. Relatedly, I wish to acknowledge two journals that published previous versions of chapters that are included in this book. A shorter portion of chapter 3 was first published in the interdisciplinary journal *CLCWeb: Comparative Literature and Culture*, and another version of chapter 5 was published in the international journal, *Otherness: Essays and Studies*.

To bring these acknowledgments to a close, I wish to express my thanks to the people who had considerable impact on this book's final steps and development. I have been inspired by the work of activists, advocates, and artists who have worked long hours to improve the lives of Latinx and lesbian, gay, bisexual, transgender, and queer (LGBTQ) peoples. The work of these unsung heroes repeatedly breathed new life into this project. Artists and poets around the world, including Gloria Anzaldúa, Audre Lorde, and Félix González-Torres, provided considerable inspiration for this book's creation. Similarly, at Rowman & Littlefield International, I wish to thank Gurdeep Mattu, Scarlet Furness, and the rest of the staff that spent numerous hours arranging this book's production. Their dedication made the last steps easier and more of a pleasure. Then in an entirely different manner, a little buddy named Rascal offered some much-needed support on occasion, encouraging me to enjoy the afternoon sunlight and take a break from work. Equally, my partner, David R. Coon, inspired me to laugh, breathe, and look at the world with a new set of eyes. David made the journey of writing a book much smoother. His support gave me strength and helped me to see that social change takes place in multiple ways across time and space. This book is dedicated to David and the many changemakers of the world. Through this book, I honor the larger mosaic of peoples who are working to create positive forms of social change and a more inclusive future.

Edward A. Chamberlain
October 2019

Introduction

Stories of Queer Latinx Intimacies and Spatial Experiences

> Fear of going home. And of not being taken in. We're afraid of being abandoned by the mother, the culture, la Raza, for being unacceptable, faulty, damaged. Most of us unconsciously believe that if we reveal this unacceptable aspect of the self our mother/culture/race will totally reject us. To avoid rejection, some of us conform to the values of the culture, push the unacceptable parts into the shadows.[1]
> —Gloria Anzaldúa

At the end of the twentieth century, diverse people across the Americas told personal stories that show a common desire for a space that they can call *home*. In one's home, the feeling of closeness and familiarity are key elements that create a sense of intimacy. This feeling is a multifaceted sensation that often is undervalued in the public sphere, even as it is fervently protected. Beneath this desire for intimacy, however, there often is a disconcerting sense of worry that one might be separated from that comfort of home. This fear of being cut off and abandoned is a common feeling among a multitude of peoples who self-identify as departing from the normalized social identities of the United States, Caribbean cultures, and Latin American nations. This fear is a paralyzing sensation for diverse communities, including Latina/o and Latinx peoples who self-identify as LGBTQ. Much as the celebrated poet and theorist Gloria Anzaldúa attests, many queer peoples experience some fear of being labeled as "unacceptable" and displaced from their home. Such fears lead people to hide queer desires in "the shadows" as Anzaldúa suggests, while others speak out in courageous acts of artistic expression such as storytelling.

Stories and artwork about these struggles have been expressed by a range of individuals and social groups, like communities of color and people who self-identify as LGBTQ. As such artists have countered social bias and questioned respectability, they have produced modern visions of the American Dream, including what it means to be a family. These visions take the shape of intimate scenes that are presented in personal accounts, imaginative poetry, non-fiction, and visual art. These imaginative scenes are discernable in the creative works of peoples who identify as Chicana/o/x, Chilean American, Mexican American, and Puerto Rican. Although the term *Latinx* is still seen as relatively new, a multitude of people have embraced this concept to refer to peoples who are Latin American in descent and self-identify in ways that go beyond the normalized gender binary. For many who identify as LGBTQ, this binary has had the effect of constraining lives in multitudinous forms.[2] In examining these phenomena, this book analyzes the connectivities of sexual identities, spaces, and storytellers that are not always included in dialogues of US family experiences—namely, Latinx artists who identify as LGBTQ. These artists have produced notable artwork and writing that reimagines well-worn visions of family and intimacy that are delineated by norms, policy, and legislation such as marriage laws. Sadly, such social and legal codes have caused the displacement of Latinx LGBTQ peoples across the Americas. Yolanda Martínez-San Miguel explains how such displacement is interwoven with colonial history and leads to the "redefinition of national identities."[3] This reshaping of human lives materializes in multiple forms that range from the personal stories of migrants to the intimate visual artwork of citizens. If we are to understand this artistry's significance, it is necessary to situate this creative work in the cultural histories of their respective spaces.

As *Imagining Latinx Intimacies* contextualizes LGBTQ Latinx experiences in the histories of the Caribbean and the Americas, I offer the perspective that although many LGBTQ stories and media may focus on ostensibly ordinary experiences such as relationships and social spaces, these representations actually function as telling responses to exclusionary dynamics and institutions. That is to say, imagining the intimate spaces of Latinx sexualities is a defiant act that lays the framework for an alternative set of politics that support interests in forging new paths and engaging in socially transgressive acts such as non-normative sexual practices and unruly gatherings. These same dynamics and interests have led Latinx queer peoples to develop an intimate spatial imaginary that is less constraining and less judgmental than that of the dominant white culture. As Deborah R. Vargas contends, there is a benefit to understanding the lives, loves, and spaces that "defy heteronormative limits of intimacy and affect."[4] Like Vargas, I envision the nomenclature of "intimate" and "intimacy" as being a helpful idiom for explaining the meaningful social relations created by Latinx LGBTQs (or "queers" as some prefer). These key relations are read as telling responses to varying kinds of displacement and materialize in a bevy of forms that are intellectual, improvised, and physical. Further, these self-expressions and interactions take place in less visible social sites, including personal and private contexts such as an apartment of Puerto Rican lesbians, virtual environments, and semipublic places like bars.

In an examination of several sites, Juana María Rodríguez provides a foundation for the study of socially constituted spaces that Latinx peoples inhabit for a spate of purposes.[5] In *Imagining Latinx Intimacies*, I extend the theoretical thinking of Rodríguez's work by examining a set of interrelated intimate spaces, and in doing so, I show how these sites can cultivate a supportive social realm for Latinx queers to develop and share their dreams, intellects, and lives. Accordingly, *Imagining Latinx Intimacies* is by no means intended to maintain a fixed set of borders but, rather, to create and honor a set of bridges between cultural contexts. To make such connections, this book offers a set of critical examinations that works with the perspectives of several theorists including Anzaldúa, who envisioned bridges as "thresholds to other realities, archetypal, primal symbols of shifting consciousness. They are passageways, conduits, and connectors that connote transitioning, crossing borders, and changing perspectives."[6] For Anzaldúa, bridges are made from more than mortar, wood, and steel. In her logic, bridges can also be imagined art forms, including books, images, and writing. These cultural creations are the connectors and meeting points that link cultures and time periods in intellectual and social forms. Although material realities frequently have been privileged as the most meaningful in some circles, the imagined spatial experiences of films and texts like poetry and novels indeed hold the potential to cultivate the needed bridge—or dream—to a more hospitable future. As such, I interpret the artistic representation of Latinx queer spaces as being important blueprints for the future—blueprints that enable people to develop a world that supports one's development, relationships, and well-being. As Marijn Nieuwenhuis and David Crouch have said, "Space is relational, subjective and personal," and thus, they are imbued with feelings that are meaningful.[7] Human feelings have been discounted again and again as being inconsequential, yet more and more scholars are regarding this interior affect as being intricately linked to spatial experience. Scholar Ernesto Javier Martínez expounds on this idea by theorizing how queers of color engage in acts of "spatial praxis that are bound up in the multiform relations of desire, identity, migration, and representation."[8] Like Martínez's research, *Imagining Latinx Intimacies* is interested in the spatial praxis of Latinx queers because it is seen as a worthwhile process for realizing dreams of creating a more egalitarian and inclusive queer world. That being said, this queer realization is an ongoing and piecemeal process taking shape in fits and starts as Latinx queers are generating a rather diverse set of cultural formations across time and space.

FORMATIVE CONTEXTS: THE CONCEPTS AND HISTORIES OF QUEER LATINX SPACES

During the 1990s, for example, there were a limited number of public spaces that resonated with queerness and foreshadowed the existence of a larger queer world. Lauren Berlant and Michael Warner speak to this world in their 1998 essay "Sex in Public," where they theorize: "The queer world is a space of entrances, exits, unsystematized lines of acquaintance, projected horizons, typifying examples, alternate routes, blockages, incommensurate geographies."[9] Like Berlant and Warner, I contend the queer world can take manifold forms, even as some queerly physical spaces such as bars and clubs are not inclusive to all folks because of marginalization that is classist and racist. In light of such displacements, Latinx queers also took to commenting on socio-spatial experiences through representation. Scholar Mary Pat Brady offers key perspective on Chicana representations of spatial experience by illuminating how spaces are made and transformed through human actions.[10] In the pages that follow, I extend the spatial praxis of Mary Pat Brady and Ernesto Javier Martínez by illuminating how a set of queer Latinx creative forms function as a notable set of "spaces" for bringing underrepresented voices into dialogue. This dialogue concerns the challenges of being queer and Latinx in a national space—the United States—where bias against queer, brown, and migrant people was inculcated in the 1990s.

The process of changing that phenomenon requires new ways of thinking about US spatial experience. Hence, this book conceptualizes "space" as being predicated on US realities, such as familial contexts, while also extending beyond such confines. These spaces materialize as imaginary scenes like those that are found in the fiction, memoirs, poetry, and visual art that convey stories of finding closeness and strength in spaces that allow for people to foster an alternative sense of family and community. Although these spatial experiences occur in several forms, I concur with Richard T. Rodríguez who suggests that many Latinx spaces hold potential to "supply a sense of familia because of the ways in which they foster a sense of Latino/a queer belonging."[11] Feelings of *familia* (or family) can manifest in several spatialized forms, thus guiding figures such as those in the art and writing. Alternatively, to be rejected by one's family or community can lead to displacement, which can be a crushing blow that affects how people envision their futures, lives, and potentials. These unsavory circumstances of unbelonging gained greater attention through an increase in media stories about such experiences during the 1990s and early 2000s—an era that came to be known as the Age of AIDS.[12] As the media presented stories about human immunodeficiency virus/acquired immunodeficiency syndrome (HIV/AIDS), the public began to learn more about queers, but not everyone empathized. A coterie of politicians and leaders continued to emit antigay and anti-immigrant rhetoric, casting Latinx and LGBTQ peoples as threats to the United States.

More often than not, community leaders and pundits have linked the spread of illness to the presence of groups that are perceived as outsiders such as migrants, people of color, and LGBTQ communities.[13] Similarly, dominant cultures repeatedly have accused Latinx and queer communities of being the purveyors of immoral ideas, thereby associating brown and Latinx bodies with contagion, physical dangers, and varying forms of impurity.[14] In a relevant study, the scholar Hiram Pérez explains, "A national unconscious seizes on the brown body as a site onto which it can project the 'unnatural' sex act it disavows."[15] This projection took several forms in the Age of AIDS and made life exceedingly arduous, if not excruciating for many queer Latinx communities and people of color who departed from ingrained gender norms. This equating of brown bodies with *the undesirable* is visible in the US government's ban on immigrants with HIV/AIDS—a ban that was imposed by callous officials in 1987 all along US borders. This ban produced even more mechanisms for stigmatizing people in the already vexed political processes of crossing borders and immigration. Over the course of its history, the United States has taken a varied approach to migration and immigration, although in recent decades the state's power has been used repeatedly to detain, displace, and keep out LGBTQ peoples from multiple countries. In these tense contexts, racism and homophobia collide because as Sandra K. Soto explains, "race and sexuality are not self-contained, discrete categories."[16] These two elements of human experience exhibit considerable overlaps that manifest in the form of racialized sexuality and double marginalization, where people are discriminated against in two forms such as racist and homophobic abuses. These discriminations have occurred through events and policies that are local, state-based, as well as national. As a consequence, artists and critics upbraided US policymakers for allowing such marginalization to occur and, in the process, have called on the public to step away from worn-out puritanical values, white supremacy, and xenophobia.

Researching such struggles from the Age of AIDS often remains a challenge because of a heap of social factors like the silence and taboos that routinely accompany sexuality and sexually transmitted infections. Just as the critic and poet Anzaldúa suggests in the epigraph at the start of this introduction, Latinx peoples routinely struggle with "coming out" as being LGBTQ in their homes because of the possibility of being cast out.[17] It is this horrifying possibility—this heart-wrenching feeling—that is most discomforting because the family sphere is believed to be a source of support when the world rejects people for being Other. This is not to suggest all Chicanx and Latinx families harbor such antigay attitudes because, in fact, a sizable proportion of families have proven accepting.[18] Yet for those facing rejection, this experience is exacerbated by the fact that Latinx peoples also face discrimination in courts of law, employment, stores, and public spaces where the dominant white cultures hold sway. Similar problems were brought to light in Anzaldúa's collection of writings *Borderlands/La Frontera: The New Mestiza*, which intervenes in these matters by linking personal experience to history. Anzaldúa's creative and critical thought about borderlands and otherness remain relevant presently as the world watches millions of people being displaced to varying degrees by community violence, civil war, and the aftermath of national policies including those of the US federal government.[19]

Imagining Latinx Intimacies expands on the creative and critical work of Anzaldúa by showing how her theories can open new ways of understanding cultural artifacts, personal writing, and related forms of visual culture.[20] Anzaldúa's insights lend an idiom for explaining social and sexual dynamics of displacement and spaces where communities and officials have created what the writer Adrienne Rich has called "compulsory heterosexuality."[21] Within many heterocentric homes, moral constraints have been the unsavory seeds that fostered the creation of alternative spaces—sites and locales that the scholar José Esteban Muñoz views as vital social "outposts" of a queer world in the making.[22] For peoples who feel that they have no place to go, alternative social spaces such as queer-friendly community groups can grant life-sustaining opportunities for connection, organizing, healing, and self-expression. Much as the artists in this book will attest, much can be done with a small amount of space. As viewers see in the short film *Small City, Big Change* by Frances Negrón-Muntaner, which is explored in the next chapter, meaningful change can be fostered by bringing together queer peoples of a small city for the larger public good.[23] Whether it is a small city's gatherings or a short film's story, such social spaces enable participants to imagine hospitable spaces that are free of bias and exclusion. Even though popular queer social spaces like Castro Street in San Francisco and Christopher Street in New York City are hailed as significant queer spaces because of their high concentrations of LGBTQ businesses and denizens, these spaces continue to be perceived as welcoming only people who fit the mainstream media's sanitized vision of sexual minorities: cisgender gay white men. To make a more equitable and inclusive set of spaces for queer people of color, a more egalitarian and socially conscious ethic of spatial creation must be imagined, produced, and set in place.

In the eyes of critics today, the physical absence of LGBTQ and Latinx populations is a telling marker of the ways that bias, privilege, and power frequently collude, making spatial creation difficult. In terms of numbers, the US Census Bureau provides some insight into Latinx spaces during the late 1990s. The bureau published a report explaining how approximately 5.8% of all US businesses in 1997 were owned by Hispanics.[24] Most likely, the bureau's study is likely underreporting the exact number because many smaller businesses go unnoticed, yet it also speaks to the small number of brown peoples that felt comfortable going on the record in a predominantly white nation that has scrutinized Latinx peoples and their presence within US communities. In contrast, for many Latinx communities, local Latinx businesses bring people together and function as

Figure 0.1. The Castro District gayborhood in the city of San Francisco, California.

sites for sharing information; however, the census officials anonymize the data so assessing these enterprises remains difficult. Further, there is no official census data for LGBTQ businesses during the 1990s, though the number is conjectured to be low, and this dearth can be attributed to the persistent homophobia of the 1990s. Latinx-owned businesses grew considerably in the years following the 1990s, showing a desire to create more Latinx-friendly spaces that would provide support to communities imperiled by prejudices.

Recognizing the desire for more Latinx-friendly spaces is an important step toward the "browning" of public spaces, including LGBTQ bars and similar sites, which would enable queer Latinx peoples to have a greater number of life-sustaining spaces. Historically, US capitalists have constructed environments that are noninclusive toward both of the aforesaid communities, and as a result, Latinx queer peoples have taken to frequenting landscapes beyond urban terrains and suburban sprawls. As shown by the researchers Catriona Sandilands, Laura Pulido, and Juan Carlos Galeano, a multitude of queer and Latinx peoples celebrate and defend their connections to the natural world through a myriad of methods that are based in both the logics of reality and more imaginative terms.[25] Nevertheless, in her study of environmentally related movements, the geographer Pulido articulates that "from the perspective of marginalized communities, environmental problems reflect and may intensify, larger existing inequalities and uneven power relations."[26] As a response to such uneven conditions, Latinx queer peoples such as Anzaldúa have developed an assortment of environmentally conscious commentaries and spaces that have served as a courageous reclaiming of land as well as a means to contest inequalities.[27]

By using inventive spatial strategies, queer Latinx peoples have created a means of making real-life spaces as well as imaginary ones that allow for the celebration and development of queer Latinx desires and passions. For those seeking a space to freely express themselves, these sites may be seen as offering a type of "oasis where shared identities and experiences thrive," though they are by no means utopian in nature or easily generalizable.[28] The multiform aspect of LGBTQ spaces can be seen in how a great many sites serve as sanctuaries for LGBTQ identities, social practices, and thought. Among the many instances of LGBTQ spaces, the more commonly known sites include bars, bathhouses, bookstores, cruises, gayborhoods, parades, resorts, websites, and sociopolitical organizations such as the now nonoperational National Latino/a Lesbian and Gay Organization (LLEGÓ), which closed its doors in 2004. Then in some more progressive neighborhoods such as the Capitol Hill neighborhood of Seattle, many people endeavor to create a more queer-friendly dynamic through programs that foster a "safe zone" through sticker campaigns and decorative projects like rainbow crosswalks.[29] Such queer spatial experiences also have been shape-shifting and on the move due to the way people hold LGBTQ gatherings in a range of spaces throughout the year such as in the case of supper clubs that move from one person's house to another, and academic conferences that move from one city to another each year. Comparably, in the case of many youth spaces, as we see in the case of the young adult novel *The Mariposa Club* from the prolific Mexican American writer Rigoberto González, some Latinx LGBTQ youths gather with friends across whatever spaces are available and offer a modicum of privacy including the local schoolyard and neighboring homes. Such privacies are sought as many sites continue to be unwelcoming to young Latinx peoples. Because many US spaces continue to uphold white-centric and homophobic views as the norm, there continues to be a need for compassionate and egalitarian spaces that foster inclusivity.

Imagining Latinx Intimacies aims to expand our concepts of queer social spaces by considering lesser-studied queer Latinx sites such as after-school programs, poetic scenes, and small towns that support queer and Latinx self-development. Already in the prior decade, a slew of studies of space have theorized the sociopolitical impact of public spaces like cityscapes and barrios. In turn, this dynamic creates a rather metronormative theory of belonging, community, and identity. In recent years however, there has been a move to focus on understudied locales like interstices (the blending of the public and private), rural areas, suburban places,

Figure 0.2. A rainbow crosswalk in the Capitol Hill gayborhood of Seattle, Washington.

evolving regions as well as locales that fall outside of binaristic thinking altogether such as transgender spatial experiences.[30] This book falls within the latter set and explores how spatial experiences such as intimate spaces are laced with problematic assumptions about migrants, Latinx peoples, and people of color. The problematic thinking of nationalism and xenophobia came to a head during the Cold War and thereafter played a role in the way that Latinx queers were perceived in the late twentieth century and beyond. Kristin L. Matthews tells that the era of the Cold War from 1945 to 1991 was a turbulent time of "struggle in postwar America" where people tried to "delineate the *good American*."[31]

For a bevy of critics in the 1980s and 1990s, the "good American" was by no means seen as LGBTQ, let alone Latinx. Ensconced in the fearful rhetoric of AIDSphobia and offensive terms like "illegal alien," queer Latinx peoples were pushed to the peripheries of the public dialogue and spaces even before the discussion began.[32] Resulting from this situation, many queer communities and Latinx peoples resisted such ideals because they demand a rigid conformity and inhibit creativity. Unsurprisingly, the mix of characters and creators examined in this study are unconcerned with assimilating to dominant standards, being proper, or developing what may be perceived as a "normal" connection to the nation-state.

The creative work considered here fosters distinctive messages, though *Imagining Latinx Intimacies* offers the viewpoint that a set of queer Latinx creators comparably capture and raise up intimate social relations of Latinx queers by emphasizing people's connections to spaces. This emphasis comes through in the imagery and stories of Latinx queer figures. Their imagery and stories are powerful indicators of the degree to which queer Latinx peoples face (un)belonging, exclusion, and a sense of otherness across the United States. In response, the imagery and stories explored in this book exemplify the critical approach that bell hooks calls "talking back," where people of color respond to the dominant culture's mechanisms of power and normativity in poetic and inspiring discourse.[33] This book contends that artists' sophisticated portrayals of intimate life offer us strategies for resisting exclusionary and oppressive structures. These strategies are born out of the hybridity and queer experiences of people who migrate across or connect multiple cultures. For this reason, *Imagining Latinx Intimacies* builds on the concept of *hybrid space*, a critical concept that has been theorized by Adriana de Souza e Silva and Sarah Whatmore. Although Whatmore and de Souza e Silva discuss this notion in contexts other than Latinx studies, this lens is helpful for explaining how social spaces such as intimate sites often involve a mix of cultures, experiences, and languages. Through this optic, I explain how artists portray hybrid spatiality in chatrooms, landscapes, and youth spaces—the very scenes that should offer a means to nurture emotional and psychological well-being, yet is jeopardized by homophobic, racist, and xenophobic acts. This kind of study grants what Anzaldúa calls "a path of conocimiento"—a means to develop knowledge and solve problems such as biases and exclusionary mechanisms that have infiltrated nearly all aspects of our daily lives.[34] Although this path-making takes many shapes, there is a common goal in the pieces examined here that is both spoken and beneath the surface: to create alternative and meaningful spaces where Latinx queers can congregate, share knowledge, and resist processes that threaten their lives.

Looking to the cultural history of queer Latinx experiences, the act of creating social spaces and intimacies takes place in a number of ways both planned and otherwise. While there are many permutations of this socio-spatial phenomena across the US mainland and beyond, one of the previous and high-profile examples of alternative space-making is a space known as "Nuyorico"—a portmanteau term that captures the alchemy of connecting New York City's geography and Puerto Rican cultures.[35] To a similar extent, queer groups of all heritages have come together to fashion alternative community spaces like those of the Radical Faeries, who instantiated shared spaces in natural settings in a kind of "back-to-the-land counterculturalism."[36] Much like the Radical Faeries and Latinx queers discussed here, I myself have found a need for queer social spaces for the sake of developing a close, intimate connection with like-minded people. After entering college for instance, I attended our campus's queer student union, which was established in the late 1970s and went by the name "Gay Union of Trenton State" (GUTS). As I attended the weekly meetings, I wished such a social space had existed at my rather straitlaced high school. The scarcity of such sites is troubling for a range of reasons and points to the value of reimagining sites that might not initially seem to have queer social potential. To fashion these social contexts is a critical and creative process that lays a crucial groundwork for new alliances and homes for ethnic and social groups such as queer Latinx peoples who are made to feel like outsiders. In looking to the extant research, forms of home have received more attention by researchers in Latina/o and Latinx studies in recent years.[37] Often such studies focus on social dimensions of Latina/o families, yet only a few of them have begun to theorize the multifaceted queer dimensions and efflorescence of Latinx intimate spaces in modern representation.

Spanning the space of the family home to more expansive social realms, this book speaks to the fraught relations that Latinx queers experience in heteronormative cultural contexts in the United States during the 1990s and early 2000s. This book largely gives its focus to examples, ideas, and theories of non-normative Latinx sexualities and spatial thinking, while also remaining attentive to the distinctive ways that notions of "place" have been envisioned by scholars.[38] The concepts of space and place are helpful tools for understanding the troubled and unique social relations produced in and around queer Latinx communities. In an article written for *Time Magazine*, the cultural historian Julio Capó insightfully comments on these troubled relations by highlighting the ways that "queer and transgender Latinos have historically fallen victim to habitual and casual violence by both the state and civilians."[39] This dismaying and painful pattern of violence takes place in innumerable landscapes, constituting an unsavory sociopolitical phenomenon that I call *spatial violence*—an ingrained predicament that is perpetrated through quotidian relations and processes of the white and heterosexual US nation-state. Disturbing forms of spatial violence occur at one of the spaces commonly explored in the field of Latina/o studies—the borderlands—resulting from various kinds of discrimination and physical violence take place at borders and within the wake of such sites.⁴⁰ Envisioned as an *herida abierta* (open wound) by Anzaldúa, this liminal kind of socio-physical space looms large in Latina/o and Latinx cultural production from the latter half of the twentieth century and into the present.⁴¹ To counter that vulnerability of being wounded, queer Latinx peoples use their creative ingenuity to imagine beneficial spaces of connectivity, including new visions of domestic life and social spheres occurring in less obvious expanses such as the Internet where the spatial dynamics of diffusion and discontinuity allow for less fixity in human spatiality.⁴² These spaces also include the geographies of coalition-building, which can take place across a range of sites and is one of the beneficial outcomes of fostering queer spaces. *Imagining Latinx Intimacies* highlights this coalition-building to speak to the positives of fostering bridges across social divides and finding common cause for the purpose of creating positive social change.

Instead of accepting the idea of the family home and one's local homeland as being the most important social space of community-building and self-creation, this book explores the manner in which queer Latinx peoples craft a variety of socio-spatial experiences. This in turn provides blueprints for living a more desirable and rewarding life that is not predicated on the structures of capitalism, which are often sexist, homophobic, and racist in their composition. I use the word *blueprint* intentionally here to speak to the belief that the caustic homophobia of the past and present necessitates the creation of new plans for inclusive and forward-thinking communities. Such blueprints can open our minds to the alternative ways of existing in a world that has taken a punitive stance against brown peoples who exhibit transgressive genders and sexualities. In looking back, the sociologist Sean Cahill expounds on these dynamics through a lens of sexuality studies by identifying how "the religious right has sought to pit gay and lesbian people against people of color and to portray the two communities as mutually exclusive."⁴³ As Cahill shows in his study of black and Latino same-sex households, the divisive acts of some traditionalists can sometimes have the effect of inhibiting the formation of coalitions that can engender positive formulations like community dialogue in socially diverse spaces.

As a part of this building of coalitions, the research collected in *Imagining Latinx Intimacies* provides a glimmer of the multiplicity of sociopolitical coalitions that can be built. This book however, has limits, too. Much of it focuses on the lives of young people and those entering midlife. More research and coalition-building must be done to support the lives of elder Latinx queers, who sometimes have been cast aside. Nonetheless, this coalition-building has been (and continues to be) crucial for creating political progress. As David Eng explains, "our historical moment is defined precisely by new combinations of racial, sexual, and economic disparities."⁴⁴ In light of ongoing inequalities, a more enlivening and thoughtful set of blueprints is necessary. Developing such blueprints can allow us to foster the more hospitable "queer futurity" that has been theorized by scholars like Muñoz.[45] Moreover, as researchers show, the real-life experiences of encountering discrimination, hate, and violence in the private and public spheres negatively affects the emotional and physical well-being of queer Latinx people as well as similarly marginalized sexual minority groups. Being displaced from one's home, as we see happen in González's novel *The Mariposa Club*, has been shown to have a profound impact on one's self-esteem, sense of self, and self-development. In studying *The Mariposa Club*, which shows a young transgender girl being forced out of her home, there is a parallel with González's own experience. In an interview, he explains, "like many gay men, I had to leave my family in order to thrive. But that lack of familial love—that emptiness—continues to haunt me."[46] Such struggles also have been explored by scholars such as T. Jackie Cuevas, whose research on gender variant critique in Chicanx communities attests to the challenges of blazing a trail beyond the gender binary.[47] In this same context, recent studies have shown that queer Latinx youths are twice as likely to feel they lack social belonging in their communities, and they are also twice as likely to be excluded in public school spaces where students bully LGBTQ students for going against the norms of gender and sexuality.[48]

Considering how queer Latinx artists have been pressed by traditionalist norms and policies of people such as the now-deceased Senator Jesse Helms, who actively fought against federal funding for art programs and AIDS research, there is a great need for spaces to connect, create, and practice forms of self-care in the 1980s and thereafter.[49] Such spaces are, like the identities that frequent them, shaped by several factors, including nonconforming experiences of gender, ethnicity, race, and sexuality. This book neither purports that all Latinx experiences are similar, nor does this project use the nomenclature of *Latino*, *Latina*, or *Latinx* to blur the many diverse lives of individuals considered here. I employ an approach that is similar to that of scholars such as Muñoz, who have articulated critiques about the manner in which the experiences of Latinx peoples are often generalized. In the past, critics spoke about "the Latino culture," which conjures to mind a monoculture that flattens the distinctiveness and multiplicity of Latinx social experiences.[50] Instead of maintaining such views, this book fosters a critical consciousness of the ways that Latinx lives and spaces intersect with a set of genders and sexualities that transgress normative constructions. Incorporated here is the thought of scholars that research intersectionality, a major critical concept that was first articulated by the US legal theorist Kimberlé Crenshaw in the late 1980s.[51] In the case of Latinx LGBTQs across the United States, a pernicious set of homophobic and racist practices continue to intersect within a slew of contexts and cause a painful double marginalization. To address the artistry that challenges this painful phenomenon, *Imagining Latinx Intimacies* takes a more socially conscious approach and builds on the concept of *Latinx* as a means of challenging the gender dichotomy implicit within the ethnonym *Latina*/o, which has been read as expressing either feminine or masculine gender experience. This binary forecloses the possibility of self-identifying in multiple ways such as nonbinary and transgender. More recently, scholars such as Catalina M. de Onís, Roy Pérez, and Juana María Rodríguez have contributed telling commentaries on the manifold ways in which Latinx writers, filmmakers, and artists have contributed to, or have participated in, the ongoing instantiation of Latinidad that extends beyond dualisms, deepening our understanding of Latino-ness.[52] While showing a spectrum of ways to perform Latinidad, their work thoughtfully illuminates the manner in which queerness informs the making of Latinx lives and spaces.

To develop this line of thinking, *Imagining Latinx Intimacies* links discussions of Latinidad to the significant scholarship of Nayan Shah, who first articulated the relevant concept of "queer domesticity," a framework that underpins the first half of this book.[53] In his study, Shah vocalizes that queer domesticity manifests as a mix of social circumstances and practices that run counter to the normalized western visions of heterosexual relations that are shored up largely by a cult of "respectable domesticity."[54] Shah uses the concept to theorize the social relations that were created and perceived within San Francisco's Chinese American population during the nineteenth and twentieth centuries. Although my study here does not examine Asian immigrant culture, I find Shah's terminology provides a useful framework for Latinx forms of culture that similarly go beyond the heteronormative spatial relations. In particular, his ideas provide a supportive lens for understanding the queer spatial relations generated by the cultural artifacts of film and literature. In the texts I study here, the "queer domestic" manifests in multitudinous ways, showing the rich diversity of possible belonging and kinship experiences. The daily lives of queer people and related circumstances, such as battles against HIV/AIDS, tend to remake spatial arrangements. By "remake," I refer to the ways that queer people's social relationships and values transform domestic and spatial arrangements for the betterment of all people, hence making the domestic sphere and other milieus more hospitable and inclusive to people existing outside the center of cultural and societal normality. Moreover, I view this "queer domestic" as being a phenomenon that extends beyond the typical home-space inasmuch as I contend the privacies of queer relationships often spill over to locales that may not be perceived as domestic per se—as I show in my discussion of school-based clubs that exhibit a domestic dimension.

The spillage of queer relationships is further explored within the second half of *Imagining Latinx Intimacies*, where I provide three case studies of queer spatial imaginings. This queer spillage of relationships takes on another dimension in the latter half of the book, where I examine how queer Latinx artistry from the early 2000s exhibit a highly imaginative approach that connects disparate elements and alternates between bizarre and playful. To explain these hybrid depictions in the second half of the book, I introduce a concept that I call the *queerly inventive,* a term that is meant to capture the fanciful, performative, and spirited way that Latinx lives are being depicted through language, imagery, and scenes. The terminology is a way of identifying a broader set of imaginative phenomena, and this neologism serves as a critical formulation that is intended to give a name to a set of cultural and artistic dynamics. In several pieces considered here, the depicted bodies are given greater emphasis and challenge US physical ideals. These cultural artifacts show bodies that are imaginary or metamorphosed into figures that are half-human and half-animal (or plants). These cultural producers' embrace of such radical imaginings is comparable to the inventive interventions of advocates and reformers such as AIDS activists late in the twentieth century. To grab the attention of the media, groups such as AIDS Coalition to Unleash Power (ACT-UP) imaginatively created direct actions such as street theater and die-ins, which ultimately were intended to foster dialogue, democratize society, and empower people with AIDS that typically were denied rights and opportunities.[55]

Although judges, the state, religious groups, and others have attempted to repress queer and Latinx communities by historically associating these groups with abjection, immoral conduct, psychosis, and Satanism (among other negatives), a cluster of queer artists and activists have built socially engaged artwork in the form billboards, fundraising, Internet campaigns, poster campaigns, demonstrations, and other forms of civil disobedience that use queer personal experience as evidence to counter problematic defamation. Hence, I read the creative work here as being artistic extensions of larger LGBTQ liberation and Latinx movements that cross the Americas in a range of sites late during the twentieth century.[56] This diverse set of printed and visual texts has much in common with the activisms of the Puerto Rican Young Lords, the Chicana/o Movement, Black Lives Matter, and UndocuQueer Movement, which similarly resisted systemic bias. This diverse set of artists likewise encourages us to throw off the constraints that hinder the expression of our personal stories and intimate spaces. As I have assembled this book's archive of art, film, and writing, it became clear that not all people identify themselves or their activities using the same terminology. Still some terms, such as the words *gay* and *queer* have managed to circulate in numerous parts of the world. In view of that, I wish to foreground my use of the term *queer* for the sake of clarifying and because it is one of the overarching concepts that animates my larger discussion of the artists' actions, lives, materials, and intellectual projects. In using the term *queer,* I remain cautious because like many other critics in the field, I believe that this term can be limiting and that it often connotes the idea of a pregiven or essential identity. However, this book does not impose a fixed identity on the characters or artwork. Instead, I endeavor to make sense of the lives, styles, and social phenomena experienced within these contexts. Siobhan B. Somerville also rightly points out that the concept of "'Queer' causes confusion."[57] Somerville's critical discussion of the term's meanings shows that although the concept can be flexible, the multiple meanings can lead to some forms of bewilderment, especially if critics disregard the need to carefully contextualize their use of the term. In part, I use the term *queer* as a way of uniting the pieces—not for the purpose of erasing their unique sense of self—but rather for the purpose of assembling a coalition of speakers who can testify about similar circumstances. In the process, my project embraces the fairly common viewpoint that these lives are shaped by sociopolitical discourses, ideology, and practices. Through this optic, I consider how the heterosexual allies of queer peoples, such as caretakers or the friends of queers, similarly can occupy a positionality of queerness when they socially align themselves in common cause with Latinx queer peoples. My queering of heterosexuals here is not meant to be assimilative in approach, but rather, this method highlights how queerness can have many valences and materialize in a slew of forms.

In part, *Imagining Latinx Intimacies* uses the term *queer* to articulate how some seemingly straight people and cultural objects, such as literature, can be said to exhibit a queer sensibility. This sensibility is—within the eyes of dominant culture and queers themselves—antinormative, irreverent, and unconventional by the often-unspoken standards of Anglophone white cultures. Similarly, I remain thoughtful about how the concept and experiences of queerness are polysemous and ensconced in multiple histories. Ultimately though, a common language can be helpful to bring these topics into dialogue. In his book *Queer Ricans*, La Fountain-Stokes insists *queer* functions as a suitable idiom to discuss Latina/o and Latinx experiences insofar as this concept has gained a currency in academia, activism, and public forums, among others.[58] Yet some strands of queer theory have overlooked some socially affirming experiences that allow for conviviality.[59] Scholars such as Michael D. Snediker theorize it is actually possible to embrace optimism and positive forms of affect in queer forms of study.[60] Hence, instead of seeing the space of home and social sites as always being ruled by heterosexism, I explain how homes and social spaces can be reimagined as queer-friendly and enable further actions like resistance and positive "emotional refreshment."[61] This idea is shored up by the scholarly work of researchers such as Lauren Berlant, Jennifer Cooke, and Ann Cvetkovich, whose research on intimacy demonstrates the usefulness of intimacy and spaces.[62] As these scholars show, intimacies can be perceived as striking political interventions. Yet these personal experiences also are already made vulnerable by social and national pressures across the United States, even in sites such as the home-space that may appear sequestered from the political fractiousness of US public life.⁶³

In contrast, creative acts can function as a means to remediating damage and generating healing forms of bridges such as those that Anzaldúa theorizes in her later anthology *This Bridge Called Home*. To extend this way of thinking, it behooves us to ponder what it takes to create these spaces that link communities and allow people to connect with one another. What does it take for diverse cultures to come together and become more socially hybridized? To theorize this situation, I turn to the research of Adriana De Souza e Silva and Sarah Whatmore. They have developed concepts of "hybrid space" that have certain commonalities with the spatial thinking of Anzaldúa, though they look at hybrid spaces in different contexts such as mobile technology.⁶⁴ Their discussions of hybrid spatial experience provide a means of explicating the links between queer Latinx spaces and those beyond their local sphere such as more public spaces like dance halls that feel intimate and have a domestic resonance. Through these lenses, I develop a notion of *queer hybrid space* to articulate the multilayered sites that queer Latinx people inhabit. The lens of queer hybrid space also gives space-makers and researchers a means of naming resistant forms of social and community investments that take shape in several spatial forms. Queerly hybrid spaces include art, texts, and contexts that not only create bridges between people but also resist deleterious imperatives for purity and separatism that lead to conflicts such as border disputes, culture wars, and community violence. In pragmatic terms, practitioners can use this framework to extend research in multiple disciplines like border studies and Latinx studies.

In studying these contexts, I reflected on my own positionality as a queer and white researcher who exists at the interstices of communities as well as outside of cultural norms. I am a queer son of a heterosexual woman who immigrated to the United States from Australia in the 1970s. As I grew up, I realized my mother was not seen as "belonging" in the United States. As a child, I helped her to practice for her citizenship test, which made me see that she was perceived as an outsider and Other. In a comparable way, I was made to feel like an outsider when my peers labeled my interests as "girly" and cast my physical mannerisms as "different." I was perceived as feminine, queer, and unathletic—three unpardonable sins that deviated from my rather traditional school's social expectations and values. As I was bullied by youths extolling such values, I also struggled with my own body image, which caused me to question the social mores that shape one's internal sense of identity and self-worth. These events led me to become more reflective and hold a deep passion for studying how ideas of belonging, normative practices of social life, and human movement shape humanity. In light of this, I have devoted my life to understanding how social problems such as discrimination, hate speech, inequality, and violence give rise to a dearth of socio-spatial possibilities for queer and brown peoples. I find a common cause with Latinx queers that show an interest in challenging biased attitudes and normative practices, which have had the effect of shoring up discrimination, otherness, and exclusion.

MAKING CONNECTIONS: METHODS FOR EXAMINING QUEER LATINX SPACES

Historically, scholars have associated the artistic and critical work of Anzaldúa with a field of thought known as Chicana Feminism; however, Anzaldúa's perspectives have much to offer to the fields of geography, queer studies, and cultural studies. Her theories about liminal worlds and nonmajoritarian sites, which she envisioned as the *mundo zurdo* (roughly translated as the "left-handed world") provides the basis for an incisive critical framework that questions the neglect and oppression of queer Latinx lives. As AnaLouise Keating has shown, Anzaldúa's contributions are still less readily embraced by queer cultural critics and other academics. Keating asks, "Are most queer theorists so Eurocentric or masculinist in their text selections that they have entirely ignored *This Bridge Called My Back*, where Anzaldúa's queer theorizing first occurs in print?"[65] The critical thought of Anzaldúa indeed has received less reverence and inclusion in dialogues of queer studies. Such exclusion could be traced to the fact that Anzaldúa often disregarded the nearly ubiquitous US expectation that scholarly writing should be written in just one language—English. In her work, Anzaldúa mixed English, Spanish, and indigenous languages in her writing, blending her critical commentaries with poetic writing, and thus she resists the imperatives of the monolingual state and a shortsighted academy. Despite the efforts of feminist studies scholars who exalted the ideas of cultural pluralism and multiculturalism late in the twentieth century, there remains a cultural myopia in academia.

Forward movement away from such shortsighted stances often feels slow, even as academics and writers like Ilan Stavans have made some progress in publishing unconventional intellectual projects. Stavans's volume, *Latino USA: A Cartoon History*, offers readers a historical commentary that is both critical and entertaining insofar as its intermedial approach links Lalo Alcaraz's illustrations with Stavans's own verbal commentary. The hybrid approach in the work of Alcaraz and Stavans is part of a larger phenomenon of cultural hybridity, a concept that has been theorized extensively by scholars such as Néstor Gárcia Canclini. Just as Gárcia Canclini shows in his research, experiences of cultural hybridity play substantive roles in the creation of artwork, popular culture, and intellectual projects across the Americas.[66] Moreover, the success of intermedial and hybrid texts is no longer a seldom occurrence inasmuch as talented writers like Cathia Jenainati and Meg-John Barker similarly are mixing genres to make innovative cerebral projects that link visual media and theoretical perspectives.[67] An analogous form of mixing also arises in intellectual projects where scholars compare and connect ostensibly disparate forms of cultural production that might not initially seem unifiable at first glance. The researcher Michelle Habell-Pallán proffers critical comparisons of performance art, music, and film that hold potential to create "a map of alternative paths that may lead to alternative futures" where social justice is not simply a dream but a reality.[68] Creating similar maps can grant opportunities like coalitions that can be used to chart socially beneficial pathways as well as generate new exemplars of creative resistance to inspire action and (re)thinking in the present age.

Imagining Latinx Intimacies celebrates and embraces the cutting-edge creativities of innovators like Anzaldúa, Habell-Pallán, and Stavans by introducing concepts that bridge fields in an interdisciplinary manner. The bridging of seemingly disparate fields may allow for new perspectives and potentialities, yet such work is not accomplished without some challenges. Considering interdisciplinarity historically, there has been a rather unfortunate trend of pathbreaking projects being rejected because they are seen as flouting the usual practices. In using interdisciplinary approaches, we can begin to transform the discussion and denormalize the underlying barriers and forces of heterosexist and white institutions that shape home-spaces. This is not to say that I read all home-spaces as similar because their social and sexual intimacies (including queer intimacies) are discussed in varying ways.[69] Carlos Ulises Decena, for instance, makes known that coming out as LGBTQ in the Latino familial home is not always a common desire for some gay immigrant men because of the possibility that such disclosures might lead to blowback.[70] For these reasons, many queer people of color build bridges to new spaces that will allow and celebrate their intimacies. These intimate spaces often are imagined beyond the domestic sphere of family. This is not to say all queers are cast out in heteronormative family contexts, but rather they are extending their social sphere's environs in queer forms.

In looking to the mainstream representation of the 1990s, Americans witnessed only a small number of Latinx queer representations such as in the case of the popular television show *Real World: San Francisco* where the Cuban American Pedro Zamora called attention to the need for social spaces that are attuned to the social struggles of being Latinx and HIV positive in the United States. Nevertheless, these TV portrayals walked a fine line between raising awareness about the social struggles of being gay and furthering practices of social marginalization such as narrating the lives of queers of color through discourses of abjection and victimization. To a limited degree, *Real World: San Francisco* began to mediate stories of Latinx queers in spaces occupied by white heterosexual people.

By taking such paths, Latinx queers paved the way for representations in film, literature, and television. In contrast to these mainstream forays, authors and artists published humanizing stories, which challenged diminishing imagery. Equally, the financial success of sexually conscious stories from Chicana and Latina feminists like Ana Castillo, Sandra Cisneros, Rosario Ferré, and Cherríe Moraga have carved out a new kind of textual space for publishing the transgressive stories of queer Latinx peoples from the twentieth century and thereafter.[71] In a comparable manner, openly queer Latinx creators like Arturo Islas, Rafael Campo, Frances Negrón-Muntaner, and Manuel Ramos Otero blazed new trails in the 1980s and 1990s by putting forth creativity that explored relations of sexuality, space, and practices like those found in the cases of patriarchal social mores, institutions, and religion.[72] In years prior, a number of scholars charted the structures where neoliberalism and socioeconomic systems like capitalism shaped the possibilities of spatial creation as well as play roles in making spatial voids. Scholars like Mary Pat Brady, Juana María Rodríguez, Marisel Moreno, and Yolanda Martínez-San Miguel contribute influential studies that illuminate Chicanx and Latinx spatial experiences like that of home-spaces.[73] Their research expands on the thought of cultural geographers such as Henri Lefebvre, Lawrence Knopp, Doreen Massey, and Linda McDowell. Akin to these scholars, I aim to theorize the imagining of alternative spaces in the representation of queer Latinx communities. In this way, I see the vicissitudes of queer Latinx experiences and spatial creativity as demanding further research, and I pursue this work with the hope that my research will illuminate a more informed pathway toward an equitable future.[74]

THE CHAPTERS AND ORGANIZATION OF
IMAGINING LATINX INTIMACIES

To understand these representations of queer Latinx intimacy, this book is organized into two major sections that altogether explore five kinds of spatial experience. These five spaces are: the domestic spaces of queer homes, the social spaces of gay and straight groups including gay and straight alliances (or GSAs), queer online spaces enabling intimacy, natural spaces including the human body, and sensational public spaces of spectacle such as beaches and theaters. These approaches are employed in recognition of the fact that Latinx queers negotiate between multiple concrete circumstances of daily labor and radical social scenes that make possible pleasure and a more inventive playfulness that is less constrained by the dominant culture's codes. The first set of studies in this book is placed under the heading of "Close to Home: Rescripting Domestic Spaces." This section offers case studies of the ways queer Latinx peoples are represented as using practical approaches such as community organizing to create inclusive spaces in the real world. These quotidian domestic spaces contrast with those of the second section "Far from Home: Alternative and Imaginary Spaces," where I examine three spatial experiences that are host to a mix of Latinx bodies, which exhibit hybrid, unusual, and virtual qualities. These latter chapters explore the relationship of nonconventional corporealities and spatiality that resist the inculcated status quo by embracing a more performative and inventive approach. Surveying these two major zones of Latinx cultural production affords readers a greater understanding of the creative breadth and intellect of queer Latinx artists from the 1990s and 2000s.

By taking these approaches, I aim to offer a more balanced and organized study of the creativities that are used to combat spatial violence like social exclusion and the diminishment of Latinx queers in homophobic spaces. To begin with the more material elements of familial life, I commence with the queer domesticity explored in chapter 1—"Reimagining the Family Home," which compares a short story by Moisés Agosto-Rosario with Frances Negrón-Muntaner's documentary titled *Brincando el Charco: Portrait of a Puerto Rican* (1994). This study of migration and home-spaces elaborates on the investigations of Lawrence La Fountain-Stokes and Radost Rangelova.[75] Using these lenses, I contend these creative narratives show a queer trajectory, which I interpret as a hybrid spatial experience that connects people and spaces in ways that often challenge facile thinking about spatial experiences. This heuristic allows us to think about how the social experiences created in dance spaces partially mirror intimate relations of kinship, yet also foster notable social dynamics such as a relationality that is more ephemeral, flexible, permeable, and unfixed. Then in chapter 2—"Enhancing Schools"—I shift from focusing on the individual's home to nearby social spaces created at schools and neighboring households for the goal of examining a set of queer writings from a popular area of writing—young adult fiction. In this second chapter, I explicate two young adult novels that depict LGBTQ youth groups. Beginning with a collection of youth-focused poetry titled *So Often the Pitcher Goes to Water until It Breaks* (1999) from the Mexican American writer Rigoberto González, I situate how questions of youth have played a key role in the making of Latinx cultural productions. Following this context, I compare González's novel *The Mariposa Club* to the novel *Getting It* by the Mexican American author Alex Sánchez. This text depicts the social challenges and achievements of creating supportive queer youth spaces during the early 2000s. Through a comparative approach, Latinx spatial dynamics are theorized as playing key roles in the emotional and psychological development of transgender and queer Latinx youths.

In the second section "Far from Home," the chapters explore portrayals of virtual and imagined life experiences that likely would resonate with readers as rather bawdy, peculiar, and just plain impossible. This move toward more imaginary spaces including performative contexts allows readers to reflect on the ways that queers move beyond the constraints of physical space and foster hybrid spaces beyond that of the home. This move beyond the physical is a means of fostering queer spaces that Deborah R. Vargas calls "alternative imaginaries" where Latinx queers may find conducive spaces for self-making, community, and radical creativity including alter egos and erotic play, which is less constrained by the rather serious and lock-step real world.[76] Building on these ideas, in the third chapter, I elucidate online forms of virtual performance through a study of two Puerto Rican texts that embed online communications in print-based books. This section illuminates how the Puerto Rican writers Rane Arroyo and Ángel Lozada fashion forms of web-conscious artistry that hybridize digital media, literary texts, and online performance of queerly social identities. With this imaginatively integrative approach, Arroyo and Lozada create a powerful set of statements about the need for social spaces, including that of technological spaces that can facilitate non-normative intimate interactions.

In chapter 4, I compare another innovative form of writing, which shows the imagined mixing of humans and non-humans including animals and natural environments. Several pieces of poetry by the Chicana writer Anzaldúa and the Puerto Rican writer Rane Arroyo focus on the experiences and spaces of nonhuman living beings. Resembling forms of therianthropy, which is a form of lived hybridity, readers observe beings that defy the ordinary physiques of our world. These imaginary scenes are compared with the artwork of the renowned Mexican artist Frida Kahlo and the Mexican American artist Tino Rodríguez, both of whom embrace a similarly imaginative form of mixing within their visual forms of artwork. I offer an analysis of these blendings by exploring Arroyo's collection *The Singing Shark* and a newly published collection of pieces by Anzaldúa that recently have been made available through the generosity and efforts of the scholar AnaLouise Keating. In reflection on these exceptional pieces of poetry, I explain how the writings' peculiar figures such as Arroyo's shark-man and mermaids mobilize challenges to the problematic imperatives of purity and the exploitation of natural landscapes. Arroyo's work also builds on the ideas of another notable narrative—*West Side Story*—to show how this half-man, half-shark figure is struggling with a body that is ill-equipped for the human environment. His text is read as an intimate allegory about the ways that Latinx queers navigate and negotiate heterosexual social spaces. To conclude the chapters, chapter 5, "Navigating Spectacular Spaces," offers an elucidation of the spaces and experiences narrated in the memoir *Madre and I: A Memoir of Our Immigrant Lives*, which was written by the Chilean American gay writer named Guillermo Reyes. Considering a range of expected sites such as theaters (and unexpected) sites such as beaches and clubs, this chapter illuminates the way that Latinx queers are using spectacular sites to contest forces that silence queer Latinx peoples.

Taken together, these final chapters show how Latinx queers are using imaginative spaces to resist dominant ideologies and foster empathetic futures. In the epilogue, I extend this set of ideas to news coverage of the 2016 massacre at the Pulse Night Club, where forty-nine people were murdered and more than fifty people were injured.[77] The majority of the dead and injured in this queer space were Latinx, hence leading us to question what progress (if any) has been made in the past several decades. Amid this moment, consideration is given to how this egregious violence displaced queer people from a community center that served to unify a mix of diverse peoples. In studying such events, I revisit what many recently have called *the myth* of the American Dream by examining how queer Latinx youths remain vulnerable because of a lack of supportive spaces, ingrained bias, and exclusionary measures. The importance of advancing such dialogues was well articulated at the 2016 American Studies Association conference, where speakers highlighted how queer Latinx studies continues to be useful for addressing a range of sociopolitical issues today.[78] Such studies yield insights on the struggles faced by displaced peoples such as peoples living with HIV and youth of color that eschew sexual normativities. With these approaches, diverse advocates and scholars can better understand the complex socialities of Latinx sexualities in spatial contexts and the value of fostering an egalitarian ethic.

NOTES

1. Gloria E. Anzaldúa, *Borderlands/La Frontera: The New Mestiza*, 4th ed. (San Francisco: Aunt Lute Books, 1987 and 2012), 42. Citations refer to the 2012 edition.

2. *Latinx* is used to speak to a range of gender experiences beyond the limitations of binaries including transgender and genderqueer experiences. See the following interview with Juana María Rodríguez: Sarah Hayley Barrett, "Latinx: The Ungendering of the Spanish Language," LatinoUSA.org, last modified January 29, 2016, Web.

3. Yolanda Martínez-San Miguel, *Caribe Two Ways: Cultura de la migración en el Caribe insular hispánico* (Ediciones Callejón, 2003), 28, 40.

4. Deborah R. Vargas, "Ruminations on Lo Sucio as a Latino Queer Analytic," *American Quarterly* 66, no. 3 (2014): 723.

5. Juana María Rodríguez, *Queer Latinidad: Identity Practices and Discursive Spaces* (New York: New York University Press, 2003).

6. Gloria E. Anzaldúa, "Preface: (Un)natural bridges, (Un)safe spaces," *This Bridge We Call Home: Radical Visions for Transformation*, eds. Gloria E. Anzaldúa and Ana-Louise Keating (New York: Routledge, 2002), 1.

7. Marijn Nieuwenhuis and David Crouch, *The Question of Space: Interrogating the Spatial Turn between Disciplines* (London: Rowman & Littlefield International, 2017), x.

8. Ernesto Javier Martínez, *On Making Sense: Queer Race Narratives of Intelligibility* (Stanford, CA: Stanford University Press, 2013), 105.

9. Lauren Berlant and Michael Warner, "Sex in Public," *Critical Inquiry* 24, no. 2 (1998): 558.

10. Mary Pat Brady, *Extinct Lands, Temporal Geographies: Chicana Literature and the Urgency of Space* (Durham, NC: Duke University Press, 2002).

11. Richard T. Rodríguez, *Next of Kin: The Family in Chicano/a Cultural Politics* (Durham, NC: Duke University Press, 2009), 173.

12. David Gere, *How to Make Dances in an Epidemic: Tracking Choreography in the Age of AIDS* (Madison: University of Wisconsin Press, 2004); Anna Kline, Emma Kline, and Emily Oken, "Minority Women and Sexual Choice in the Age of AIDS," *Social Science and Medicine* 34, no. 4 (1992): 447–57; Edmund White, *Loss within Loss: Artists in the Age of AIDS* (Madison: University of Wisconsin Press, 2002).

13. John Mckiernan-González, "Health," *Keywords for Latina/o Studies*, eds. Deborah R. Vargas, Nancy Raquel Mirabel, and Lawrence La Fountain-Stokes (New York: New York University, 2017), 79.

14. Amy L. Fairchild and Eileen A. Tynan, "Policies of Containment: Immigration in the Era of AIDS," *American Journal of Public Health* 84, no. 12 (December 1994): 2011–22; Cathy Lisa Schneider, "Racism, Drug Policy and AIDS," *Political Science Quarterly* 113, no. 3 (Autumn 1998): 427–46.

15. Hiram Pérez, *A Taste for Brown Bodies: Gay Modernity and Cosmopolitan Desire* (New York: New York University Press, 2015), 19.

16. Sandra K. Soto, *Reading Chican@ Like a Queer: The De-Mastery of Desire* (Austin: University of Texas Press, 2010), 1.

17. Luis H. Román Garcia, "In Search of My Queer Aztlán," *Queer Aztlán: Chicano Male Recollections of Consciousness and Coming Out*, eds. Adelaida Del Castillo and Gibran Guido (San Diego: Cognella Academic Publishing, 2015), 317–18.

18. Anthony C. Ocampo, "The Gay Second Generation: Sexual Identity and Family Relations of Filipino and Latino Gay Men," *Journal of Ethnic and Migration Studies* 40, no. 1 (2013): 155–73.

19. Alia Malek, "Moving Beyond the Label of 'War Refugee,'" *The New York Times Magazine*, May 17 2019. Web.

20. Elisa Garza, "Chicana Lesbianism and the Multigenre Text," *Tortilleras: Hispanic and U.S. Latina Lesbian Expression*, eds. Lourdes Torres and Inmaculada Pertusa (Philadelphia: Temple University Press, 2003), 196–212.

21. Adrienne Rich, *Blood, Bread, and Poetry* (New York: W. W. Norton, 1994).

22. José Esteban Muñoz, *Cruising Utopia: The Then and There of Queer Futurity* (New York: New York University Press, 2009), 49.

23. Von Diaz, "How Latino Activists Fought for Transgender Rights in Massachusetts," *Colorlines.com*, November 15, 2013, Web.

24. US Census Bureau, "Census Brief: Hispanic Owned Businesses," October 2001.

25. John Galeano, "On Rivers," *The Environmental Humanities*, eds. Serpil Oppermann and Serenella Iovino (London: Rowman & Littlefield International, 2017), 331–38; Laura Pulido, *Environmentalism and Economic Justice* (Tucson: University of Arizona Press,1996); Catriona Sandilands, "Queer Ecology," *Keywords for Environmental Studies*, eds. Joni Adamson, William A. Gleason, and David N. Pellow (New York: New York University Press, 2016), 169–71.

26. Pulido, *Environmentalism and Economic Justice*, xv.

27. Christina Holmes, *Ecological Borderlands: Body, Nature and Spirit in Chicana Feminism* (Urbana: University of Illinois Press, 2016).

28. Oskaras Vorobjovas-Pinta and Brady Robards, "The Shared Oasis: An Insider Ethnographic Account of a Gay Resort," *Tourist Studies* 17, no. 4 (2017): 383.

29. Sami Edge, "SPD Sets National Example with LGBTQ-friendly Safe Haven Plan," *The Seattle Times*, Crime, August 10, 2015, Web.

30. Trystan Cotten, "Introduction: Migration and Morphing," *Transgender Migrations: The Bodies, Borders, and Politics of Transition*, ed. Trystan Cotten (New York: Routledge, 2012), 1–8.

31. Kristin L. Matthews, *Reading America: Citizenship, Democracy and Cold War Literature* (Amherst: University of Massachusetts Press, 2016), 5.

32. Ricardo L. Ortíz, "Diaspora," *Keywords for Latina/o Studies* (New York: New York University Press, 2017), 50.
33. bell hooks, *Talking Back: Thinking Feminist, Thinking Black* (Cambridge: Between the Lines, 1989), 5.
34. Gloria Anzaldúa, "Now Let Us Shift . . . the Path of Conocimiento . . . Inner Work, Public Acts," *This Bridge We Call Home*, eds. Gloria Anzaldúa and AnaLouise Keating (New York: Routledge, 2002), 540–78.
35. Lawrence La Fountain-Stokes, *Queer Ricans: Cultures and Sexualities in the Diaspora* (Minneapolis: University of Minnesota Press, 2009), 132.
36. Scott Morgensen, "Radical Faeries," in *LGBTQ America Today: An Encyclopedia*, ed. John Hawley (Westport, CT: Greenwood Press, 2009), 1012.
37. Katie Acosta, *Amigas y Amantes: Sexually Nonconforming Latinas Negotiate Family* (New Brunswick, NJ: Rutgers University Press, 2013), 1–3; Marisel Moreno, "Revisiting la Gran Familia Puertorriqueña in the Works of Rosario Ferré and Judith Ortíz Cofer," *CENTRO Journal* 22, no. 2 (Fall 2010): 76.
38. Michel de Certeau, *The Practice of Everyday Life*, trans. Steven Rendall (Los Angeles: University of California Press, 1984).
39. Julio Capó, "Pulse and the Long History of Violence against Queer Latinos," *Time Magazine* (June 17, 2016), Web.
40. Nicole M. Guidotti-Hernández, "Borderlands," *Keywords for Latina/o Studies*, eds. Deborah Vargas, Nancy Raquel Mirabel and Lawrence La Fountain Stokes (New York: New York University Press, 2017), 21–24.
41. Anzaldua, *Borderlands/La Frontera*, 25.
42. Michael Brown and Larry Knopp, "Queer Diffusions," *Environment and Planning D: Society and Space* 21 (2003): 409–24.
43. Sean Cahill, "Black and Latino Same-Sex Couple Households and the Racial Dynamics of Antigay Activism," *Black Sexualities: Probing Powers, Passions, Practices and Policies*, eds. Juan Battle and Sandra L. Barnes (New Brunswick, NJ: Rutgers University Press, 2010), 244.
44. David Eng, *The Feeling of Kinship: Queer Liberalism and the Racialization of Intimacy* (Durham, NC: Duke University Press, 2010), 5.
45. Muñoz, *Cruising Utopia*, 18.
46. Bernard Lumpkin, "Rigoberto González: Populating Bookshelves," *Lambda Literary*, May 4 2013, Web.
47. T. Jackie Cuevas, *Post-Borderlandia: Chicana Literature and Gender Variant Critique* (New Brunswick, NJ: Rutgers University Press, 2018).
48. Human Rights Campaign, The League of United Latin American Citizens and the Human Rights Campaign, "Supporting and Caring for Our Latino LGBT Youth," accessed 2012, Web.
49. Steven A. Holmes, "Jesse Helms Dies at 86; Conservative Force in the Senate," *The New York Times*, last modified July 8, 2008, Web.
50. Harold Augenbraum and Margarite Fernández Olmos, "Introduction: An American Literary Tradition," *The Latino Reader: Five Centuries of an American Literary Tradition from Cabeza de Vaca to Oscar Hijuelos* (New York: Houghton Mifflin, 1997), xix.
51. Kimberlé Crenshaw, "Demarginalizing the Intersection of Race and Sex: A Black Feminist Critique of Antidiscrimination Doctrine, Feminist Theory and Antiracist Politics," *University of Chicago Legal Forum* 1 (1989): 140.
52. Catalina M. de Onís and Roy Pérez, "What's in an 'x': An Exchange about the Politics of 'Latinx,'" *Chiricú Journal: Latina/o Literatures, Arts, and Cultures* 1, no. 2 (Spring 2017): 78–91; Juana María Rodríguez, "The Ungendering of the Spanish Language," interviewed by Sarah Hayley Barrett and Oscar Nñ, *Latinousa.org*, January 29 2016. Web.
53. Nayan Shah, *Contagious Divides: Epidemics and Race in San Francisco's Chinatown* (Berkeley: University of California Press, 2001), 77–104.
54. Shah, *Contagious Divides*, 77.

55. Amid the civil rights and justice movements of 1960s, diverse groups of people spoke out against the longstanding inequities. My project builds on the critical and intellectual projects of these movements. See for instance, Mark Hamilton Lytle's *America's Uncivil Wars*.

56. Deborah R. Vargas, Nancy Raquel Mirabal, and Lawrence La Fountain-Stokes, "Introduction," *Keywords for Latina/o Studies* (New York: New York University Press, 2017), 2.

57. Siobhan B. Somerville, "Queer," in *Keywords for American Cultural Studies*, eds. Bruce Burgett and Glenn Hendler (New York: New York University Press, 2007), 187.

58. La Fountain-Stokes, *Queer Ricans*, 1–5.

59. Lee Edelman, Tim Dean, et al., "The Antisocial Thesis in Queer Theory," *PMLA* 121, no. 3 (2006): 819–28.

60. Michael Snediker, *Queer Optimism: Lyric Personhood and Other Felicitous Persuasions* (Minneapolis: University of Minnesota Press, 2009).

61. Glenna Matthews, *Just a Housewife: The Rise and Fall of Domesticity in America* (New York: Cambridge University Press, 1989), xiv.

62. Lauren Berlant, "Intimacy: A Special Issue," in *Intimacy*, ed. Lauren Berlant (Chicago: University of Chicago Press, 2000), 1–8; Jennifer Cooke, "Making a Scene: Towards an Anatomy of Literary Intimacies," in *Scenes of Intimacy: Reading, Writing and Theorizing Contemporary Literature*, ed. Jennifer Cooke (New York: Bloomsbury, 2013), 3–22; Ann Cvetkovich, *An Archive of Feelings: Trauma, Sexuality and Lesbian Public Cultures* (Durham, NC: Duke University Press, 2003).

63. Elizabeth A. Chauvin, Heidi S. Kulkin, and Gretchen A. Percle, "Suicide among Gay and Lesbian Adolescents and Young Adults: A Review of the Literature," *Journal of Homosexuality* 40, no. 1 (2000): 2.

64. Adriana De Souza e Silva, "From Cyber to Hybrid: Mobile Technologies as Interfaces of Hybrid Spaces," *Culture and Space* 9, no. 3 (2006): 261–62; Sarah Whatmore, *Hybrid Geographies: Natures Cultures Spaces* (Thousand Oaks, CA: Sage Publications, 2002).

65. AnaLouise Keating, "Introduction," *The Gloria Anzaldúa Reader*, ed. AnaLouise Keating (Durham, NC: Duke University Press, 2009), 5.

66. Néstor Gárcia Canclini, *Hybrid Cultures: Strategies for Entering and Leaving Modernity*, trans. Christopher Chiappari and Sylvia L. Lopez (Minneapolis: University of Minnesota Press, 2005).

67. Cathia Jenainati, *Feminism: A Graphic Guide* (Lanham, MD: Icon Books, 2010); Meg-John Barker, *Queer: A Graphic History* (Lanham, MD: Icon Books, 2016).

68. Michelle Habell-Pallán, *Loca Motion: The Travels of Chicana and Latina Popular Culture* (New York: New York University Press, 2005), 14.

69. Marivel T. Danielson, *Homecoming Queers: Desire and Difference in Chicana Latina Cultural Production* (New Brunswick, NJ: Rutgers University Press, 2009); Albert T. Hurtado, *Intimate Frontiers: Sex, Gender and Culture in Old California* (Albuquerque: University of New Mexico Press, 1999); La Fountain-Stokes, *Queer Ricans*, 133.

70. Carlos Ulises Decena, *Tacit Subjects: Belonging and Same-Sex Desire among Dominican Immigrant Men* (Durham, NC: Duke University Press, 2011), 29.

71. Sandra Cisneros, *The House on Mango Street* (Houston: Arte Público Press, 1984); Rosario Ferré, *Sweet Diamond Dust and Other Stories* (New York: Plume, 1996).

72. Rafael Campo, *What the Body Told* (Durham, NC: Duke University Press, 1996); Manuel de Jesús Vega, "Chicano, Gay and Doomed: AIDS in Arturo Islas's '*The Rain God*,'" *Confluencia* 11, no. 2 (Spring 1996): 112–18; Frances Negrón-Muntaner and Peter Biella, *AIDS in the Barrio: Eso no me pasa a mi*, Cinema Guild, 1985; Lawrence La Fountain-Stokes, "Autobiographical Writing and Shifting Migrant Experience," *Queer Ricans: Cultures and Sexualities in the Diaspora* (Minneapolis: University of Minnesota Press), 19–22.

73. Brady, *Extinct Lands*; Rodríguez, *Queer Latinidad*; Martínez-San Miguel, *Caribe Two Ways*.

74. Carol Reisen, Miguel A. Iracheta, Maria Cecilia Zea, Fernanda T. Bianchi, and Paul J. Poppen, "Sex in Public and Private Settings among Latino MSM," *AIDS Care* 22, no. 6 (May 2010): 697–704.

75. La Fountain-Stokes, *Queer Ricans*, 95; Radost Rangelova, *Gendered Geographies in Puerto Rican Culture* (Chapel Hill: University of North Carolina Press, 2016).

76. Vargas, "Ruminations on *Lo Sucio* as a Latino Queer Analytic," 718.

77. Nick Madigan, Benjamin Mueller, and Sheryl Stolberg, "49 Lives Lost to Horror in Orlando: Mostly Young, Gay and Latino," *New York Times*, June 13, 2016, Web.

78. Erotic Geographies: Sensation and Transnational Latina/o Queerness, American Studies Association Conference, Friday, November 18, 2016, Hyatt Regency Denver, Colorado. Conference panel.

I

Close to Home:
Rescripting Domestic Spaces

ONE

Reimagining the Family Home

The Queering of Domesticity in Puerto Rican Storytelling

> In fact, alternative, new family configurations are a major component of queer world-making.
>
> —Lawrence La Fountain-Stokes[1]

In 1994, the Puerto Rican filmmaker and scholar Frances Negrón-Muntaner presented her second independent film *Brincando el charco: Portrait of a Puerto Rican*.[2] The film's main title *Brincando el charco* ("Jumping the Puddle") refers to the ongoing migration and travel of people from the US commonwealth of Puerto Rico to the mainland United States (and the reverse). For the film's main character—Claudia—this travel is a part of her exile from Puerto Rico after she is cast out of her family's home. This expulsion occurs after her father—Papí—learns of his daughter's desire for another woman. After arguing with her, the father hits Claudia multiple times and uses a threatening tone. He shouts at her "*Vete!*" which translates as "Get out!" Her father also labels her intimacy with a woman as "*suciedades*" (dirtiness), which drives Claudia to critique her conservative Christian father for his intolerance. Shown in a dramatic and emotional style, the black-and-white flashback of Claudia's expulsion alludes to the gloomy reality that LGBTQ peoples across the Americas have been displaced—banished from their home—for vocalizing their desires openly in a place where heterosexuality and patriarchy are the norm. Following this interaction, her mother and brother defend their kin Claudia, yet Papí remains the arbiter of who can live in the domestic sphere. This moment concludes with the young Claudia walking backward out of the family's bright kitchen, dissolving into the hallway's darkness.

As Claudia's body dissolves into the backdrop, *Brincando el charco* suggests that the family's close-knit intimacy also comes apart, thereby inviting viewers to reflect on the film's portrayal of family relations. Although such relations may appear simplistic, Claudia's previous query to her father "*¿Qué clase de Cristiano eres tú?*" (What kind of Christian are you?) points to the idea that this family is not only ruled by the patriarch but also by the religiosity instilled by the original colonizers of Puerto Rico.[3] The family sphere often is imagined as *separate* from the public sphere, but as poet and scholar Gloria Anzaldúa reminds us, powerful institutions such as US companies (and their ideologies) tend to cross borders and thereby enact a colonization that is "coupled with exploitation."[4] People and places in various parts of the world have been used by US capitalists to make a profit, and in the process, these colonizers' ideologies become the new norm. In the aftermath of colonization, Latinx queers often have been driven into "sexile"—a term that is used for explaining the movement of queer peoples who have been displaced by homophobic ideology.[5] For Claudia, her dissolving into the dark is where her sexile commences, yet as the film attests, this dissolving is not the end. Instead, *Brincando el charco* suggests her sexile is a starting point for Claudia's process of constructing an innovative family configuration and intimate space with her partner Ana on the US mainland. Notably, such ideas are echoed in the storytelling of another Puerto Rican author

Figure 1.1.   Claudia is pushed into darkness and out of the family's home by her father in Brincando el charco.

named Moisés Agosto-Rosario, whose collection of stories *Nocturno y otros desamparos* (*Nocturnes and Other Neglects*) depicts queer Puerto Rican characters engaging in a similar process of connecting intimately and politically with friends. Much like viewers see in Negrón-Muntaner's film, Agosto-Rosario's stories suggest that the process of imagining the *family space* as an integrative and sociopolitical undertaking enables queer Latinx peoples to accomplish several things besides solely having a family life.

Reimagining the family sphere in new ways allows for the beneficial creation of community spaces, networking, and self-development. The storytelling of Negrón-Muntaner and Agosto-Rosario provide blueprints for fostering a more inclusive spectrum of domesticity by showcasing scenes that critique social problems such as homophobia and patriarchal culture, which concatenate to create social displacement and exclusion. *Brincando el charco* calls attention to these problems by portraying how Claudia considers what it means to be a lesbian Puerto Rican living on the US mainland. Over the course of the film, Claudia's reflections on identity are woven together with personal story, stock footage, and interviews with a slew of Puerto Rican people including a young activist Moisés Agosto-Rosario—the aforementioned author. During the film, Agosto-Rosario comments on Puerto Rican lived experiences in New York state, saying that a town there is "*como otro pueblo más de Puerto Rico*" (like another town of Puerto Rico). His words indicate how a space like Puerto Rico can *travel* and stretch out through people's recollections of the past as well through the movements of bodies across vast distances. In this way, Puerto Rican spatial experience is by no means static, and as Jorge Duany explains, Puerto Rican peoples continue to be "on the move," crisscrossing the Western Hemisphere and linking cultural contexts into a hybrid space.[6] In effect, the concept of space here can be understood as a flexible phenomenon that manifests in a myriad of forms. This flexible spatial concept has much in common with the epigraph, in which La Fountain-Stokes suggests that family spaces can indeed manifest in alternative forms and be read as "queer world-making."[7] Creating a *queer world* involves a mixed coterie of people, the implementation of inventive approaches, and a more diverse set of spaces that intertwine, shadow one another, and recreate prior sites.

Among these spaces, we observe sites that take the shape of intimate and social milieus from representation such as Negrón-Muntaner's experimental film *Brincando el charco* as well as Agosto-Rosario's eclectic short stories. As these pieces show us, several Puerto Rican people find a social intimacy with a domestic sensibility in sites that might not appear domestic at first glance such as a dance floor. Still, their relations instantiate a meaningful connectivity. Starting with a bird's-eye view, this chapter introduces the reader to several key ways of understanding representations of queer Puerto Rican domesticities in the 1990s and early

2000s. Such domestic contexts are nonuniform in their visual and textual formulation, even though this representation also demonstrate a pattern in which intimacies are formed through shared desires, friendship, physical closeness, and social resistance. This pattern of socially alternative and queer forms of domesticity became more prominent and visible in stories and media forms as diverse reformers such as AIDS activists pressed for fair treatment and justice. Along with these sociopolitical factors, I conjecture that twentieth-century migration also played a substantive role in changing how people thought of family, home, and homeland. Hundreds of thousands of Puerto Rican peoples migrated to the US mainland during the twentieth century with the hope of procuring new employment opportunities and a higher quality of life. The most sizeable waves of migration occurred after World War II—a moment when commercial air travel became easier and the US government program called "Operation Bootstrap ultimately "displaced thousands of rural workers,"[8] bringing a sizable number of Puerto Rican people to the US mainland.

Although there are many reasons for queer Puerto Rican people to migrate to the United States, there exists a strand of discourse—or a *dream*—that suggests the United States offers an inclusiveness for LGBTQ peoples more than most Caribbean terrains. This fantasy of the United States being "safer" for queer Latinx peoples sadly was shattered in June 2016 when a man used semiautomatic weapons to kill forty-nine people and injure fifty-eight (many of whom were Puerto Rican and Latinx) at the Pulse Nightclub in Orlando, Florida.[9] To the horror of queer communities and their allies, this attack exhibits an eerie resemblance to a previous act of arson in 1973 that killed thirty-two people at a gay bar called the Upstairs Lounge in New Orleans, Louisiana.[10] Such attacks are part of a widespread, yet underreported pattern of violence against queer spaces, which speaks to the necessity of research and queerly supportive initiatives. The attacks contrast with the dance spaces shown in the storytelling of Negrón-Muntaner and Agosto-Rosario, who depict dance spaces as a locus of intimacy that has the comforts of the domestic sphere (albeit in another form). Given the lack of public support and safety, queer Latinx peoples have taken it on themselves to create their own spaces that might not look like their prior homes per se, yet still provide feelings of safety, which is viewed as being a human necessity across cultures.[11]

Social spaces such as dance halls can become the helpful *home away from home* for queer people who experience deleterious forms of social persecution and violence within the homes of their biological families. To deal with this challenging social dynamic, the characters in the aforementioned creative works craft alternative interpersonal relations that mix the ideas of biological family with that of one's social intimates, creating a *queer family of friends*. This queer family finds comfort in the apartments and dance halls beyond the biological family's home. To be more precise, the characters' own personal interiors—their queer sense of self—is nurtured by the interiors and spatiality of queer sites. This parallel of the queer self and spatiality alludes to the primacy of space in the making of queer identities. Such queer connections of self and space arguably involve what Yolanda Martínez-San Miguel identifies as *"poder transformador"* (transforming power) insofar as these queerly inclusive spaces can enable queers to become themselves.[12] This idea of queer *becoming* is shown prominently in *Brincando el charco*, which presents several "portraits" of Puerto Rican people that are developing their own creative talents as well as their social environs. In the case of the photographer Claudia (who is played by Negrón-Muntaner herself), viewers are led to consider how Claudia's camera work is a means of visualizing her worldview including sociopolitical perspectives. Claudia's poignant photography is depicted alongside an equally potent amorous relationship with a stateside Puerto Rican woman named Ana, who is played by the charismatic actress Natalia Lazarus. As the film's viewers learn, Ana is working to formalize a Latino district in Philadelphia—a space where Latina/o and Latinx people can join together for community and socializing. Interestingly, some of the film's most powerful scenes take place indoors or in close contact, which generates a feeling of immediacy. Viewers are treated to sites such as apartment spaces, building entrances, dance halls, and studios that bring people of color and languages into close contact. This integrative approach of uniting people reads as a subtle form of resistance to what scholar Ricardo L. Ortíz calls "queer- and trans-phobic violence in both home- and host-lands."[13] In this way, I interpret the spatial imaginaries of Negrón-Muntaner and Agosto-Rosario as providing a means to counter the ongoing sociopolitical negativities of displacement and sexile in a similar, yet distinctive manner. These storytelling counterpoints depict processes of incorporation and hybridity that deviate from US normalized processes that tend to exclude difference, thus resonating in a queerly social manner that informs observers' critical faculties. Culminating as hybrid in approach, these pieces challenge embedded drives for purity as well as misconceptions like the idea that all Puerto Rican people are light-skinned or white. By contesting such views, the storytelling of queer Puerto Rican film and writing leads observers to rethink the relation of identity to influential spaces such as domesticity, communities, and the nation.

CONTEXTUALIZING THE QUEER INTERIORS OF PUERTO RICAN LIVES AND STORYTELLING

Radost Rangelova historicizes her research of Puerto Rican lives by relating how the family home traditionally has been understood as a site of "patriarchal control" that has been shaped by gender and nationhood.[14] Such controls seldom leave little room for genders that depart from normality; but instead of abandoning the home-space altogether, some scholars have encouraged a reconsideration of "home." The researcher Nayan Shah hypothesizes, "exploring deviant sexualities and queer domesticities allows us to conceive of alternatives that do not funnel all valued sensual relations into heterosexual marriage and reproduction."[15] Just as Shah suggests, imagining alternatives to dominant domestic relations can grant a productive lens for developing understandings of how human beings experience desire, sensations, and spaces that mainstream Western society has labeled as ineffable, mysterious, taboo, and unspeakable. Yet in Negrón-Muntaner's narrative and that of Agosto-Rosario, we see Puerto Rican queers fostering meaningful intimate relations such as those with same-sex partners and community members. These relations exhibit a significant degree of personal connectivity that is found among people who are related by blood, and this relationality becomes a rewarding and guiding principle in their lives. This connectivity manifests across Puerto Rican social practices like dance, which serves as a meaningful social connection in the storytelling of both *Brincando el charco* and *Nocturno y otros desamparos*. Like Frances Aparicio has shown, myriad researchers have neglected to honor and recognize the broad diversity of cultural influences that constitute such intimate dance experience.[16] Honoring these diverse cultural influences not only grants an understanding of the storytelling but also serves as a reminder of the way in which intimacies at home and dancing in public are in fact social constructions predicated on a mix of social values and ideologies. Putting these experiences to paper or film can grant us a preliminary set of blueprints to deconstruct underling extant social problems like homophobia and racism that prevent queer Puerto Rican people from achieving a full sense of belonging and citizenship.

Relatedly, José Esteban Muñoz explains that the predominant US notion of citizenship involves a form of "national affect"—a sort of national sentiment—that is largely white-centric and remains rather undertheorized. In a parallel to Muñoz's work, this chapter aims to intervene and cultivate alternative ways of doing connectivity and sociality such as intimacies that arise in non-normative domesticities. Further down the line, I hope that these non-normative spatialities allow us to dream of and create more inclusive (and less constraining) kinds of social belonging that ameliorate limited notions of citizenship, hence moving beyond exclusionary paradigms.[17] *Brincando el charco* functions as a way of redressing problematic unbelonging including the way that Anglophone white notions of domesticity have dominated the social sphere. To begin, Negrón-Muntaner subverts the idea that relationships must lead to the often-idealized arrangements such as the monogamous heterosexual married couple that procreates to continue a familial legacy.[18] *Brincando el charco* conveys several relationships, including brief intimacies that emphasize the value of exploring intimate connections within social spaces like dance halls. In a related piece of scholarly writing, Negrón-Muntaner emphasizes how queer Latinx peoples have valued alternative sites for intimacy such as dance clubs. She writes:

> It is thus not surprising that for Latino queers finding a hospitable place to dance has frequently been a top priority in the United States. In fact one of the first items on the agenda for Fuego Latino, a Philadelphia gay and lesbian group that I joined in the summer of 1992, was precisely pressuring the local club owners for "Latin Nights." The desire for a different dancing space stemmed from a sense that Latino queers in Philadelphia were homeless, for convergent if not identical reasons.... And for those who, like myself, had recently arrived directly from Latin America or the Caribbean and were used to a vibrant club scene, there was an acute need for a home outside of home.[19]

In Negrón-Muntaner's personal testimony, her commentary on spaces of dance stand out insofar as she codifies *dance spaces as home*, suggesting they engender meaningful forms of intimate and familial feelings that sometimes are difficult to find. In a comparable way, Puerto Rican writers such as the gay short-story writer Agosto-Rosario also depicts dance spaces that challenge ingrained forms of familial and monogamous homelife.[20] Agosto-Rosario's story collection *Nocturno y otros desamparos* from 2007 shows a mixed set of characters who feel varying emotions such as grief, isolation, and release amid the social connectivities arising on the dance floor. Such feelings partly resemble the way that many more Puerto Rican peoples have felt frustrated by the distancing that is experienced between the US mainland and the island of Puerto Rico. Critics today perceive the US political governance of Puerto Rico as modern-day colonialism where the island's residents are ruled by a distant authority on the US mainland. For instance, critics and scholars have called for a revision of the Jones-Shafroth Act of 1917, which remains a controversial act that speaks to matters of domesticity. Though the act granted citizenship to the peoples of Puerto Rico and made migration to the US mainland possible, there continues to be a feeling of inequality and exclusion from the larger national conversation.

Since 1898, the US government has kept Puerto Rico at a distance insofar as the US has denied Puerto Rican people on the island the right to participate in national processes such as presidential elections and congressional meetings.[21] This political distancing has perpetuated a disparity and unfair power dynamic that permeates Puerto Rican lives. This mixed relationship brings to mind the contradictory idea that although the island is a "possession" of the United States, the island's status largely is one of unbelonging and subordination. Kept in a state of political limbo by the US government, Puerto Rico is a space with neither sovereignty nor statehood. This lack of autonomy mirrors the powerlessness that many queer Puerto Ricans feel when they are displaced from their homes for being LGBTQ. As a result of becoming a "DiaspoRican" who is part of the larger diaspora of Puerto Rican migrants, multiple geographical influences play a role in the creative work of the artists that I consider here. This multiplicity of influence has been characterized by scholars such as Marisel C. Moreno as "transinsular."[22] Such attention is given to queer DiaspoRicans because this grouping has faced considerable hardship inasmuch as they have been perceived as neither belonging on the island nor belonging on the US mainland, thus experiencing a double exclusion. This idea of exclusion is brought to the fore in *Brincando el charco*, where Claudia thoughtfully inquires "what escapes the 'us' in *nosotros*," which begs the question of who is included in the social spaces of family homes and polity. As her film shows, queer Puerto Ricans are pushed to work through miscellaneous forms of social displacement and exclusion by connecting with queer people and taking pride in their bodies and traditions like public displays of queer selfhood, dance, and public parades. This idea is further emphasized in Negrón-Muntaner's film where the film's intertitles suggest Claudia has "a body with multiple points of contact," suggesting she is tied to various sites. At the same time, the film *Brincando el charco* also suggests not all people are so easily connected because of stereotypes and ideologies such as white supremacy that maintain an exclusive notion of domesticity.

In examining the nineteenth-century United States, Nayan Shah insightfully demonstrates how Americans strived to police the boundaries of "respectable domesticity" as migrants were moving to the US mainland.[23] As a part of this phenomenon, powerful white groups attempted to police the ways that ethnic groups fostered social arrangements of domestic life. Sadly, a sizable number of traditionalists in Puerto Rico and the United States have eschewed the idea that queer Puerto Ricans deserve a space at the table of the *Gran Familia Puertoriqueña*, which is the mythical idea of a unified Puerto Rican culture. Yet Agosto-Rosario and Negrón-Muntaner *queer* domestic arrangements of the family home by expanding its narrow confines into the exterior worlds, hence creating an alternative domestic landscape that is—as Jorge Duany and Augustin Laó suggest—"translocal."[24] For Duany and Laó, the *translocal* speaks to the interconnectedness of Puerto Rico and the United States that defies simplistic categorization and remains emotionally charged because of the variety of perspectives about Puerto Rico's status as an "*Estado Libre Asociado*" (Associated Free State) or commonwealth. In this way, queer Puerto Rican domesticity and its underlying intimacies are by no means settled or static; rather, these texts largely suggest that we must read domestic phenomena as more fluid in nature. Situating this fluidity, the researcher Mary Pratt Brady shows how a wide array of human spaces including vast parcels of land are perceived as "processual," or *in-process* because of how sites demonstrate the capacity to change as a result of geopolitics and cultural shifts.[25] The family home is one such processual space because of the way the home may start as a hospitable place for a young person (before they reveal themselves to be queer), but later the home becomes socially toxic because of the antigay animus that propels young people like Claudia into a position of sexile.

NEGRÓN-MUNTANER'S PORTRAYALS OF SOCIAL DOMESTICITY AND DANCE SPACES

Along with filming *Brincando el charco*, Negrón-Muntaner has produced notable queer-centric films such as *AIDS in the Barrio* (1985) and *Small City Big Change* (2013), developing an integrative documentary style that gives voice to queer Latinx peoples when there are few documentarians making such efforts. *AIDS in the Barrio* and *Small City, Big Change* respond to ignorance about HIV/AIDS and transgender lives respectively, yet notably they also function as artistic devices that unify, building communities through linking voices and viewers. In *Small City, Big Change*, Negrón-Muntaner brings together the voices of multiple Latinx people, who testify on camera about the bias and struggles that transgender and nonbinary Latinx peoples were facing in the city of Chelsea, Massachusetts. Following a set of cruel and physical attacks against transgender people, the residents of Chelsea felt compelled to organize their community and convince their representative to support the Transgender Equal Rights Bill of 2012. Using a documentary approach, Negrón-Muntaner weaves together a set of interviews with transgender Latinx women and community organizers to tell the city's story. In addition, the film's down-to-earth feel is generated through the use of soft background music and a mix of local landscape shots to create a feeling of connectedness, which I perceive as a notable intimacy that arises between biologically unrelated people who gather in a common cause. Told in both Spanish and English, *Small City, Big Change* creates a bridge or meeting point between several contexts of Massachusetts to halt the pernicious pattern of transphobic violence.

A similar gathering of people takes place in the 1994 film *Brincando el charco*. Gilberto M. Blasini speaks to this element of unification in his assessment of the film when he explains that *Brincando el charco* "suggests the possibility of creating alliances with other groups."[26] To a similar degree, Lawrence La Fountain-Stokes praised Negrón-Muntaner's film-making as a major step forward in queer Puerto Rican representation, though he views it as teetering on the edge of "overintellectualization."[27] Much as these critics suggest, the film exists at the crossroads of creative storytelling and experimental intellectual critique. The film *Brincando* further builds on this hybrid mode by reflecting on the intersections of gender, nation, race and sexuality. Yet in the critical appraisals of the film, it appears that few critics have substantively pondered how *Brincando el charco* presents the aforesaid pattern of intimate spatial arrangements where community-building and the chance of attaining personal well-being are highlighted.[28] To understand this emphasis on queer bodily comfort and safety, let us consider how many queer people encounter sharp disapproval, outright hostility, and violence when they hold hands or kiss in public.[29] Responding to negativities like these, the creative filmmaking of Negrón-Muntaner intervenes by unabashedly depicting queer intimate practices such as extended kiss scenes between women without the camera shying away in both their own home-spaces as well as on the streets in places like San Juan, Puerto Rico.

At the midpoint in her life, viewers observe Claudia as an experienced photographer, who shares her life with a long-term partner named Ana. Much like Claudia, Ana self-identifies as Puerto Rican, and as a result of living most of her life on the US mainland, she has come to use Spanish less often. This point is explored in an emotive moment where Ana tells Claudia about her relatives mocking her for not speaking Spanish fluently. Claudia responds to Ana's anecdote of being ostracized in her own family by embracing Ana physically and calling her relatives "jerks." In a reciprocal manner, Ana helps Claudia work through the tensions that arise when Claudia learns of her father's death. The two women discuss whether Claudia should attend her estranged father's final moment: the family-organized funeral in Puerto Rico. Claudia laments to Ana: "I thought he would never really die. . . . He owed me an apology." Claudia's morose statement reveals the perception that patriarchs are immortal, though not infallible. In this moment, the viewer sees the flashback that shows how Claudia clashed with her father when he learned of her love for women. Although she could have chosen to not attend—as retribution—she finally decides to return to Puerto Rico. As in the other moments of the film, Claudia chooses to build bridges and reunite with her family, emphasizing the value of connecting, forgiving, and creating social alternatives. She takes the moral high road in this moment, suggesting that she is a more empathetic family member than her father, yet still paying him tribute and including him as a part of her family. Remarkably and sadly, this particular return to the island intimates that the space of death—the funeral—is one of the only possible realms in which the restrictive sphere of heterosexual life can create bridges to new landscapes of queer domesticity.

In researching stories of migration, Irene Mata examines the significant oppositional quality of Latina narratives that "offer decentralized accounts of power."[30] Like Mata suggests, many Latina narratives such as Claudia's story promulgate a new take that moves beyond that of traditional hierarchies. This situation is the case in *Brincando el charco*, which moves on from the father being the center of the story and instead

Figure 1.2. Claudia and her partner Ana share an intimate moment in their home in Brincando el charco.

creates a space for women's stories. Similarly, as the death of Claudia's father already has been the subject of much scholarly discussion, this chapter gives more emphasis to the interactions with Claudia's partner Ana, who occupies a considerable role in the film's narrative. Shown as the dependable professional and breadwinner in the two women's apartment, Ana dresses in business attire, connecting her to a world run by heterosexual male officials. But this dynamic does not preclude the possibility of equality in their own domestic sphere. From their interactions, it becomes clear that Ana works long hours in a traditional position of employment, while the photographer Claudia meets with queer and Puerto Rican people for photoshoots. When Ana requests that Claudia be present for taking pictures at one of her events in Philadelphia, Claudia balks at the idea because she feels that people assume her schedule is always flexible, saying "I hate that." In response, Claudia remains firm, which stands in contrast to her argument with her father previously in the film where Claudia melts in the background. Her stance also mirrors the stalwart position of Philadelphia's earlier inhabitants: the rebellious colonists that signed the US Declaration of Independence and the US Constitution to affirm nationhood. Philadelphia also has a long history of being home to Puerto Rican migrants, bespeaking the importance of cultural history in shaping their pathways and domestic lives. The film's focus on domestic life is shown in several more ways such as when the answering machine's message alerts us that Claudia and Ana share the same phone line, suggesting they are "out" to the community. Their friends additionally stop by the house and loaf with Ana and Claudia, connoting that although the women are homebodies, their home is an integrative site—a hybrid space—where people crisscross the intimate and the public.

Above all, the character of Ana provides the greatest amount of emotional and social support to Claudia, however throughout much of the film, Claudia still appears uneasy. Even as Claudia appears comfortable in her domestic sphere with Ana, viewers see she is still critical and reflective about her relationality with US dominant culture. Claudia's (dis)connection to the ingrained cultural practices is shown through both her on-screen research about Puerto Rican history as well through dialogue and interactions with others in the film. Her physical stance, forward persona, and vestment stand out as different from those around her. Queer audiences likely will note that Claudia's propensity to don a leather jacket and boots marks her as a sexual Other—one who lives outside the gendered social boundaries of straight America. This idea is reified in a series of scenes where Claudia provides a voice-over that narrates her status as an "outsider," which has transpired on moving to the US mainland and rejecting straight norms. She ostensibly prefers such a move to the other option—being an "insider" in Puerto Rico who must, as she says, "swallow broken records" and accept the hackneyed, constraining axioms of heteronormative daily practices. In saying that she is an outsider with "her guts showing," she makes a graphic, strong statement about the powerful role that her interior and physical life plays in constituting her daily existence. This image of personal embodiment suggests her sexual orientation is so central to her identity that she has located it in her "guts," which some critics say is the site of all intuitive thinking.[31] To liken her inward cultural life to the inner physical body suggests that her cultural and social life is vital to her, but this portrayal also hints at abjection because of its decidedly raw and visceral qualities, which people keep hidden in their bodies. Yet to create the kind of queer domesticity Ana and Claudia seemingly desire, this eroticism and attendant feelings must be brought outward to each other and beyond, which places both women in physical peril as a result of antigay violence perpetrated in daily forms.

Alongside its rumination on outsiders, Negrón-Muntaner's film intrepidly explores the physical eroticism of queer Puerto Rican domesticity by showing both the intimate relations between Claudia and her partner and between several unnamed women. *Brincando* depicts brief bedroom scenes in which Claudia and Ana are shown canoodling and kissing. With this moment, viewers are led to ponder women's desires and sexuality in other contexts such as interviews and imagined scenes such as an erotic montage of various women embracing, kissing, and removing clothes. This montage is a sequence of soft-core scenes, in which we see passion and urgency in the women's physical movements. What these scenes accomplish is make visible the paramount role that physical pleasure plays in the lives of queer women. Instead of sweeping the topic of eroticism under the rug, Negrón-Muntaner's film becomes an occasion to (re)consider the significance of lesbian eroticism. La Fountain-Stokes characterizes the aforesaid scene as a "seminude lesbian erotic sequence," yet its spatial dynamics are noteworthy, too.[32] The women's bodies are pressed up against one another in medium shots, while several close-up shots bring a woman's breasts into view. The scene takes place in what seem to be a person's bedroom, and the camera work establishes a subject shot, which makes it appear that the viewer is involved. Although the shot remains wholly centered on them, it is clear that the women are enjoying themselves. Viewers discern a sense of physical urgency in the women's expression—as if the dominant culture has denied them these important pleasures for too long. Negrón-Muntaner further involves the audience watching at home by breaking up the action with intertitles that question "¿Qué miras?" (What are you watching?). This query calls out the viewer, questioning them about their purpose in watching. Is it pleasure that the audience derives from seeing women engage in erotic play? As observers never learn whose home is the actual backdrop, viewers are led to consider that it could be anyone's home, thereby shortening the distance between the physical taboos of lesbian sexuality and common household spaces.

Creating such a bold film was not a simple and untroubled process for Negrón-Muntaner because of the influence of several sensitive issues. On the subject of sexuality, Negrón-Muntaner has openly expressed her hesitation and commented on the self-reflective process she experienced as she conceptualized the film's larger approaches and narrative. This hesitation, however, did not prevent her from presenting the intimacies between women as a positive phenomenon that merits a place in the film. In an interview on this matter, she explains:

> Toward the end of the film's production, I was faced with the question of whether I was practicing self-censorship by not representing lesbian sex. By ignoring sex, was I implying that sexuality is not important to Puerto Rican lesbians? Or was I censoring myself because this is a film that has public television funding and, arguably, my parents were going to watch it at some point? At the same time, does every single film with a lesbian as a main protagonist need sex? I wavered on that issue. But the idea, the thought, the horror that there had never been a film by a Puerto Rican woman representing lesbian sex—or any sex!—as an enjoyable representation won me over.[33]

Negrón-Muntaner's interior turmoil about whether to include same-gender eroticism speaks to the immense power and repercussions that come with showcasing the realities that go on behind the closed doors of lesbian Puerto Rican women's homes. However, in the film, there are several scenes in which the main characters engage in forms of eroticism. In a key scene, the protagonist Claudia approaches her bed—the bed in which Ana is sleeping. The film then treats viewers to a moment where a longer kiss between Ana and Claudia suggests their deep commitment to one another. In so doing, the film *Brincando el charco* speaks to the ways that lesbian eroticism can be a constitutive element in the daily social practice of making queerly domestic spaces.

The constitution of one's home (and homeland) are further explored in Negrón-Muntaner's film as it leads viewers to examine the social problems caused by racism and white privilege in the US mainland and Puerto Rico. In the process of telling the protagonist's own story, *Brincando el charco* shows viewers a related interview of a Puerto Rican woman of color named Sandra Andino who explains that people have expressed shock that a Puerto Rican woman could have dark skin. The woman explains that in discussions with some uninformed people, she has been asked "*¿de dónde yo soy?*" (where am I from?), implying that she is unusual or fails to fit preconceived ideas. The implication is that people assume Puerto Rican people look just one way (white), and furthermore, this moment speaks to the problematic nature of US assumptions about race as well as sexuality. The same woman of color mentioned previously explains how she regards these people's reactions as an "*insulto*" (insult), speaking to the way in which feelings play key roles in discussions of body and identity. The film develops this idea by pointing to racist phrases commonly used in Puerto Rican communities such as "*es negro pero buena gente*" (he is black, but good people). Such statements reveal underlying assumptions that circulate, yet Claudia stops short of lambasting particular people or groups who use these cruel statements. In showing these scenes, Negrón-Muntaner exposes the assumptions that negatively affect social relations and people's opportunities across social landscapes. As Claudia herself ruminates on these situations in her voiceover, she is shown washing her skin in her home's shower, where she reflects on her identity. The camerawork brings in viewers to inspect Claudia's skin, creating a physical closeness that is contrary to the seemingly distant violence of colonialism and slavery that has given rise to Puerto Rican notions of ethnicity and race in centuries past. Instead of pointing fingers at a single group, this moment urges reflection about the ways our bodies and homes are tied intricately to previous ideas, policies, and strife.

Alongside these historical examinations, Negrón-Muntaner's *Brincando el charco* provides some levity by showing how Claudia frequents queer-friendly spaces such as jovial discos. For Claudia, these entertainment spaces create an alternative domestic sphere—even though they may not seem domestic at first sight. Despite the fact that these spaces might not initially appear domestic, they still hold the potential to foster a social connection like the sort that people experience in their more traditional homes. The film explores this dimension of Claudia's character by exploring another one of Claudia's memories. When she begins to pack for her trip back to Puerto Rico to attend her father's funeral, Claudia finds an earring in her suitcase that belonged to a former girlfriend. In the flashback that follows, Claudia dances with a woman who wears the aforesaid earring in a Puerto Rican disco. As the two dance, Claudia states in voice-over, "The disco was home. Every Friday and Saturday night, it was the space I felt safest, the only space I could openly love my wanted." In contrast to Claudia's expulsion from her originary domestic home, this disco scene connotes the meaningfulness of having a comfortable, safe haven to express one's desires. The rhythms are familiar, and she appears "at home" in this dance space. On the other hand, *Brincando el charco* never suggests all discos are queer utopias because, as the film shows, Claudia is at first uncomfortable in the new discos she visits on the mainland United States. Indeed, when she first arrives in the United States she explains, "After landing, the disco ceased to be home. It became alien. The body movements, the gazes of the women that shaped my desires were absent. The monotonous music cornered me." Claudia's thoughtful voice-over highlights her self-reflective and critical-minded approach to understanding social and spatial experiences.

Accompanying her voice-over is a medium shot of Claudia standing away from the dance floor and looking markedly despondent and disconnected from the space. Claudia's own physical countenance is stiff and awkward, telling that she feels unsure and this space is unfamiliar to her; however, her dejected demeanor changes when a trio of men walk into the disco. The men catch her attention and, in her narration, she says, "But if I was to survive here, I would need to claim the bar, and one night, a group of men helped. Securing the spotlight as they walked, the disco became theirs." As the three men dance collectively, a space opens on the dance floor. Although they dance a little apart from one another, their bodies evince a cohesive choreography that reads as confident, intimate, organized, and familiar. Their dance is not overtly sexual, yet their plan is preconceived and performed in sync. Their bodies are covered fully by clothes. But as the three men dance to the music, their unity connotes ties of affinity that differ from the rest of the dancers, suggesting a familial dynamic. With this dance, the men alter the space, making it a queerly connective space for same-gender dance experiences. Here Claudia's face is one of awe and fascination. After reflecting on this moment, Claudia says, "They allowed me to imagine a space for the body that had no image." This *dancing family* reroutes the social pathways and normative practices that have become associated with the traditional heteronormative family, engendering another set of social possibilities for Claudia on the unfamiliar US mainland.

Figure 1.3. Claudia happily dances with her girlfriend at a brightly lit disco in *Brincando el charco*.

To highlight the various kinds of dance—or movement—that are done across the film, *Brincando el charco* employs widely used film techniques that emphasize the corporeal, erotic, and sensual experience of the dance space. In this way, I use a broad notion of dance to speak to the physical movements that Claudia and her fellow characters create in the film. Further, the film intensifies its focus on dance and embodiment by making use of well-chosen camera angles, color, lighting, and music that accentuate the body's prominent role in the film's storytelling. To be specific, the film uses bright light and vivid color to dress the body and code it in noteworthy ways. The film scholar Louis Giannetti explains that filmmakers use color as a device to create symbolism and stylization. This idea is apparent in *Brincando* insofar as it visually shows the disco in a much more colorful, celebratory way, thus contrasting with Claudia's prior home, which was depicted in gray, white, and black.[34] As a result, the film's juxtaposition of the disco's colorfulness and her father's dreary home only intensifies the meaningfulness and socially vibrant dynamic of the disco space. Thus, the disco becomes a means of letting go and joining with others, including her girlfriend. She and her girlfriend — "her wanted" — dance closely in this space. Accordingly, these dance spaces provide a means of moving beyond some negativities of the past. Moreover, the use of bright colors in the disco also connotes this space is open to the broader spectrum of people instead of just a select few. Rather than being a space of constraint or worry, the disco evokes the feelings of energy, freedom, joy, and a sense of human multiplicity. In reality however, not all discos can be construed as such socially ideal spaces because of how they historically have tended to exclude groups who are regarded as different from ingrained norms. As Richard Dyer shows, discos have a history of being perceived as mere products of capitalism, an economic system that has maintained limited notions of gender and bodily acceptability.[35] Despite such negativity, Dyer illuminates how queer peoples have reimagined the cultural spaces of disco in new ways, suggesting a malleability that allows for new possibilities. Recreating the dance-space means bringing in the physical dance moves of Puerto Rico and mixing them with the sonic experiences occasioned by the discos on the US mainland.

A similarly notable recreation of dance experience is shown when Claudia reads a letter from a friend who continues to live on the island of Puerto Rico. Claudia receives the missive from a close friend named Maritza, who writes about a gay pride parade that took place on the island. Maritza narrates the parade experience in a voice-over, while the film showcases video footage from the event, ranging from people marching with signs, to interviews conducted on the streets, to colorful costumes, and people dancing together. Through the film's framing, viewers note that Claudia holds an active interest in these sociopolitical matters. Through these elements, *Brincando* generates an awareness of the struggles LGBTQ peoples are facing in Puerto Rico and speaks to the benefits of queer socializing for forming coalitions. Within the narrative's voice-over, Claudia's friend Maritza explains how the parade takes place across open streets:

> *Hubo una parada gay en Puerto Rico. Aunque los cuentos son muchos, déjame darte los titulares. Lo organizó un travestí americana. La policía no quería protegernos. El alcalde negó los permisos hasta lo último. Los comerciantes se oponían a que pisáramos sus aceras.*
> (There was a gay parade in Puerto Rico. Although the stories are many, let me give you the headlines. An American transvestite organized it.

> The police didn't want to protect us. The mayor denied the permits until the last moment. The business owners opposed our walking on their paths.)

As Maritza's letter suggests, the local people of San Juan exhibit some degree of discomfort with the idea of allowing queer people to occupy these public spaces; however, despite the uneasiness, these brave queer Puerto Ricans proceed with their parade, becoming a more visible constituency in the public cityscape of Puerto Rico. In this manner, the parade-goers display a sense of pride and raise awareness by making themselves noticeable on the streets. In dancing and marching, these social practices provide a means of reconceptualizing an alternative queer experience in Puerto Rico, thereby contrasting with the previous heterocentric domesticity.

The sexual self-expressions in *Brincando el charco* modify the ordinary spaces of the city streets and transform them into queer spaces—albeit temporarily. Nevertheless, the film depicts varying kinds of anti-queer critique from religious people, and thus the film enables all people to have a say. People from various walks of life are interviewed, creating a record of the views of the time. This chronicling of such queer experiences also helps to challenge negative stereotypes about queers and educate people, creating greater tolerance for such marginalized communities.[36] Although the effectiveness of such activism remains unclear, critics such as Paul R. Brewer point to the positive and negative media coverage of events such as the murder of Matthew Shepard in the 1990s and the bullying of a college student named Tyler Clementi in the 2000s as being causes of increased tolerance of queer people.[37] In this light, Negrón-Muntaner's film does double-duty because, while it depicts activists who aim to disrupt the unwritten visual ban on queer expression, the film itself furthers that aim by making queer Puerto Ricans visible to a larger audience.[38] Like the media scholar Mary L. Gray, I believe this action of making gays visible has the effect of creating a greater sense of "familiarity." By openly showing themselves as queer to the businesses, mayor, police, and people on the street, these queer individuals lessen the so-called strangeness of queerness, rendering them understandable.[39] Focusing on business owners, mayor, and police are significant insofar as they are the ones exerting influence and sociopolitical power. In learning of these scenes, Claudia ponders their significance and makes no additional comment on them. Yet by embedding these scenes in Claudia's story, Negrón-Muntaner connects activism and Claudia's day-to-day experiences, suggesting she is a part of this hybrid community and the work these activists do. Though she is a US-based photographer, the implication is that Claudia is still a part of the island. Despite her distance, she inhabits a hybrid dimension with these activists through ties of family, communication, and memory.

Scholars who work in the field of queer studies such as the sociologist Suzanna Danuta Walters have claimed visibility projects such as parades in public spaces, function as a key form social rebellion.[40] In this manner, instead of trying to win over straight people, the parade can be interpreted as a *revolution* that claims space and takes a more forthright approach for the sake of creating a more egalitarian way of life for Latinx LGBTQs. Such processes of gathering together for the sake of challenging the heterocentrism are by no means limited to Puerto Rico either. For instance, in their discussion of queer cultural spaces, critics Lauren Berlant and Michael Warner explain that such sites exist in manifold forms like "mobile sites of drag, youth culture, music, dance, parades, flaunting, and cruising—sites whose mobility makes them possible but also renders them hard to recognize as world-making because they are so fragile and ephemeral."[41] The delicate and fleeting qualities of parades may encode parades as minor in terms of impact, but they have an effect of linking parade participants and onlookers in meaningful sociality. Even by tolerating a parade begrudgingly (as several witnesses verbalize), these onlookers' recognition of the event as a part of their world has the effect of dignifying the parade's politics as meaningful. Akin to the men dancing at the disco, the sizable parade of queer marchers becomes an eye-catching spectacle that cannot be disregarded by the heteronormative glance of Puerto Rico's public. By way of this relationality, a sensibility of queerness spreads across the city's landscape, permeating the island and sowing the seeds of sociopolitical change.

AGOSTO-ROSARIO'S SHORT STORIES OF DANCING, DEATH, AND QUEER RELATIONALITY

Like the filmmaker-scholar Negrón-Muntaner, the activist-author Agosto-Rosario is a socially conscious writer who demonstrates substantive concern about the well-being of LGBTQ people throughout his work. This effort is shown in his 2007 collection of writings titled *Nocturno y otros desamparos* (*Nocturnes and Other Neglects*) as well as pieces like *Los otros cuerpos: antología de temática gay, lésbica y 'queer' desde Puerto Rico y su diáspora* (*The Other Bodies: Anthology of Gay, Lesbian and "Queer" Themes from Puerto Rico and Its Diaspora*), which he coedited with David Caleb Acevedo and Luis Negrón in 2007.[42] Agosto-Rosario's creative work interestingly mirrors the artistry produced by Negrón-Muntaner. As in *Brincando el charco*, readers discern a manifestation of translocal domestic experience that materializes in physical and sonic forms. Prior to the present study, the social phenomena of queer Latinx bodies and intimacies has been theorized substantively by Juana María Rodríguez, who elucidates the roles of "reading practices" in how we understand queer physical gestures and sexual contexts.[43] Such critical perceptions of corporeal acts are indeed crucial to theorizing how Agosto-Rosario's writing constructs an alternative form of domestic spatial experience through stories of music and dance. To understand these pieces' subtext, we must read queerly, which involves a careful consideration of how the stories' characters enact dance and intimacy in ways that extend beyond that of the ritualized heteronormativities.

In Agosto-Rosario's *Nocturno y otros desamparos*, readers are required to read between the lines of physical moves and mortality permeating these queer spatial experiences. Mortality and death loom large, which is the antithesis of physically intimate action on the dance floor and in other concrete spaces such as apartments. Agosto-Rosario's scenes of dance and physical domesticities are also distinctive from that of Negrón-Muntaner's film where less time is spent pondering the meaning of a particular home, yet their creations share emphases on the ways that the death of a loved one affects domesticity, interior feelings, and social relations. Not all of Agosto-Rosario's stories concern the experience of dying, but two of them stand apart because they call on readers to embrace a sensibility of carpe diem with the message being: explore inner desires in the here and now because life is short. These drives for intimate relationality emanate in Agosto-Rosario's narratives as the stories portray emotional experiences of AIDS, powerful drugs, and social support for those in strife. Dancing and listening to music become a means of escaping from strife as well as a route to exploring one's inner self. Accessing such inner spaces becomes possible through musical engagement that conjures memories of sites and spatial sensations, including the warmth of crowded dance halls. In her study of Chicana music, Deborah R. Vargas reminds that there are meaningful "alternative notions of *comunidad* and 'home'" where "place is sonic."[44] Just as Vargas suggests, the writing of Agosto-Rosario illustrates how dancers and listeners can be taken to a time and place of comfort or inspiration where they first fell in love with a melody or partner. Ideas like these are shown in Agosto-Rosario's story "Incesante" ("Relentless"), where a character explains that a new song "*me elevó a un tipo de viaje místico . . . a un lugar en el que nunca había estado*" (raised me to a kind of mystic trip . . . a place in which I have never been).[45] In these scenes, dance and music have the effect of connecting the characters to otherworldly spaces as well as stirring physical sensations.

Agosto-Rosario's addition of such sensational memories is legible as a counterbalance to the weighty subjects of mortality that often have the effect of dampening a storyline. Instead of suggesting that death ends all, Agosto-Rosario's stories connote the idea that the dead remain with us in memory because of how the living continue to be the stewards of the past. Through community-based memories that take the shape of shared stories, queers keep their connections to those that have been lost during the age of HIV/AIDS. Several of the queer male figures within this narrative are shown as migrating to the United States from the island of Puerto Rico; moreover, the stories suggest that some of these characters have contracted HIV. This idea is also reinforced within the author's biography on the book's inside flap, which tells Agosto-Rosario is a poet, novelist, and activist who advocates for people living with HIV/AIDS.[46] Yet notably, these stories do not focus entirely on the multifaceted subjects of HIV/AIDS, and so these texts may be interpreted as being a part of a growing body literature known as post-AIDS writing. Agosto-Rosario's collection *Nocturno y otros desamparos* may remind readers of Negrón-Muntaner's film because like her film, this collection depicts dance scenes that have the feeling of a friendlier space. Much like the spaces portrayed in the creative work of Negrón-Muntaner, these dance scenes offer a more hospitable milieu for two Puerto Rican queer men named Antonio and Miguel. These two queer men find the dance scene to be a meaningful outlet insofar as these spaces provide pleasures that the dominant culture usually denies them in the public sphere, a place where men commonly cannot dance with one another without risking the possibility of being displaced, stigmatized, taunted, or threatened with heterosexist violence.

To the men in Agosto-Rosario's writing, music and dance serve as a means of queer conviviality whereby they can feel safe and capable of expressing themselves openly.[47] This point is visible in Agosto-Rosario's story "Incesante" in which a single song titled "Relentless" becomes a source of obsession for the two queer men. Antonio's love interest Miguel introduces the song while the two men have breakfast at a table together. This common familial scene is made queer as one of the men describes hearing a song at the disco and *"medicamentos"* (medicines) lie upon the kitchen table, suggesting the man is seropositive. Miguel explains, *"esta canción toca un lugar que duele, Antonio. Me duele, me duele, me duele tanto"* (this song touches a place that hurts, Antonio. It hurts, it hurts, it hurts so much).[48] This feeling of pain, which appears to be both emotional and physical, is also spatial. Antonio explains, *"Sin darme cuenta, ya estaba en los lugares más oscuros del alma"* (Without realizing it, I was already in the darkest places of the soul).[49] The song "Relentless" resonates powerfully with the two men, figuratively taking them to imagined spaces within themselves. To understand this song better, the two men depart from the New York area and travel to Montreal, Canada, for a trio of dance parties that actually take place each year in that city. It remains one of the largest and most popular queer dance festivals in the world. On arrival, the two men begin to notice *"cientos de hombres"* (hundreds of men) who are seemingly everywhere, engaged in various activities such as *"besándose en las mejillas"* (kissing each other on the cheeks) and *"comprando ropa para completar sus outfits"* (buying clothes to complete their outfits).[50] These phrases speak to the way that queer visitors can *remake* city landscapes in varied forms that can resonate as queer because of the preponderance of LGBTQs who regularly attend such sites.

Approximating a form of migration, the travel of Antonio, Miguel, and their brethren mirrors the movement of diverse LGBTQs who transport themselves on a temporary basis for a plethora of reasons such as escaping from the doldrums of homophobic spaces, the desire to visit family, the want of a brief respite from work, or the urge to connect with fellow queers, who are referred to as *family* at times. In this same area of thought, the researcher Ernesto Javier Martínez theorizes a storytelling motif that he called "queer exodus," which is discernible in Latinx stories from the 1980s and 1990s.[51] His study reveals how LGBTQ peoples often have felt pressed to move to new and seemingly more openminded sites. Although some queer peoples might imagine this move to be liberatory, Martínez negates such idealistic and simple characterizations of this pattern because there has been, and forever will be, a range of results in such acts of movement. Feelings of belonging, happiness, and safety may be the intended goals of such movement, though a number of queer people of color frustratingly still experience classism, heterosexism, racism, and sexism after landing in their much-desired destinations. Patterns of conformity and common practice materialize across all sexualities, stories, and spaces in both accepted and demonized forms, including at the dances that Antonio and Miguel attend.

After Antonio and Miguel arrive in Montreal, they get dressed for the first dance party of their trip—"*la fiesta de cuero*"—the leather party where everyone dons their favorite leather garb. In studying this scene, the two characters' leather clothing marks their bodies as queer because, in many queer communities, leather is a common fetish that brings diverse people together, creating what is called "leather communities."[52] Leather-related dances and contests continue to be a popular form of queer bonding and celebration in many cities throughout the world. In large cities such as Seattle, organizations hold contests to determine who deserves the title of "Seattle Leather Daddy." In the process, the organizers of these events are actually remaking the figure of the family patriarch by refiguring the "daddy" as a distinctly gay or queer personage. Like a neighborhood block party, many leather gatherings unite people, thereby mirroring the social gatherings that Claudia attends in *Brincando el charco*. This is not to say that such gatherings are always idyllic scenes because, as researchers such as Yvette Saavedra and Deena J. González have noted, white gay men historically have exhibited prejudice against Latinx peoples in queer communities.[53] Such social divides have led to the creation of Latina/o-centered organizations—intimate gathering spaces—for advancing a queerly Latina/o and Latinx agenda. Such divided politics are underscored in the film *Brincando el charco* where a gay white publisher says to Claudia, "I don't understand why you would start your book with an image of a seemingly straight man carrying an American flag. What does that have to do with you as a lesbian?" The publisher's statement shows a lack of awareness about the way that straight-acting men are perceived as the norm within the androcentric US society at the end of twentieth century. In contrast to such norms, Agosto-Rosario's story narrates how the main characters Antonio and Miguel depart from social standards by attending a large queer gathering where they bring their *"boletos"* and *"drogas"* (tickets and drugs) for an evening where they can express their desire for one another openly through physical expression. As these men leave the hotel in leather, their showy vestment marks them as "different" in the eyes of fellow tourists:

> *Salimos de nuestro dormitorio encuerados de la cabeza a los pies. Tomamos el elevador, llegamos al vestíbulo del hotel y las puertas se abrierion despacio, igual que se abren las cortinas de un teatro. Los otros turistas miraron nuestra indumentaria. Nos reimos y salimos a la calle.*[54]
>
> (We left from our room dressed in leather from head to toe. We took the elevator, we arrived at the lobby of the hotel and the doors of the elevator opened slowly, similar to that of the curtains of a theatre. The other tourists looked at our clothing. We laughed and left to the street.)

The men's leather-clad bodies mark them as unusual in the tourists' eyes. As the elevator doors open above—like that of a theater's curtains—the story suggests that these men create a visually spectacular occurrence in what is usually a heteronormative environment. Their appearances challenge the dominant US cultural scripts, yet once they arrive at the queer dance party they seamlessly fit in, connecting with the crowd. What Agosto-Rosario's text shows is that although spaces such as hotels are ostensibly unscripted, they nonetheless rely on a particular set of social and cultural codes that instills normativity.[55] At the conclusion of "Incesante" for instance, the two men who had traveled together and shown affection for one another for the duration of the story, they appear ultimately to separate and experience loneliness. Hence, while the text offers no simple palliative for the intimate challenges that many Latinx LGBTQs often encounter in relationships, it nonetheless describes an alternative and compelling form of domesticity—one that provides for meaningful social connectivities and long-lasting, sustaining memories.

Even though the men actually leave New York to travel to Montreal, Canada, their experience on the dance floors still exhibits some of the markers associated with the domestic milieu. As in *Brincando el charco*, we observe dances are a means to have fun, but these sites also function as a way of garnering the comfort and inclusivity that most domestic realms offer. These sites also are exclusive (like actual homes) because we can see the dances are not open to the public. The two men must purchase boletos to enter.[56] Although this may seem at odds with the usual notion of a home, these situations do have a parallel because people must pay exorbitant prices for homes in many geographical regions now. Thus, buying tickets for a dance might be read as having a parity with the costs of renting a home. Likewise, the dance allows these men to be themselves (and express their desires) openly—something that is not easily accomplished in the public eye of the dominant culture due to fears about the possibility of homophobic retribution. In this case, the threat of antigay violence in public effectively causes their domestic dynamic to travel. As was suggested previously, domesticity can be read as a portable or transferable personal condition that need not remain static in its spatial dimensions. In effect, the comforts and pleasures of intimate domestic arrangements traverse borders because of the way that domestic circumstances tend to resemble an exercise in memory and feeling. As these cultural artifacts suggest, queer Puerto Ricans constitute their domestic worlds through a mix of memories and sensations, such as the comforting fragrance of a partner's home cooking or the heartening feeling created by the embrace between queer peoples. In the story "Incesante," the comfort of seeing other queer couples out in the open is a reassuring experience that one is not alone. On several occasions at these dances, Antonio finds "*amistades*" (friendships or friends) and "*gente que conocía*" (people that I knew), thus finding familiarity among the "*selva de cuerpos*" (forest of bodies).[57] In pointing to the gente que conocía and selva, there is an implied unity in this social gathering where people are bonded like a family by physicality and desire.

For Antonio and Miguel, dancing at the parties of Montreal is a moment of escape from the social and sexual boundaries that the dominant US culture attempts to place around them. It is also the physical embodiment of self-expression and a chance to embrace another openly as they would at home. As they explore the dances, Antonio explains that "*Me encontraba con gente que conocía*" (I found myself with people that I knew), which brings to mind a convivial and familiar closeness.[58] Then at the Black and Blue dance party, Antonio and Miguel dance to their song, "Relentless." Once they dance together, Antonio still feels an interior physical ache, which appears to stem from persistent loneliness, despite Miguel's affection. Antonio is unable to suppress this ache, and Miguel's noncommittal stance suggests that there is no definite future for the two becoming more than close friends. Antonio explains the situation in the following:

> *Era Relentless. Nos miramos. Sin tener que decir nada, comenzamos a dejar que la música nos entrara al cuerpo. En cuestión de segundos los dos volábamos con la piel erizada. Sin misericordia alguna nos retorcíamos el uno contra el otro, compartiendo la piel pero también un dolor. . . . Miguel se fue en silencio. La puerta se cerró y abrí la cajita del disco.*[59]
> (It was Relentless. We looked at each other. Without having to say anything, we began to let the music enter our bodies. In a matter of seconds we were flying with our hair standing on end. Without any worry, we became entangled with each other, sharing a skin but also a

pain. . . . Miguel left in silence. The door closed and I opened the box of the disc.)

Agosto-Rosario's depiction of Antonio and his boyfriend Miguel suggests that dancing and music gives them a decidedly physical pleasure as the music envelopes their bodies. But it is also evocative of a pain. Dancing to their favorite song is freeing and sensual, yet at the same time a reminder of some unidentified trouble in the text. Even though the text never states what these woes are, I contend that this *"dolor"* (pain) is connected to both the emotional loneliness that queers often feel, as well as their bodily vulnerability. On two occasions in the text, the narrator Antonio speaks of the *medicamentos* and *"pastillas"* (pills) that he has to take.[60] These treatments imply that Antonio and Miguel have a serious ailment, such as some physical condition relating to HIV/AIDS, that threatens their lives. Nevertheless, the dancing at a queer party space momentarily offers an escape from the woes of illness and the constraints of heteronormativity that frequently feel like an oppressive weight on one's shoulders.

Like Negrón-Muntaner's film, Agosto-Rosario's *Nocturno y otros desamparos* shows how familiar relations like those of domesticity can manifest in unexpected places. In Agosto-Rosario's two short stories *"Sombrillas rosadas"* ("Pink umbrellas") and *"El baile de las rosas"* ("The dance of the roses"), dancing at clubs similarly brings queer people together. That is, these stories similarly point to the dancers' common bonds, mortality, and vulnerability. In the story "Sombrillas Rosadas," the primary queer male protagonist, who is simply referred to as Nene (boy), confronts a symbol of his mortality after visiting a nightclub.[61] Nene enters a club in Los Angeles, thinking *"Iba a encontrar unos amigos"* (I went to find some friends). This reflection comes about after Nene makes a new acquaintance at a dance club. When Nene becomes rather attracted emotionally with this new suitor (who remains nameless), he visits his apartment and they become physically intimate. After the two young men make passionate love, Nene notices a painting. When he inquires about the painting, the new friend explains that it has a sentimental value because it has the name of his now deceased, former companion—Alfredo—inscribed on it. The painting's artist (who also goes unnamed) has listed "Alfredo" alongside the names of other friends who spent the summers with Nene's new friend on the queer-friendly location of Fire Island in New York.[62] Nene's friend states that Fire Island was a special place in which, *"bailábamos en la playa, gozándonos el sol, el mar, los hombres bronceados paseándose todos hermosos sin miedo a disfrutar la vida. Era el único lugar en donde podíamos crear nuestra familia"* (We danced on the beach, enjoying the sun, the sea, the tan men passing all beautiful without fear to enjoy life. It was the only place where we were able to create our family).[63] As in the case of *Brincando el charco*, readers observe that a queer space and acts of dancing play prominent roles in bringing people together in a way similar to that of a traditional family reunion where people generate meaningful social bonds through physical closeness.

Further, it is significant that the Agosto-Rosario's character highlights Fire Island as creating a notable space because Fire Island has been known as a popular queer locale for queer entertainment and recreation for many decades. As in the prior cases, this site carries several of the markers that define most domestic constructs, such as an intimacy in relationships, elements of trust, close spatial dimensions, and feelings of love, among other things. However, this almost idealistic image of familial togetherness contrasts with Alfredo's death, which overshadows the prior happiness. Nevertheless, the nostalgia of dancing and family creation in "*Sombrillas rosas*" produces a more positive and upbeat portrayal than Agosto-Rosario's prior short story about dancing. In this narrative, the story focuses on a queer nightclub where a queer Puerto Rican writer named Daniel observes and reflects on a man's solo dance moves. This solitary man always holds a rose while he moves to the club's pervasive music. He becomes a source of curiosity for Daniel because he moves with impressive style, "*como si fuese la corriente de un rio, resbalaba con el ritmo de la música*" (As if he was the current of a river, he was sliding with the rhythm of the music).[64] These words suggest to readers that the man is full of life, brimming over with a significant energy. Likewise, the man's body fascinates the main character Daniel, and as a result, Daniel becomes the man's audience every time he dances at the club. As Agosto-Rosario's story develops, the social relationships are highlighted further, suggesting the socially meaningful quality of branching outward and meeting new people. The story's protagonist Daniel eventually learns the aforesaid man's identity when he helps a friend named Salvador.

Salvador asks Daniel to accompany him in retrieving a small religious altar that a recently deceased friend named Dimitri had borrowed. On entering Dimitri's apartment, Daniel quickly realizes that the recently deceased Dimitri was the man who had always danced with a rose at the nightclub. In listening to Salvador, Daniel learns that Dimitri's friends all had self-destructed by excessively using drugs and exhausting themselves by partying too much. Daniel explains that in Dimitri's apartment, he sees: "*cuatro fotos. Frente a cada una, una vela encendida alumbrada un pétalo de rosa y un tallo seco desflorado*" (Four photos. In front of each, a lit candle was shining light on a rose petal and a dry, deflowered stalk).[65] From the narration, it appears that Dimitri's dancing, roses, and photographs are a way to honor his friends, who not only lost themselves but also each other. These roses are striking too because they confer the idea that like roses, lives are beautiful, but also fragile and short-lived. The men's photographs are likewise powerful images because they provide an earthly, physical connection to the men who died. Through this homage to the four friends, readers observe Dimitri's desire to honor "the family" they created. By holding up their likenesses in this tribute, the photographs function as a symbol of their past and remembered connection. In emphasizing these portraits of the men, the story shows how significant a queer family can be to those who need it, even though the new form may not resemble that of the conventional notion of domesticity. These last remnants of Dimitri's improvised queer family provide Daniel (as well as the reader) with an understanding of the importance of men's relationships, while also memorializing those lost to AIDS.

At the very end of Agosto-Rosario's story, Daniel decides he must write about it as a means of exploring and reconciling the tense situation in which he finds himself. He says, "*Entré a mi apartamento, busqué mis cuadernos y me puse a garabatear de nuevo. Me di otro pase y un estirón de conciencia hizo que la neblina se esfumara*" (I entered into my apartment, searched for my notebooks and dedicated myself to scribbling anew. I gave it another try and a growth of conscience made the fog evaporate).[66] "*El baile de las rosas*" shows that Daniel writes down Dimitri's personal story, thus suggesting himself to be the author of this short story we have been reading up until now. In these stories, men find an unorthodox intimacy in the spaces of music and dance, where death even as numerous positive feelings begin to take shape. Agosto-Rosario and the visual art of Negrón-Muntaner recognize the benefits of supporting the social relations that take place in intimate queer spaces. In doing so, we can arrive at an informed perspective about the roles that the queer body, ethnicity, and interior feelings have in creating domestic sites.

A WORLD REIMAGINED: THE SOCIAL MIXING AND MIXED METHODS OF QUEER DOMESTICITIES

In a short chapter for the illuminating *Keywords for Latina/o Studies*, the researcher Richard T. Rodríguez highlights that a considerable number of Latinx queers both hold ties to their biological families as well as "create family with strangers."[67] The inclusion of strangers in acts of family-making may appear counterintuitive, yet for many queer people of color, family is created in a wide range of forms beyond the normative models held up by white family-makers. This mix of methods in kinship production allows more people to generate safer spaces for the pleasures of dancing, gathering, and surviving in a world that often has been unkind to queer Latinx peoples. The similar, yet distinctive trajectories of domesticity in Agosto-Rosario's stories and Negrón-Muntaner's film reveal the potentialities of gathering to dance when the heteronormative spaces fail to create inclusive atmospheres for Puerto Rican queers and their allies. Meaningful social change, however, is taking place. From dancing in Puerto Rican streets to dance festivals in Montreal, queer peoples are crafting alternative trajectories of sociality that (re)create the quotidian sensations of family and home in a more accessible formulation.

Despite that the common familial paradigm of domesticity generally is seen as being entrenched in constraining discourses of normativity, Latinx queers have reimagined the sociality of a household. This reimagined framework of domestic life is a flexible blueprint that holds potential to unite, even as it remains flexible for individuals who eschew more durable and concrete notions of domesticity. Posited as a bigger tent now, queer Latinx domesticities are sites where more people can gather to exchange ideas, mix in nontraditional ways, and question the dampening effect of the status quo. Such questioning similarly comes through in the next chapter where two young adult novels portray youths as fostering gay-straight alliances at high schools for the purpose of creating sociopolitical support. Much like coalitions, these social groups draw on a longer history of LGBTQ activism and advocacy, creating the conditions for queer people to make a space for themselves. In bringing these forms together, we discern how they call out for a new ethics of dealing with queer domestic experiences and life beyond the traditional space of family. As these pieces attest, greater time and support must be given to fostering the formation of queer hybrid spaces that interconnect the sociality of public life and homelife in inventive ways. In studying these contexts of physical and emotional closeness, we discern such gatherings as playing salient roles in shaping the futures of Latinx youths who are finding their queer way.

In sum, the artistic materials of Negrón-Muntaner and Agosto-Rosario suggest that queer spaces can empower peoples to feel affirmed and thus survive the emotional turmoil they are subjected to by a hostile, uncaring public sphere that historically targeted their assemblies. These survivals are made possible by the creators' integrative approaches, and they function as an entreaty to think more critically about how families and homes are constituted in a variety of social and physical forms. In particular, the spatial creativities of Agosto-Rosario and Negrón-Muntaner enable observers to empathize more easily with queer populations as well as rethink the ways we attach importance and meanings to space, particularly spaces that grant feelings of peace, release, safety, and togetherness. This rethinking comes about through alternative dreams, in which we reimagine the space of home, suggesting a myriad of benefits come with studying alternativities produced by queer populations in both reality and culture. Reconsiderations like these similarly help to clear the mind of limited forms of thinking that hinder self-actualization, self-expression of interior feelings, and a greater sense of well-being. Such fostering of mixed (or hybrid) spaces like queer domesticities are pivotal because they hold potentialities for enlivening our socialities and creating new spatial experiences that can enhance the futures of diverse populations.

NOTES

1. Lawrence La Fountain-Stokes, *Queer Ricans: Cultures and Sexualities in the Diaspora* (Minneapolis: University of Minnesota Press, 2009), 121.
2. Frances Negrón-Muntaner, dir., *Brincando el charco: Portrait of a Puerto Rican*, Film, Women Make Movies, 1994.
3. Juana María Rodríguez, "Sexuality," in *Keywords for Latina/o Studies*, eds. Deborah R. Vargas, Nancy Raquel Mirabal, and Lawrence La Fountain-Stokes (New York: New York University Press, 2017), 199.
4. Gloria Anzaldúa, *Borderlands/La Frontera: The New Mestiza*, eds. Norma Cantú and Aida Hurtado (San Francisco: Aunt Lute Books, 2012), 32.
5. Yolanda Martínez-San Miguel, "Female Sexiles: Toward an Archeology of Displacement of Sexual Minorities in the Caribbean," *Signs* 36, no. 4 (June 2011): 813.
6. Jorge Duany, "Nation and Migration: Rethinking Puerto Rican Identity in a Transnational Context," in *None of the Above: Puerto Ricans in the Global Era*, ed. Frances Negrón-Muntaner (New York: Palgrave Macmillan, 2007), 51.
7. Lauren Berlant and Michael Warner, "Sex in Public," *Critical Inquiry* 24, no. 2 (Winter 1998): 558.
8. Jorge Duany, *Puerto Rico: What Everyone Needs to Know* (New York: Oxford University Press, 2017), 138–41.
9. Lawrence La Fountain-Stokes, "Queer Puerto Ricans and the Burden of Violence," *QED: A Journal in GLBTQ Worldmaking* 3, no. 3 (2016): 99–102.
10. Liam Stack, "Before Orlando Shooting, an Anti-Gay Massacre in New Orleans Was Largely Forgotten," *The New York Times*, 14 June 2016, Web.
11. Jason B, Whiting, Douglas B. Smith, Megan Oka, and Gunnur Karakurt, "Safety in Intimate Partnerships: The Role of Appraisals and Threats," *Journal of Family Violence* (April 2012): 314.
12. Yolanda Martínez-San Miguel, *Caribe Two Ways: Cultura de la migración en el Caribe insular hispánico* (San Juan, Puerto Rico: Ediciones Callejón, 2003), 355.
13. Ricardo L. Ortíz, "Diaspora," in *Keywords for Latina/o Studies*, eds. Deborah R. Vargas, Nancy Raquel Mirabal, and Lawrence La Fountain-Stokes (New York: New York University Press, 2017), 50.
14. Radost Rangelova, *Gendered Geographies in Puerto Rican Cultures: Spaces, Sexualities, Solidarities* (Chapel Hill: University of North Carolina Press, 2015), 84.
15. Nayan Shah, *Contagious Divides: Epidemics and Race in San Francisco's Chinatown* (Berkeley: University of California Press, 2001), 78–79.
16. Frances R. Aparicio, *Listening to Salsa: Gender, Latin Popular Music and Puerto Rican Cultures* (Hanover, CT: Wesleyan University Press, 1998), 9.
17. José Esteban Muñoz, "Feeling Brown: Ethnicity and Affect in Ricardo Bracho's The Sweetest Hangover (and Other STDs)," *Theater Journal* 52, no. 1 (March 2000), 67–79.
18. Kimberly A. Freeman, *Love American Style* (New York: Routledge, 2003), 10.
19. Frances Negrón-Muntaner, "Comment: Dance with Me," *Gay Latino Studies: A Critical Reader*, eds. Michael Hames-García and Ernesto Javier Martínez (Durham, NC: Duke University Press, 2011), 313.
20. Moisés Agosto-Rosario, *Nocturno y otros desamparos* (San Juan, Puerto Rico: Terranova Editores, 2007).
21. On three separate occasions, the Puerto Rican people have voted on their island's political status in plebiscites, and in each case, a majority of people have stated that they prefer no change in their affiliation with the United States.
22. La Fountain-Stokes, *Queer Ricans*, x; Marisel C. Moreno, *Family Matters: Puerto Rican Women Authors on the Island and Mainland* (Richmond: University of Virginia Press, 2012), 26.
23. Shah, *Contagious Divides*, 12.
24. Jorge Duany, *Puerto Rican Nation on the Move* (Chapel Hill: University of North Carolina Press, 2001), 4.

25. Mary Pat Brady, *Extinct Lands, Temporal Geographies: Chicana Literature and the Urgency of Space* (Durham, NC: Duke University Press), 5.

26. Gilberto M. Blasini, "Hybridizing Puerto Ricanness," *Caribbean Studies* 36, no. 1 (2008): 198.

27. La Fountain-Stokes, *Queer Ricans*, 106.

28. The critic, Alberto Sandoval-Sánchez asserts that the film *Brincando el Charco: Portrait of a Puerto Rican* has a "queered notion of home" (153). See Alberto Sandoval-Sánchez, "Imagining Puerto Rican Queer Citizenship: Frances Negrón-Muntaner's *Brincando el charco: Portrait of a Puerto Rican*," *None of the Above: Puerto Ricans in the Global Era*, ed. Frances Negrón-Muntaner (New York: Palgrave MacMillan, 2007), 153.

29. Guy Trebay, "A Kiss Too Far?" *The New York Times*, February 18, 2007, ST1.

30. Irene Mata, *Domestic Disturbances: Re-Imagining Narratives of Gender, Labor, and Immigration* (Austin: University of Texas Press, 2014), 6.

31. My thanks go to Dr. Vivian N. Halloran for helping me to think through the social complexity of this scene.

32. La Fountain-Stokes, *Queer Ricans*, 107.

33. Frances Negrón-Muntaner, "Frances Negrón-Muntaner," in *Women of Vision: Histories in Feminist Film and Video*, ed. Alexandra Juhasz (Minneapolis: University of Minnesota Press, 2001), 286.

34. Louis Giannetti, *Understanding Movies*, 9th ed. (Upper Saddle Creek, NJ: Prentice Hall, 2002), 26.

35. Richard Dyer, "In Defense of Disco," in *Out in Culture: Gay, Lesbian, and Queer Essays on Popular Culture*, ed. Corey K. Creekmur and Alexander Doty (Durham, NC: Duke University Press, 1995), 408–10.

36. See, for instance, the following resources, Paul R. Brewer, "The Shifting Foundations of Public Opinion about Gay Rights," *The Journal of Politics* 65, no. 4 (Nov. 2003): 1208–20; Mary L. Gray, *Out in the Country: Youth, Media and Queer Visibility* (New York: New York University Press, 2009), 59; Rosemary Hennessy, "Queer Visibility in Commodity Culture," *Cultural Critique* 29 (Winter 1994–1995): 31–76.

37. Beth DeFalco and Geoff Mulvihill, "N.J. Student Kills Self After Sex Broadcast," *Washington Post*, 30 September 2010, Section A, Page 3; "Vote to Repeal 'Don't Ask, Don't Tell' a Win for All," *Arizona Daily Star*, 21 December 2010. http://azstarnet.com/news/opinion/editorial/article_7fde0fa5-9d7d-5350-a122-88f7f81c16ca.html. Patrick Healy, "Laramie Killing Epilogue a Decade Later," *New York Times*, 16 September 2008: Section A1.

38. Negrón-Muntaner's film has been shown at film festivals, as well as screenings around the world. According to the film's distributor, Women Make Movies, more than 463 copies of the film have been purchased.

39. Gray, *Out in the Country*, xi.

40. Suzanna Danuta Walters, *All the Rage: The Story of Gay Visibility in America* (Chicago: University of Chicago Press, 2001), 28–29.

41. Berlant and Warner, "Sex in Public," 561.

42. David Caleb Acevedo and Luis Negrón, *Los otros cuerpos: Antología de temática gay, lésbica y 'queer' desde Puerto Rico y su diaspora* (San Juan, Puerto Rico: Editorial Tiempo Nuevo, 2007).

43. Juana María Rodríguez, *Sexual Futures: Queer Gestures and Other Latina Longings* (New York: New York University Press, 2014), 29–68.

44. Deborah R. Vargas, *Dissonant Divas: The Limits of La Onda in Chicana Music* (Minneapolis: University of Minnesota Press, 2012), 147.

45. Agosto-Rosario, *Nocturno y otros desamparos*, 55.

46. "Awards of Courage: Moisés Agosto-Rosario," *AMFAR: The Foundation for AIDS Research*, 2002, 15 October 2010, Internet, www.amfar.org/spotlight/article.aspx?id=4508.

47. The study of the interplay between dance and gender is a well-developed field of research; yet, the study of such interplay in texts appears to receive little attention. Critics such as Douglass Crimp, Richard Dyer, and Gillian Frank have critiqued the

relations of queer culture to disco, showing certain musical styles have attracted queers. See Douglass Crimp, "DISS-CO (A FRAGMENT): From *Before Pictures*, A Memoir of 1970s New York," *Criticism* 50, no. 1 (Winter 2008): 1–18; Dyer, "In Defense of Disco," 407–15; Gillian Frank, "Discophobia: Antigay Prejudice and the 1979 Backlash against Disco," *Journal of the History of Sexuality* 15, no. 2 (May 2007): 276–306.

48. Agosto-Rosario, *Nocturno y otros desamparos*, 65.
49. Agosto-Rosario, *Nocturno y otros desamparos*, 58.
50. Agosto-Rosario, *Nocturno y otros desamparos*, 59.
51. Ernesto Javier Martínez, *On Making Sense: Queer Race Narratives of Intelligibility* (Stanford, CA: Stanford University Press, 2013), 89.
52. Peter Hennen, *Faeries, Bears, and Leathermen: Men in Community Queering the Masculine* (Chicago: University of Chicago Press, 2008), 136–37.
53. Yvette Saavedra and Deena J. González, "Latino/Latina Americans and LGBTQ Issues," in *LGBTQ America Today: An Encyclopedia, Vol. 2*, ed. John C. Hawley (Westport, CT: Greenwood Press, 2009), 650.
54. Agosto-Rosario, *Nocturno y otros desamparos*, 59.
55. For more of a discussion of habitus, see Pierre Bourdieu, *Outline of a Theory of Practice*, trans. Richard Nice (Cambridge: Cambridge University Press, 1977), 72–78.
56. Agosto-Rosario, *Nocturno y otros desamparos*, 59.
57. Agosto-Rosario, *Nocturno y otros desamparos*, 60, 63, 64.
58. Agosto-Rosario, *Nocturno y otros desamparos*, 63.
59. Agosto-Rosario, *Nocturno y otros desamparos*, 64–65.
60. Agosto-Rosario, *Nocturno y otros desamparos*, 63, 66.
61. In Spanish, the term *Nene* can signify a variety of words, such as "darling" or "honey" or "little boy."
62. See Beth Greenfield, "Gay Getaways: The New Wave," *The New York Times*, 14 July 2006, Section F, Page 1, 12; and Esther Newton, *Cherry Grove, Fire Island: Sixty Years in America's First Gay and Lesbian Town* (Boston: Beacon Press, 1993).
63. Agosto-Rosario, *Nocturno y otros desamparos*, 43.
64. Agosto-Rosario, *Nocturno y otros desamparos*, 76.
65. Agosto-Rosario, *Nocturno y otros desamparos*, 80.
66. Agosto-Rosario, *Nocturno y otros desamparos*, 81–82.
67. Richard T. Rodríguez, "Family," in *Keywords for Latina/o Studies*, eds. Deborah R. Vargas, Nancy Raquel Mirabal, and Lawrence La Fountain-Stokes (New York: New York University Press, 2017), 62.

TWO
Enhancing Schools

Creating Social Alliances and Queer Spaces in the Young Adult Fiction of González and Sánchez

> A home affords its inhabitants a sense of emotional and geographical groundedness. Something homemade connotes authenticity and loving intention. Home is coalition and commonality.
> —Marivel Danielson[1]

In the preceding chapter, Latinx queer peoples created domestic spaces beyond the traditional family home in apartments and dance spaces; however, this phenomenon of domestic reimagining also takes place in similar forms across a range of other sites, including schools and neighborhoods. The Mexican American author Rigoberto González portrays this phenomenon in his young adult novel *The Mariposa Club*, which portrays the story of four youths who aim to create an LGBTQ club at school, which "will be a place for future students who feel as displaced as they do."[2] Displaced by homophobia to varying degrees at home and school, three queer Latinx youths named Maui (Mauricio), Trini (Trinidad), and Lib (Liberace) band together with a white youth named Isaac to create a group they call the "Fierce Foursome," which also resembles a family because of its social closeness. This family took shape when a bold Trini "sashayed into freshman algebra class with faint traces of makeup," and Maui thought, "I knew I wanted to be just like her."[3] Trini was born as a biological male named Trinidad but outgrew the imposed male status, displaying a more feminine sense of self and embracing the pronouns of "she" and "her." Maui's admiration for Trini's bravery leads to a meaningful social relationship, which enables these youths to counter the bigotry of the fictional town Caliente Valley, California.

In contrast to their town, the Fierce Foursome collaborate to create a school club that resembles a *home away from home* for "mariposas," which is the term that Latinx peoples often use to identify butterflies as well as queer peoples. This term also alludes to how these youths are growing and entering adulthood; however, they remain vulnerable to bullies and people who supposedly guard the youths' well-being. The youths' support for one another is invaluable because their high school neither counsels nor protects LGBTQ students. This precarious social position has been documented by researchers, who find that "LGB students were almost five times as likely as heterosexual students to have missed school because of fears about safety."[4] Addressing the safety concerns of LGBTQ students requires more than simple admonishments, detentions, or suspensions for students who harass queer students. As Gloria Anzaldúa argues, a "cultural shift" is needed in US public spaces such as educational systems that continue to allow bullying and other unequal treatment.[5] Schools, for instance, can prioritize new teacher trainings that show promise in improving the educational experiences of queer students of color. It is also necessary to rethink our schools' architecture because such spatial designs affect the daily lives of students in simple and complex ways. This necessity for change comes through in the novels of the early 2000s that depict US student groups like gay-straight alliances (GSAs), which are alternative social spaces that function as incubators for supportive social structures. These alternative support systems are the necessary blueprints for creating more queerly inclusive schools for our contemporary period as well as the future. González's *The Mariposa Club* (2009) and Alex Sánchez's novel *Getting It* (2006) map out these student groups' positive impact in similar and distinctive forms. That is to say, both texts show how queer and gender nonconforming youth navigate the uneasy process of creating social spaces that "memorialize their friendships" and create more engaging learning environments.[6] Though their narrators tell stories from distinct perspectives, both texts suggest that US educational environs and domestic spaces are enhanced when we honor the dignity, humanity, and lasting contributions of queer and transgender Latinx youths.

As the gay Mexican American youth Maui narrates his experience with Trini in *The Mariposa Club*, readers receive a comparable, yet distinct perspective in *Getting It*, where a heterosexual Mexican American youth named Carlos relates how he met Sal, a gay youth who seeks allies to create a GSA at their high school in Texas. In *Getting It*, readers learn GSAs are meant to "build understanding" and "address homophobic name calling."[7] Such efforts are necessary when we consider the multitude of violent acts that are perpetrated against LGBTQ youths, which shows how queer lives are devalued. These actions illustrate a need for more socially conscious spaces—a subject that is highlighted in *The Mariposa Club*, which shows how the character Trini is attacked at a school

Figure 2.1. The repetitive and uniform architecture of U.S. schools leaves little room for diversity and uniqueness.

dance for dressing in a gown.[8] In the narrative, the school's jocks terminate Trini's strut on the catwalk by "breaking her arm and two ribs."[9] Though this disturbing scene is fictional, it mirrors the fatal attack on the US teenager Lawrence (Larry) King. It is believed that King was shot in the head because of antigay animus at his school. González pays a tribute to King near the start of his book, writing "For Lawrence King, our fiercest mariposa."[10] This dedication honors the memory of a young person, while speaking to the precarious social positioning that young queer and transgender (or trans) people inhabit. González's concern about youths' experiences also is visible in his 1999 poetry collection *So Often the Pitcher Goes to Water until It Breaks*.[11] His poems "Abuelo Photographs," "Growing Up with Goya's Saturno," and "Sinister Hand" bespeak several sufferings of young figures. In this mix of free verse, González depicts a young person haunted by a threatening figure, a father who disciplines his child for using his left hand, and a mother who abandons her child. These poems' sympathetic and gloomy portrayals suggest a pattern of concern for youths much like those in *The Mariposa Club*. Like the writing in the novel, González's poems shed light on the way that youths feel neglected, stigmatized, and traumatized in the seemingly safe home-spaces created by some US nuclear families.

Similar to that of González, the writing of Sánchez has given particular attention to the conflicts of young people by depicting queer Latinx youths in several popular novels. Along with *Getting It*, Sánchez has published young adult stories like *Rainbow Boys*, *Rainbow High*, and *Rainbow Road*. His novel *Getting It* is legible as groundbreaking because its main character Carlos is a young heterosexual male, who works with a gay youth named Sal to create their high school's first GSA. Throughout these cases, readers discern that students want to be recognized as human beings, feel respected, and have safer spaces to gather with people important to them. Cultivating such social spaces allows students to nurture the deep friendships that evolve between youth—a form of connection that I call *social intimacy*. Although intimacy has been conceptualized as amative, or based in love and desire historically, the idea of intimacy has been expanded to capture the emotional closeness and feelings of safety that arise between friends and groups such as coalitions. As Marivel Danielson attests in this chapter's epigraph, coalitions instantiate the social closeness of home, but creating such homelike spaces in schools remains a challenge because of the antigay objections expressed by heterosexual parents and erotophobic leaders who try to create a sexless, yet still heterocentric learning environment. Despite such moves, we can look to some positive examples of the 1970s and 1980s that have allowed queer youths to reimagine educational systems and create new approaches that extend beyond the simple "inclusionary strategies" that have been critiqued by the researcher Karma Chávez.[12] As she illustrates, mere efforts at creating inclusion often fail to address the way that mainstream gay political efforts are seen as participating in normative societal processes. Like Chávez, I contend that US systems such as schools can do more to create alternatives where Latinx queers are not just solely "included" or assimilated into ingrained normativities.

To understand these contexts, it is beneficial to recognize early efforts such as a queer college group called the Lambda Student Alliance, which was established at the historically black Howard University in Washington, DC, in the 1970s. Equally in the following decade, a secondary school instructor named Kevin Jennings lent his support to students for the creation of the first GSA in the US state of Massachusetts.[13] These groups and several more paved the way for schools to imagine safer social spaces for youth to gather. Predictably, these social developments led to a myriad of debates, policies, and even court cases across the United States.[14] To address these subjects, advocates and legal critics have looked to the Equal Access Act (EAA), which was passed by the US Congress in 1984 and stipulated all federally funded schools must allow students to create extracurricular groups. Most notably, this act served the purpose of guaranteeing students the right to organize prayer groups at schools, however a set of figures including advocates, judges, and lawyers also have interpreted this law as protecting the First Amendment rights of LGBTQ students at schools. In response, some conservative schools voiced objections to such groups on moral grounds and sought to challenge the EAA so they could try to prevent open dialogues about queerness. This set of actions is lamentably consistent with a larger sociopolitical phenomenon that has been carried forth by the powers of the US federal government as well as state governments. The researcher M. Jacqui Alexander speaks to these traditionalists' efforts in her examination of the modern "neocolonial state," which she has theorized as advancing "heterosexual imperatives of nation-building" in several localities and forms.[15] Alexander's commentary illuminates one of the persistent mechanisms of the nation-state: an effort to normalize heterosexuality as pure and superior, though on further inspection, these imperatives are largely the by-product of oppressive logics from the colonial age.

Heterosexual imperatives have shaped the multiple laws, practices, and priorities of US public school systems in a myriad of contexts. As an extension of the neocolonial state, many US school boards, administrative staff, and teachers have become the technologies for policing behaviors in schools and indoctrinating young minds into a limited set of gender normativities and ideologies. Nonetheless, these mechanisms have not hindered the pursuit of alternatives. Contrary to the traditionalists' efforts, prohibitions on GSAs only intensified some communities' desires to generate safer spaces for queer-friendly and gender nonconforming students. Safe spaces are still needed across the United States as bullies continue to harass queer and transgender students. However, as scholars Brian Arao and Kristi Clemens suggest, there are problems that come with keeping *everyone* safe.[16] Allowing bullies to be "safe" can ultimately enable the bullies to *continue* bullying, necessitating a rethinking of safety. Studying popular texts such as these novels can grant inspiring ways of thinking about youth spaces so students can find chances for personal growth, building bridges, and engaging in helpful social practices of civil dialogue. Important work of this nature is taken up within the narratives of González and Sánchez, although some questions remain about how these books seemingly downplay certain identity-based issues like the political marginalization of queer people, which manifests in contexts such as law, policy, and social life.[17] Rather than narrating the multiple thorny issues throughout the storylines, González and Sánchez only highlight violence on a few occasions and mostly focus on the daily conversations of youths and adults. Even so, by taking such approaches, these two youth narratives humanize the youths as real people and cultivate a more well-rounded approach to supporting queer and transgender youths.

UNDERSTANDING THE REALITIES AND REPRESENTATION OF LGBTQ STUDENT SPACES

To explain the novels, this chapter theorizes how González and Sánchez narrate youth spaces at US public schools as being sites that *can become* conducive to self-expression and student development. In the novels, the school grounds become the means for creating hospitable social spaces that their own families often lack because of extant homophobia. In this fashion, school clubs provide the grounds for reimagining the domestic ideal that emanates from the American Dream. Yet such acts of spatial creation often are complicated by administrators and community leaders, who are beholden to the whims of community, parents, and officials, many of whom remain antagonistic to LGBTQ students. Far from being places of "purity" as some parents might like, we should consider how the spaces of school can be recognized as hybrid spaces where a variety of ideas and people are interwoven—even if they are not seen as such at first glance.[18] The hybrid nature of contemporary schools is visible in the mix of "myriad currents" and "hypercomplexity" of forces that shape schools' daily operations.[19] To deny these intersecting flows is to ignore the diverse assets that students bring to class. Appreciating the actual hybrid dimensions of educational spaces is a step toward greater learning. Such flows, which include social practices and thought are theorized by Henri Lefebvre, yet their interlocking (or hybrid) nature remains less studied. To be more precise, we should observe how socially and politically traditional views of the community intersect in schools where a many students often exhibit a forward-thinking politics, which often leads parents to mislabel queer youths as troubled radicals and rabble-rousers. Sadly, such acts of labeling are evocative of another era when racial segregation and racist violence was normalized across US public schools. To counter that trend, intrepid teachers labored to make space for groups like the Mariposa Club. In González's novel, an older white chemistry teacher named Ms. McAllister agrees to serve as the group's adviser, explaining, "It's about time the school joined the rest of enlightened society in the new millennium."[20] The novels' Latinx queer youths celebrate upon hearing her words, signaling the importance of hiring empathetic and open-minded educators in US public schools.

Although their adviser Ms. McAllister may be shown as an unlikely ally, her support reifies the idea that the social mixing of various ages, ethnicities, genders, and sexualities is beneficial for vulnerable youths. As a diverse mix of youth and adults band together, more stakeholders can lend their varying skills, knowledges, and strengths for purposes such as creating a safer space where more people can experience the feeling of being *at home*. This hybrid social space made by the queer Latinx youths also registers as a hospitable *alternative* to the space maintained by purists who uphold normative practices of heterosexuality as the proper pursuits in life. To a similar extent, the stories' privileging of alternatives also is mirrored in the protagonists' homes in both *The Mariposa Club* and *Getting It*, where the main protagonists are shown as living in single-parent homes. The youths long for their second parent, though these texts never diminish single-parent structures. Instead, this familial dynamic is shown as a normal part of social reality. Latinx literature of the past frequently has held up the two-parent home as the domestic ideal, yet there is movement toward embracing alternative Latinx narratives beyond the canon. In a pertinent study of such storytelling, Ralph E. Rodríguez underscores the "limiting preconceptions about just what it is we talk about when we talk about *Latinx literature*."[21] His scholarship permits critics, scholars, and readers from all over to imagine a greater number of texts such as young adult narratives including that of González and Sánchez as being significant contributions to the continually expanding sphere of literary arts and intellectual production.

On closer study, the novels exhibit a configuration resembling an "extended family" of friends, which mirrors the more encompassing and far-reaching forms of horizontal kinship that have been theorized by researchers in anthropology and family studies.[22] *The Mariposa Club* and *Getting It* portray extended families that are integrative and thus mirror the alternative domestic sensibility shown within the storytelling of Puerto Rican queer artists such as Frances Negrón-Muntaner, Moisés Agosto-Rosario, and many more. Although the youths in *The Mariposa Club* and *Getting It* do not migrate across borders, these novels point to the fact that a considerable number of queer youths of color feel alone, bullied, and need a supportive home. These circumstances have been addressed by real queer-supportive groups, including those inspired by an independent organization that is known as the Genders and Sexualities Alliance Network.[23] This nation-wide group provides information to youths and their families about the best practices of creating LGBTQ social spaces in public schools. In a comparable fashion, I view *Getting It* and *The Mariposa Club* as providing the frameworks for queer Latinx youths to make a space for themselves and allies at schools. Equally, the researcher Daniel Enrique Pérez sees González's *The Mariposa Club* as a "how-to manual for young queer Chicanos" so that they have a means of empowering themselves.[24] Pérez's work points to the transformative power of homoeroticism and queerness that scholars such as Yolanda Martínez-San Miguel has articulated in research on displacement.[25] In this sense, queerness can be understood as a lens for looking critically at the larger straight world—an alternative means of seeing and addressing the troubling underbelly of many educational spaces where youths spend much of their time. This alternative vision enables Latinx queers to further the process of decolonizing spaces codified as heterosexual and white.

Addressing such challenges will enable a better quality of life in what many advocates say is the most crucial time of one's personal development—the years of being an adolescent or teenager. In the case of *The Mariposa Club*, most of the students are shown to be approximately seventeen years of age (at the edge of graduating high school), while the youths in *Getting It* are shown to be about fifteen years old. For this age group, the inner feelings of being scrutinized and self-conscious is acute because of the ways that bodies are changing at different rates and thus physical insecurities become heightened. The underlying popularity contests at schools also contribute stress that is exacerbated by antigay sentiment and racist harassment, which can lead students to skip school. This self-exiling parallels the manner in which queers experience a form of social exile, or as critics now say, "sexile" from their homes because of homophobic parents and relatives.[26] Even as this displacement is intelligible in several parts of the novels, the texts also show the hybrid spaces of GSAs hold promise for countering systemic bigotries. Whereas these novels' scenes are fictional, they nonetheless mirror a number of real-life experiences. In a critical exchange about a similar spatial dynamic in an organizational context, Marcia Ochoa converses with the social organizer Alexandra Rodríguez de Ruíz, where they both reflect on their personal experiences with an organization named El/La Para Translatinas, which largely operates a "social justice and HIV prevention program for transgender Latinas."[27] Reflecting on their history with the group, Ochoa and Rodríguez de Ruíz explicate the importance of their organization's support for transgender Latina people in San Francisco, California. Maintaining supportive spaces for marginalized populations like transgender Latinas, or *translatinas*—as Ochoa and Rodríguez de Ruíz explain—is a vital social effort because numerous US communities, families, public services, and institutions have a history of transphobia. Organizations such as El/La are evidence of the need to enhance institutions and systems through education and the development of helpful social spaces, including GSAs, which can take varied forms depending on their context.

GSA and gender and sexuality alliances hold significant potentials, but they are by no means utopic sites that are free from the problems and stresses of the larger heterosexual world. Truth be told, researchers have found that a bevy of GSA student groups continue to be subject to community-based expectations, forces, and negativities, which affect the multitude of experiences that occur within GSA events and meetings.[28] For instance, L. T. McCready explains that queer youth groups and programs sometimes inadvertently reify social problems including exclusionary patterns where "whiteness was normalized."[29] In light of these unsavory dynamics, this second chapter reads GSA spaces as being a social space that is *in-process* because of the way that attitudes and competencies are still evolving toward a state of greater understanding and allyship. Such spaces are budding possibilities for granting students a means for expressing their inner selves more easily (without self-editing) as well as recourse for addressing hostilities like shaming and stigmatizing. At the same time, it is worth noting that the research on GSAs has shown that creating a GSA group in the school environment can lead to fewer instances of harassment and violence in schools.[30] Making new spaces for queer and trans students helps to dignify a vulnerable population. Yet making such spaces is by no means easy. According to the writings of González and Sánchez, queer social spaces come about through the work of courageous individuals and innovative acts of self-fashioning. As a starting point, we can consider the manner in which some Chicanx and Latinx peoples have embraced acts of self-fashioning including "dress with bodily performance."[31] Acts of self-fashioning can involve bold acts of individual creativity, which take place in notable ways in the novels of González and Sánchez insofar as several of the queer youth stylize their bodies and restyle their surroundings to ensure their well-being and circumvent the heterocentrism that often feels stifling.

FROM HOME TO SCHOOL: FORGING ALLIANCES IN GONZÁLEZ'S *THE MARIPOSA CLUB*

Near the beginning of *The Mariposa Club,* the narrator Maui explains how Trini moved from her own residence to her aunt's home for the purpose of transferring to a more hospitable (or queer-friendly) school system. She begins living with her Aunt Carmen, who was once "an actress in Mexican movies back in the sixties."[32] Carmen is shown as more openminded and thus reveals how family spheres need not be limited by the exclusionary binaries of gender. In an inspiring manner, Trini resists simplistic categorizations of gender that often feel reductive and limit personal expression. Carmen's house also is depicted as being a space of compassion and love for the young Trini, whose father "all but disowned her," suggesting that Trini needs a space that is conducive to her uncompromising individuality.³³ Maui and his father recognize the importance of caring for Trini when Aunt Carmen becomes ill—a subject I take up in the pages that follow. Maui's family hosts Trini, displaying how Maui's domesticity becomes mixed by welcoming Trini into their home in southern California, a place known as "Mexican country."³⁴ In this manner, Maui's home becomes a means of supporting Latinx LGBTQ peoples on an intranarrative level as well as *beyond* the book's narrative because of the way it signals that families should not be placing vulnerable queer and transgender youths into a precarious social exile.

Within these depictions, Trini and her friends contest the idea that youths must fit into the limiting binaristic ideas that undergird much of our world's sociopolitical fabric. A bevy of scholars including Jack Halberstam, Omise'Eke Natasha Tinsley, and Susan Stryker have posited persuasive studies of the ways that transgender social experiences are being felt and narrated within US cultural production.³⁵ To a similar extent, La Fountain-Stokes's research on transgender Latinx people has paved the way for the study of circumstances like those daily animosities, challenges, and ongoing struggles that Trini encounters within the Mariposa Club. La Fountain-Stokes illustrates how Latinx and Latina/o people are forced to reckon with the traditions of a largely macho Christian society, though not all community members are hostile toward transgender people. New approaches, such as the concept of "translatina/o," give a name to intersectional and Latinx lived experience. La Fountain-Stokes states that "*translatina/os* is of recent coinage and has been employed to identify transgender, transsexual, and transvestite individuals in Spanish-speaking parts of the Latin America and elsewhere."³⁶ As La Fountain-Stokes tells us, there is an ongoing evolution and proliferation in identifications, practices, and terminology that allows people to communicate their existences. The explosion of terminology and experiences can be empowering for people who exist beyond binaries, although these dynamics can overwhelm people too.³⁷ Nonetheless, in the past decade, there has arisen an increase in the representation of genderqueer and transgender peoples in various media, ranging from television programs like *Transparent* to the major motion picture titled *Trans America*; however not all stories are told equally. In the aforesaid examples, mostly white transgender stories are mediated, while transgender people of color are elided. In the few instances where transgender people of color are represented in media and storytelling, they often have been relegated to minor roles and seldom the story's lead. In the small number of more mainstream media representations, certain problematic stereotypes often are reinforced. Nevertheless, the continually popular television program *Rupaul's Drag Race* often shows people of color who push the boundaries of gender, including several performers who self-identify as queer, trans, and Latinx, however critics also express frustrations over RuPaul's use of offensive words like *tranny*, which has been deemed as being transphobic.[38] Further, *RuPaul's Drag Race* has maintained a rather narrow ideal of beauty and glamour that demands the performers to spend excessive amounts of money that overburden people. In more recent times, the television show *Pose* has garnered considerable attention for humanizing the lives of trans people of color, where several young people live with an mother-like figure who guides and shelters young people.[39] Both *The Mariposa Club* and *Pose* mirror the real-life experiences of the past, and this realistic portrayal creates a space that spotlights the humanity and complexity of these lifeworlds.

As for Trini's queer family of friends in *The Mariposa Club*, the characters never enter into an extended dialogue about how Trini evades binaries, and hence, this approach lets Trini be as fluid as she wishes. Such approaches may read as a cop-out to those in the know, though this strategy is in keeping with the cultures of the early 2000s where people are creating and using their own self-concepts and language that are more conductive to their personal sense of self. Understanding these gender nonconforming experiences and Trini's sexile beyond her parents' home requires us to think beyond ingrained paradigms. Trini defies simplistic notions of gender and sexuality, which requires us to theorize in a more integrative (or hybrid) way where we weave together bits and pieces of knowledge to foster understanding. It is thus necessary to expand our thought process by expanding beyond prior constraints and theoretical models that are mainly extensions of white queer approaches. Omise'Eke Natasha Tinsley blazes such a trail by examining representations of people of color who are pushing the boundaries of gender and sexuality within US popular culture as well as Haitian and Vodou cultural contexts. In particular, her research on the many cultural manifestations of Ezili—a feminine spirit in the Vodou belief system—provides an alternative critical framework for theorizing nonwhite lives and experience as well as creating new solidarities. Instead of reifying simple categories, Tinsley urges readers to "find new ways to make sense."[40] This alternative framework allows the long-term work of decolonizing and expanding on the preestablished perspectives of queer studies so that there are more ways of speaking of the non-normative practices of gender and sexuality. Instead of expecting Trini to fit within preestablished theories and models, we must embrace the evolving knowledges and sociality that Tinsely calls "creative genders and sexualities."[41]

This chapter intervenes in such matters by exploring how these authors' texts lead us to ponder the potentiality of alternative gender expression as well as the social impact of privileging certain gender identities, which has the effect of downplaying additional categories such as ethnicity and race. Similarly, the attention given to these subjects' spaces has been minor historically, but this topic has been a growing area of concern for scholars within the field of transgender studies or trans studies. In a recent collection, Yolanda Martínez-San Miguel and Sarah Tobias queried, "how can one find a space beyond the heteronormative and the homonormative? Most likely, what is important about the space beyond the normative that is invoked here is not its particular location but the traversing and mobilization through which that space can become possible for all of us."[42] It is this "traversing" and "mobilization" in educational environs that serves as my focal point and sets the stage for imagining queer-oriented and trans-affirmative learning environments, whereby more students can live their lives and passions. Much is gained by reflecting on existing scholarship, though there is equally a benefit to examining how path-breaking representation is conveying the affective and social dimensions of Latinx queer spatiality. The popular book *Sirena Selena Vestida de Pena* from the Afro Puerto Rican author Mayra Santos-Febres is one such text that shows the way that discourses of music and performance spaces can become a means for gender nonconforming and transgender Latinx peoples to develop themselves.[43] In a similar context of music, the value of having trans-inclusive and queer-friendly spaces was dramatized powerfully in the popular television US show *Glee*, although the program focuses largely on the stories of heterosexual and queer white people.[44] Despite that limitation, the number of representations about trans and queerly positive groups has been increasing in US popular culture as well as abroad—much like the actual number of GSAs across the US mainland. It is this pushing of boundaries that grants many of us hope for a better life.

At the present moment, however, the research concerning gay-straight student spaces has largely sidestepped the question of how ethnicity and space play roles in these student groups' day-to-day processes such as the functioning, production, and social meanings of queer spaces. A recent issue of the *Journal of Curriculum and Pedagogy* offered a cogent set of scholarly views about some of these matters, making a compelling argument for the expansion of research about how today's LGBTQ students and extracurricular groups are motivated and shaped by the sociophysical experiences of injustice, inequality, and spatial arrangements.[45] More research is needed for the sake of finding ways of breaking the silence on the intersections of ethnicity, sexuality, and space, including the ways that school spaces are assumed to be heterosexual and white. Developing inviting ways of discussing these subjects is also needed in school districts where parents have balked at the idea of supporting a notion of queer childhood or queer youth. In the introduction to their thought-provoking volume *Over the Rainbow*, the critics Michelle Ann Abate and Kenneth Kidd explain that there exists a substantial amount of "homophobia and erotophobia surrounding (often structuring) the discourses of youth."[46] These dynamics become apparent in González's novel *The Mariposa Club*, where the young Mexican American male character named Maui continues to feel frustration about his powerlessness as a young queer person. As a result, he decides to collaborate with friends Isaac (a white gay male), Liberace (a goth queer Latinx male), and Trini (a trans Latinx person) to create a social club for LGBTQ students. Set in the deserts of Southern California, *The Mariposa Club* leads us to imagine the town of Caliente Valley as being removed from the hypothetical metropole, small in size, and politically traditional especially in terms of moral values and social belief systems.[47]

Instead of showing locations that often are assumed to be the bastions of many queer populations, such as cities, these texts show more amorphous towns that are neither rural nor urban. The novels of González and Sánchez more so present stories in small towns outside the big cities' limits, yet these sites are not entirely rural in their makeup. Consequently, I interpret these texts' locations as being like a middle ground: liminal and untethered to particulars. Like the spaces I examine in the rest of this book, the settings in *The Mariposa Club* resist facile attempts at classification. Instead they place the emphasis on social dynamics and spaces that resemble palimpsests—sites that are reimagined through quotidian acts and locales that hold varying purposes. Such forms of unfixing make these sites more fluid much like the identities of the youths themselves. Although González's text is set in a more politically progressive state, the students still face an uphill battle in receiving the final approval for their GSA through the application process. In *The Mariposa Club*, we hear Trini elaborate on her ideas for some of the possible upcoming events, yet in the eyes of the somewhat more conventional Maui, Trini goes overboard at a pivotal moment when the group is trying to convince the school's key administrator that the Mariposa Club should be approved. In a fleeting burst of reverie, Trini shares a vision of what the school would be like once the Mariposa Club is permitted:

> "I see a red carpet rolled out across the entirety of the main mall," she continues. "And the yearbook paparazzi blitzing us from both sides as we catwalk up to the auditorium, which will be decked out in gold lame and just gushing with strings of silver tinsel. It will be glitz, glamour, and gourmet aperitifs. Ginger ale in champagne glasses and a large fountain filled with glazed strawberries and naked apricots. Pucker up, my love."[48]

Charming as this scenario may be, Trini's reimagining of the auditorium as a stylish party with Hollywood fanfare is read as excess and goes beyond the plans of the rest of the group. As Trini remakes the classic, heteronormative Hollywood story into an intimate queer scene where she and her date "pucker up," she also allows readers to have a moment of limitless imagination where they push beyond ingrained social boundaries. After these youths deliver their vivacious pitch for a GSA club, the principal only says "I'll mull it over" and shows little support for this group.[49] Nevertheless, Maui, Trini, and their queer friends continue the rough slog onward, believing this social club would provide them with a means to have an affirming, open, and queer-friendly space for students like themselves. This experience takes place over the course of González's narrative, suggesting that such processes require fearlessness and persistence.[50]

Unlike *The Mariposa Club*, which is told from the viewpoint of young Latinx queers, Sánchez's *Getting It* is told from the perspective of a heterosexual young Latino named Carlos, who befriends a queer classmate named Sal for the purpose of trying to improve his public image at school where he feels unpopular, physically unattractive, and lacking in stature. Carlos hopes his queer classmate can help him to improve his style and persona so that he can "get the girl"—a beautiful high school classmate named Roxy—thus mirroring a pattern created on a humorous and popular television program called *Queer Eye for the Straight Guy* during the early 2000s. Developed by the Logo Network, this cable television show has been alternately critiqued and lauded. At its core, the premise of the television show involves several gay men that help a style-less heterosexual male to improve his image and become a suave Romeo. In this storytelling, Sánchez's portrayal of transformation makes possible new avenues of development in a way that mirrors Trini's situation where she challenges gender norms. Sánchez's larger narrative signals to readers that as queers, straights, and trans people band together to create a blueprint, they can find ways to create coalitions and thereby transform their school into a more supportive space. Henceforth, innovative social possibilities can be actualized for the sake of expanding minds and improving more lives both presently and further down the road. González employs this theme of transformation near the start by creating a special spot at the school where these queer students meet: a place they call "the Queer Planter."[51] With its capital letters, this spot is marked as having great importance, even though they show that much more is desired.

In the voice of the main character Maui, González describes the planter as being: "This generic block of cement with nothing planted in it because we live in the desert and the school needs to conserve water has been our gathering spot."[52] As Maui alludes to, this space is located on school property, yet on the peripheries of the normative social circles. Despite the planter's uninteresting qualities and so-called lifelessness, this site provides a space for dialogue and uninhibited self-expression, which is exemplified by several moments such as where Isaac is "ogling the jocks."[53] Through this use of language, the youths resignify this everyday space, adding a new layer of meaning to the scene. Through invoking these words, Isaac, Lib, Maui, and Trini create an imaginary refuge that functions as a space for discussing and sharing ideas. In this site, readers see the four talk about topics such as whether to "highjack the Prom Committee or the Senior Trip Committee," but overall it is a means of harnessing their faculties for the sake of resistance.[54] Such resistance is desirable because of the nonqueer nature of their homes, town, and high school. This text's inner world mirrors much of the United States where departures from norms are frowned on generally. The text nonetheless exhibits an existing pattern in some contemporary Latinx storytelling where deviations from normative practices of gender and sexuality serve as a key plot point. Current writers such as Manuel Muñoz and Rita Indiana depict such departures, and accordingly, the stories allow readers to envision alternatives beyond exclusionary normativities.[55] Such exclusion is depicted in *The Mariposa Club* where the drama club is the "only theater company in the history of the world not to welcome fags."[56] Rather than dwelling on the exclusion, Maui says "Screw the Drama Club" and presents his idea for creating their own group—The Mariposa Club. By creating a club, these students produce a new space and opportunity for themselves in the school's social hierarchy. Although one of them—Trini—suggests this new social group at school may enable them to grab some spotlight in the yearbook, Trini also suggests that this goal is a matter of being *remembered*. Trini says that if they sit on the sidelines, "no one will remember we were even here."[57] Hence while this key social group enables the Fierce Foursome to create a transformative space, they also make their mark in a more visible way and break the pervasive silence about queer youth experiences.[58]

However, this shared ideal of transformation is far from simple because as González's *The Mariposa Club* shows, these students will encounter several problems. To form this school club, the Fierce Foursome will need a fifth member. The four approach an independent-minded black student named Maddy, who they believe to be lesbian. When asked to join their nascent LGBT club, Maddy responds by saying, "Do I look queer to you?" and "I ain't no damn lesbo."[59] Although she initially rejects the idea, the white gay male Isaac finds a way to win her over. He uses some reverse psychology by suggesting that Maddy seems uninterested in creating a club that will send an "F.U." to the school, which causes her to form a "sheepish grin," and she states, "I'm in."[60] Her rebellious personality aligns her with the queers' goals, yet in the process, Maddy is depicted as embodying some well-worn US stereotypes including the tough-talking and insubordinate black woman. Maddy only shows up infrequently in the text, leading readers to wonder why this fifth member of the group is absent. In this manner, the text suggests that these young queer people are using Maddy's name (or image) without actually involving her. Nevertheless, in the few interactions we see of these youths, we see that they do build some new social bridges through challenging the ingrained system of heterosexism. Although less prominent in the story, she nevertheless lends crucial support as an outspoken heterosexual that helps in the creation of radical groups (or spaces) at the conservative Caliente Valley High School.

Strikingly, González's scene of recruitment mirrors the strategies employed by queer movements where leaders typically conduct efforts to extend their cause's dialogue. However, the minimal role of Maddy in the story understandably may raise questions and also rile readers who desire a more egalitarian representation of women of color. *The Mariposa Club* more so leads its readers to ponder the social and cultural dimensions of gender, even as it builds on outdated imagery of gender. This dynamic is not uncommon, yet some scholars such as Ana M. Lara have questioned how experiences of blackness and race continue to be omitted from the discussions of Latinidad. In her reflection, Lara asks "How do we 'queer' Latinidad and extend its boundaries while still preserving the ways in which Latinidad offers a social and political places to rest for bodies engaged in multiple struggles in multiple places?"[61] Although the texts considered here extend the boundaries of Latinidad to some degree, they spend relatively little time focusing on the intersectionalities experienced by queer and transgender Latinx youths such as how nonconforming queers of color often become targets because of the systemic problems of homophobia, racism, and transphobia. Nevertheless, the stories of young feminine queer men such as Lib and transgender women such as Trini allow readers to begin the process of critiquing and rethinking the boundaries of Latinidad. González's characters offer an opportunity to extend the boundaries through their gender performance. Along with the feminine Trini, one of the more femme members of Fierce Foursome is Lib, who is described by the main protagonist Maui as being a "delusional overweight beauty queen."[62] His family intended to name him "Libérate" in reference to the ideal of "achieving spiritual liberation," yet his name is finalized in a more queer way through the name "Liberace," which alludes to the flashy and famous piano player that mirrors his outspoken sense of self.[63] Despite chiding him, Maui recognizes that Lib is also talented in activism and math; although some might read Maui's words as denigrating, these two youngsters are emotionally bonded and enjoy exchanging sassy repartee in a familial way.

At the start of the novel, Maui explains that the group has an intimate bond and share a common understanding of their identities. Maui explains, "The girls—yes, it's what we gay boys call each other—are already sitting on our designated planter, the one farthest from the Senior Quad, which was our choice and not anyone else's."[64] Instead of envisioning *the feminine* as something to avoid, these young ones embrace their performance of the feminine and a non-normative way of regarding each other. As such, these youths authorize readers to engage in a variety of gender experience and become close allies to people who shift beyond normative identities. Nevertheless, the close friendship between the lead character Maui and his close gay friend Isaac is shown to be more than simple camaraderie when Isaac *plays house* with Maui at the familial home. By starting with this depiction of young love between Maui and

Isaac, the novel establishes a longing that will be continued over the course of the storyline. Maui explains "there was a strange sense of intimacy that night, me in the kitchen keeping an eye on the microwave popcorn and Isaac fumbling with the remote, a can of soda in his hand. I couldn't help myself from checking him out."[65] In this scene, Maui becomes the partner who prepares the couple's food, while Isaac fiddles with technology, reifying certain social roles that repeatedly play out in the contexts of many heteronormative experiences. Although somewhat conventional, this moment of friendship between the two young men exhibits "a strange sense of intimacy," which resonates as having a resonance of queer sensibility. Through this ostensibly ordinary night together, the two youths change the home of Maui's father into a queer abode, rescripting the norms and expectations of this commonplace site. Although this moment is fleeting, this queering of Maui's home provides a pathway for thinking about alternative ways of life (beyond that of heterosexuality) and, therefore, creates an inspiring means to imagine (as well as produce) some new meaningful social intimacies and hospitable spaces in quotidian contexts of life.

Maui's imaginary domestic space with Isaac and the aforementioned queer planter are examples of the ways that queer youth are reimagining spaces for the sake of finding some sense of contentment and safety. Unfortunately, not all queer youths have been as fortunate as Maui. This idea is reinforced in additional queer narratives such as that of the bisexual writer Daisy Hernández, in which she describes her life and her thoughts on the murder of a transgender woman—a person who was assigned the gender of male and later transitioned to female. When one of Hernández's students asks whether she wants to "marry a guy or a girl," she responds to the student by saying "For me, gender doesn't matter."[66] However on further reflection, she admits her feelings are indeed shaped by the flesh, stating "it does matter—gender, sexuality, desire, all of it. If it didn't, I wouldn't be here talking about it, and Gwen Araujo would still be alive."[67] In a follow up to these words, Hernández explains how Gwen Araujo was killed and buried after it was revealed that Gwen was actually born a man.[68] The murder's exact details remain unclear, but this situation mirrors a pattern of killings in which queer and transgender people of color are frequently devalued and thus lack safe spaces.

In contrast to the macabre scene presented by Hernández, the inclusive social dynamic of Maui's house proffers a more inspiring paradigm for youth, parents, and domestic spheres, where youths like the Trini can find a way to let off steam, refresh themselves, and enjoy another *home away from home*. In *The Mariposa Club*, Maui's socially progressive father figure counters the more stereotypical machismo that Latino fathers are assumed to exemplify. On realizing that Trini has no place to go, the father states, "your friend needs us right now."[69] Through these scenes,

González's narrative counters the heteronormative expectations that the Puerto Rican lesbian Claudia (and her family) faced when their father figure cast her out within the film *Brincando el charco*. In addition, the mother figure in Sánchez's novel *Getting It* similarly shows care, thoughtfulness, and inclusiveness toward the young gay man Sal when he visits their apartment, hence suggesting that Latinx families are indeed more diverse and embracing of sociosexual differences. Yet Maui's father is a particularly intriguing exemplar as numerous parents continue to struggle to come to terms with having a son or daughter who self-identify as genderqueer or transgender. Even though the father struggles to articulate of these differences verbally, he makes an effort to protect youths, who might feel forced to leave—as we are shown in the case of the white gay male youth Isaac, who will ultimately leave home before graduating. Maui's family blazes a trail for others to follow, instructing us to protect all young people.

González's representation of Maui's flexible and inclusive home demonstrates that not all spaces in this narrative are inflexible. Because when Maui describes his talk with Lib halfway through the narrative, we see that their original hangout takes on another dimension. Maui explains, "How the Queer Planter became Lib's office is beyond me, though the space has been up for grabs since we stopped hanging around it ever since Isaac left."[70] This revisable quality becomes clear as Maui and Lib revisit the idea of creating a queer student alliance, which seemingly fell by the wayside around the middle of the text. To be concrete, Lib proposes the idea of making their queer alliance into a more heterosexual-friendly space. When Maui asks why they should consider dropping the term "LGBT" from the name of their club, his friend Lib comments, "Let's face it, an LGBT club in *this* school, in *this* town, was only going to corral the Fierce Foursome a few photo-ops. But an alliance—that's revolutionary! . . . An alliance at the high school level is that important first step towards educating the future voters of America about *every* queer person's rights."[71] Lib's idea of creating a more revolutionary space, which moves beyond the perceived separatism of some student groups, engenders an intellectually expansive set of possibilities. *The Mariposa Club* reifies this notion when Lib asserts "we need to have a space to have these difficult conversations."[72] In these words, Lib spells out the value of creating a space where they can continually work on solving the question of their time—how can a group of queer students create a socially conscious space for themselves if no one else will? Ultimately, Lib's fervent interest in creating an official GSA is finally granted later within the story where readers learn that the Mariposa Club is "here-to-stay," which offers an inspirational statement that it is possible to create such innovative social spaces despite the existing obstacles.[73]

Although Lib, Maui, and Trini attain a modicum of safe space, their gay white friend Isaac never returns home to his homophobic family after they argue with one another. In a similarly unfortunate turn of events, a young man from their school, who is believed to be queer, is killed when he aims a gun at himself in an act of suicide. These dramatic endings convey a memorable statement about the destructive nature of antigay sentiment, homophobic negativity, and other forms of silencing. Still, the text's denouement is not entirely without hope or positive elements, and in fact, the author González found sufficient reason to craft a sequel—*The Mariposa Gown*—in which the lives of the same characters are explored in more depth.[74] This textual continuation reinforces the original text's central drive of creating a future for this set of vulnerable youths. Near the end of González's first novel, the youths' social space takes the shape of an improvised ceremony where the youths reflect on the challenges they encountered as well as celebrate their strength in surviving the conflicts before them. In this moment, Trini makes an effort to dress beautifully for her impromptu ceremony, and Maui characterizes her garb as "a black blouse and a red skirt," which Trini describes as "my Sunday go-to-church attire with a little cocktail dress thrown in."[75] While Maui counters he'll always be a "jeans and t-shirt kind of guy," the two honor each other's uniqueness in the ceremony where they clink glasses of ginger ale and toast to those who have been lost including their schoolmate Tony who "didn't make it out of closet or Caliente."[76] These words speak to the way that Tony never had the public opportunity to fully realize his interior sense of self because of pervasive heterocentrism, and hence to dignify his presence, the group members of the Mariposa Club decide to make Tony an honorary member.

The group's sense of togetherness enabled these youths to create social spaces that provided a sense of protection for especially vulnerable youth like Trini to exist without having to compromise on her personal values. However, for some youths like Isaac and Tony, the public and domestic pressures to conform become too much to bear. In this regard, the novel suggests that social spaces must be developed that invite all peoples to partake in creating safe spaces. Though Trini may lack the conventional academic abilities of Lib, Trini's sensibility of limitless imagination serves the purpose of creating new pathways. This imaginative element proffers the idea that acumen, bravery, and passion are an integral part of creating inclusive social change. By refusing to adhere to the numerous codes of daily life, the character of Trini enables readers to dream, play, and perform in ways that ordinarily are eschewed by much of the US population and the dominant powers that be. In embracing this limitlessness, Trini furthers the belief that social difference and uniqueness need not be perceived as a threat, but as an alternative. This limitless imagination offers *another route* that is consistent with the US notion of free expression. In this manner, Trini and her friends enable a new vision of social life that is not predicated on constrained thinking but rather based in the freedom to create rewarding and unique lives.

THE CRAFTING AND STYLING OF QUEER ALLIANCES IN SÁNCHEZ'S NOVEL *GETTING IT*

Much like we see in the writing of González's *The Mariposa Club*, the story of Sánchez's *Getting It* takes place in a small town in the US state of Texas. Little is said about the exact location of the town, but the description and statements suggest it is a more politically conservative town with a high population of Latinx residents. In sidestepping the geographical coordinates, the book directs the reader's attention to the main character's apartment, school, and other social spaces. This approach places the spotlight on the characters' personal relationships such as the friendships of the main character, Carlos. While the text begins with the inner desires of a young heterosexual named Carlos, who wants to have a relationship with a girl, the book ultimately turns to focus on the friendship of Carlos and a gay youth. This focus on queer life is not surprising when we consider the narratives of Sánchez, who has written several books addressing the subjects of how queer youth traverse the challenges of unbelonging and coping with exclusion in the contexts of educational social landscapes. One of his early books, *Rainbow Boys* led to sequels and has brought him accolades and respect among contemporary youth fiction writers.[77] The researcher Thomas Crisp explains Sánchez's success by stating, "To say that the books are beloved almost seem an understatement: readers across a range of sexual identities and ages and from a variety of professional backgrounds (i.e., students, critics, scholars) have affirmed them as both realistic in their portrayals and positive in their content."[78] Such positive responses seem striking, especially to readers of prior generations who remember a day when queer writing was perceived as a social threat and never incorporated into schools in any manner. Hiding one's unconventional sexuality was a prerequisite for previous generations that aimed to realize the American Dream, which had excluded queer people in multiple contexts.

In building on the success of his prior narratives, Sánchez has written *Getting It*, which explores similar questions of youth and other less explored social challenges such as coming out as an ally to queers. Much as González shows readers in his own youth novel, we see a similar difficulty of forging publicly sanctioned groups because of a lack of support for queers and some conservative community standards. Although the youth in Sánchez's story wish to place queer lives on equal footing in the school, there is tension among the school's community concerning this public mixing of queerness with the conventional heterosexuality. In this way, using the term *community* may be a bit of a stretch in this case as so many of the high schoolers shown in these texts have their own self-centered agendas and diminish queers. The idea of community is certainly a much romanticized concept that brings to mind cohesion, organization, and peace. And in a counterpoint to such romanticized notions,

Getting It shows there is no such idyllic community where everyone does their part and the community's boundaries are clearly defined. Instead, these books' locations are much more amorphous and unintelligible at times. This portrayal is unsurprising when we consider how many pieces of art, design, and fiction from the early 2000s are asymmetrical and unconventional in approach. Queer critics such as Karen Tongson has commented on this pattern by calling attention to the way our societies have come to resemble "seemingly 'centerless' landscapes" that require us to rethink how we categorize and explicate human spaces.[79] This idea of irregularity is reiterated in Sánchez's novel through its suggestion that there is no single, straightforward way to build a GSA. As I will explore, new routes will have to be imagined—as we see the characters do. Much of the narrative explores just that—how do students start such a club when it will likely face blowback? As the subheading suggests, there is considerable emphasis on the idea of *how* these kinds of alliances are created, and this emphasis on technique (or style) is reified by the ways that the lead character, Carlos, will undergo a set of changes that are both physical and intellectual in nature.

During the course of Sánchez's novel, Carlos Amoroso will become more empathetic and compassionate, which is hinted at through his last name, which translates to English as "loving" and "affectionate." In particular, he moves from being uncomfortable around queers to becoming an open-minded ally to LGBTQ people. This transition toward an ally begins when Carlos hits a low point in how he views himself, and he feels like a drastic change—"a makeover"—is needed to obtain the ideal life that he envisions at school.[80] This idea of a makeover is captured in the cover art of the book, which depicts Carlos as a lean, shirtless, and perplexed figure on the front cover, while the back cover depicts a stylishly dressed and happy young man. In this manner, the book leads its readers to question the need to shed certain aspects and take on new qualities to fit into social environments like schools. Latina/o and Latinx students face pressures to conform in a multitude of forms. In a discussion of how Latinx students engage in educational contexts, Angela Valenzuela builds on ideas of Robert Blautner and Joel Spring to underscore how some "Latinas/os and other minority groups are forced to shed their languages, cultures, and community-based identities and adopt cultural ways of speaking, behaving and interacting that mirror the mores, values, and interaction styles of the dominant, Anglo majority group."[81] Even as her work largely focuses on the pressures that Latinx students experience as a whole, her view speaks to the suffocating realities of queer Latinx students who similarly are expected to act straight and conform to preformulated notions of gender. In another way, we can extend this idea to the heterosexual Carlos in *Getting It*, who gets the idea that he is expected to associate solely with fellow heterosexuals within the storyline.[82] His association with a queer peer leads to life-altering conflicts that shows heterosexuals can be friends with queers in high schools.

Before Carlos arrives at that point of building coalitions and cultivating his social awareness, *Getting It* illustrates how Carlos faces additional stresses within his familial sphere—another site in which he desires change. Like many families in the early twenty-first century, Carlos's mother and father have divorced, creating tension. Carlos's frustration at home also is based on the fact that his mother has begun dating a new man (Raul), who stays over and makes audible coital sounds, which motivates Carlos to play loud music and avoid his mother. This situation stands in stark contrast to Carlos's own loveless and sexless life, which catalyzes a desire for an intimate connection with a beautiful girl at school named Roxy Rodriguez who has "ruby lips" and the "graceful nose of an Aztec princess."[83] This high level of physical perfection intimidates Carlos, which contributes to his own sense of insecurity. In Carlos's mind, he faces multiple social and physical barriers that stand in his way of winning over Roxy. The storyline of *Getting It* illuminates how the young Carlos experiences stress and aggravation from his teenage acne and other physical characteristics that he perceives as flaws. These feelings of aggravation are exacerbated by social-media sites. In one website that comes up repeatedly in the storyline, participants will upload a photograph of themselves, and doing that allows the user—Carlos—to rate the physical beauty of other participants. However, in the process, Carlos constantly frets about his ratings because he desires to become more popular and be seen as desirable.

In Sánchez's writing, this website is described as a "teen hookup site where your photo could be rated on a scale of one to ten by anyone who saw it. Anything over five meant you were hot. But under five, you may as well crawl beneath a rock and die."[84] This website's name "Hot-or-Snot.com" bespeaks a highly problematic system of bodily classification, which enables the marginalization of people who exist outside the majority's ideal of conventional beauty. This website surfaces in the youths' conversations repeatedly, showing how the media and online sphere perpetuates stress for a vulnerable population that already faces substantial pressures to conform. Carlos's experience mirrors what queers often go through as they face the scrutiny of a mainstream media and public that regularly put down queers. Alternative narratives provide a helpful counterpoint, though Carlos and his friends never locate such alternatives. Relatedly, popular media in the form of televisual storytelling began to offer queer-friendly productions during the 1990s and 2000s; specifically, television programs like *In the Life* on PBS conveyed stories about how LGBTQ people live their lives, but these TV programs frequently struggle to maintain themselves for various reasons such as budget cuts.[85]

Alternative televisual programs are needed for youth because they allow another means of looking at the world, in which youths may find more socially positive and inspiring imagery. Such alternative narratives may also help to keep youths from falling into ruts where they feel what the young Carlos experiences: fears of inadequacy, lack of self, and the desperation to be popular. By surfacing these feelings, Sánchez shows Carlos to be a more sensitive and thoughtful persona than many might assume male youths to be. Although Carlos might outwardly appear to be a so-called typical heterosexual youth, his inner sense of self and homelife shows that he actually experiences a positionality of social difference. As the storyline progresses, he realizes his own struggles, which lead him to recognize his own ignorance about sexual diversity and thus becomes more empathetic toward queer students. This growth shows him to be an ethical and caring human being; however, before he arrives at this evolved state of being, he experiences several difficult and educational moments that teach both Carlos and the book's readers to be more mindful of extant social problems such as the harmful effects of homophobia.

Like many young men commonly do, Carlos eschews the support of his mother and instead seeks out the advice of one of the more *out* queer people at his school—a young gay man named Salvador Encarnación, who is simply referred to as "Sal."[86] In translating Sal's last name—Encarnación—readers discern the idea of creation and birth, which speaks to the ways that he will help Carlos to grow and transform into someone new. At first glance, Carlos notices how Sal wears clothing and adorns his body in ways that come across as *different*, saying "Sal's bold-colored shirts—magenta, turquoise, pink—and shiny hoop earrings made him easy to follow."[87] Although Sal's bold styling reverberates as queer, Carlos is also surprised by how Sal fails to conform to several other gay stereotypes. In their first one-on-one meeting, Sal pins Carlos to ground, and Carlos thinks, "If Sal were gay, why wasn't he acting weak and girly? What if he wasn't gay? Clearly, Sal could beat the *caca* out of him."[88] Through this scene, Sal disproves preconceived ideas, and the two begin a friendship. Sal agrees to help Carlos improve his image in exchange for Carlos's help in founding the first LGBTQ group at the school. Through this deal, the two become closer, and Sal provides Carlos with various social and styling lessons, yet these lessons ultimately make him conform to the popular tastes of the day. Sal helps Carlos to buy new clothes and style his hair by placing highlights in his hair and finds him a belt buckle that says "sexy."[89] This approach contrasts with the writing of González, whose work positively presents genderqueer and non-normative styling forms such as Goth fashion. Developing the friendship of Sal and Carlos comes with the cost of reinforcing norms that maintain several questionable ideas such as the belief that consumerism is an acceptable route to contentment.

However, while Sal makes good on his end of the bargain, Carlos struggles with being more public about his support for the queer students in his high school. This struggle plays out in spatial ways as Carlos comes to realize that Sal wants the GSA to have a more public face, and Carlos sees that he cannot sit on the sidelines. The school's lunchroom, library, and principal's office proffer readers telling examples of ways in which ingrained policy and underlying norms make public spaces into heterocentric sites. For instance, after Sal and Carlos establish their agreement to help one another, Sal visits Carlos at his lunch table at school, which leads to a heightened sense of social anxiety because Carlos is concerned about what his friends will think of him associating with someone who is openly gay. This issue comes to a head in Sánchez's novel during a moment in the school cafeteria when Carlos's friends harass Sal. As we see with the queer planter in *The Mariposa Club*, the cafeteria is a crucial social space that has its own set of social mores, which resonate as decidedly patriarchal, cisgender, and heteronormative. This harassment is seen through the eyes of Carlos when Carlos's ultramasculine friend Playboy is walking with his friends, and they pass Sal. Playboy states, "Watch your backsides," and in response Sal says "Screw you."[90] This casual homophobia is worsened when their friend Pulga responds to Sal with a snicker, saying, "Yeah you'd like that." Sal then stands up for himself at the boys' table in a following chapter when he says to Carlos, "You tell your creep friends here not to give me shit—ever again."[91] In this scene, Sal's confident and strong approach in front of the cafeteria seemingly short-circuits the boys' typical insulting demeanor, shocking them in a dumbstruck state. This moment embarrasses Carlos however, causing him to reflect and then empathize with Sal, thus creating a stronger social connection between the two youths.

The narratives of *The Mariposa Club* and *Getting It* tell stories that suggest high school environments are comprised of varying kinds of friendships and social distances between youths. Social distances are created through the use of harsh insults and slurs like *faggot* or *fag*, which diminish LGBTQ youths. In a scholarly discussion of the epithet *fag*, the researcher C. J. Pascoe explains how one high school student understands the term: "Jeremy, a Latino junior, told me that this insult literally reduced a boy to nothing, 'To call someone gay or fag is like the lowest thing you can call someone. Because that's like saying that you're nothing.'"[92] Jeremy's statement certainly cannot represent all young people's feelings, though his comment mirrors a larger pattern where toxic language diminishes and marginalizes young people. Pascoe develops this discussion by explaining how this homophobia is in fact *gendered* because while the boys were more accepting of lesbians, they remained hostile toward boys who self-identified as gay, bisexual, or queer. Despite this dynamic, which sometimes prevents queers and straights from becoming friends, Sal and Carlos develop a social bond that resembles brotherhood.

When a youth joins the two one day, Carlos become pensive. Carlos thinks, "He didn't want to share Sal. He'd grown to enjoy his time with Sal alone."[93] This closeness shows a kind of social intimacy that suggests queer and straight youth can get beyond the walls placed between them. Together, these two youths share a brotherly dynamic and will go on to fight the heterosexist powers of their school, which is described as being intimidating and highly masculine. This idea is evident from the start when Carlos visits the principal's office with some queer students. He describes the principal's desk and office as being "some sort of battle tank, armored with papers."[94] The militaristic language conveys a markedly traditional and heterosexual connotation owing to the way many militaries historically have been unwelcoming to queer people. Despite the unfriendly atmosphere, the youths persist in petitioning their principal to allow the club to exist. When the principal resists the idea of a GSA, Carlos (who had remained largely quiet till then) speaks up in support of the idea, showing that *even heterosexual students believe* there should be more inclusive social spaces for the students at school. Sánchez writes:

> Carlos jammed his hands into his pockets, trying to keep from trembling. "But, um, according to the ACLU.org site—that's the American Civil Liberties Union—because of, um, a Supreme Court decision about something called the Federal Equal Access Act, you have to allow the club." Carlos swallowed the lump in his throat. "Even if you think it's immoral." . . . Sal stared at Carlos, his frustrated scowl slowly turning upward into a smile. Then we triumphantly pivoted to face Mr. Harris.[95]

In this scene, Carlos's actions effectively make him into a solid ally and hero—much to the chagrin of his fellow heterosexual Principal Harris. However, this image of allyship is thwarted when Carlos fails to show up for the next GSA meeting, causing strife between himself and the queer community. Nevertheless, near the end of *Getting It*, Carlos calls another meeting of the GSA, but notably his friend Sal is missing from the meeting as a result of some quarrelling that took place between them previously. Yet the friendship forged by these two youths is shown as meriting a second chance. Through these developments, Sánchez replaces the heterosexual love story that generally is portrayed in much youth fiction with another storyline that is largely a combination of a few different stories, which revolve around friendship and growth.

Most obviously, Sánchez builds on what is generally called the *buddy genre*, in which two friends work together to solve problems that neither can solve alone. This plot manifests in numerous popular Hollywood films, and in particular, *Getting It* resembles a particular strand of buddy-based storytelling known as the *interracial buddy movie*, which includes films such as *Lethal Weapon* and *Rush Hour*. But instead of showing two men of different ethnic identities, Sánchez's novel showcases two youths who have claimed dissimilar sexual orientations. The two youths also exhibit personal growth during the course of the stories, suggesting a coming-of-age narrative. By mixing this coming-of-age narrative with the buddy genre, Sánchez has latched onto popular US interests and shows the beneficial support systems that can take place between two people who might seem incompatible prima facie. As the narrative progresses, a reconciliation between Carlos and Sal is implied through their gathering in a space of learning—the school's library. Positioning the two teens' reconciliation in the library is symbolic because it correlates the inquiry and learning of traditional academic learning with Other forms of social learning, which is constructed through interpersonal communication and social dynamics.

This library scene suggests that learning about Others like Sal and his queer friends actually is in keeping with academic learning that students conduct in secondary schools. This concept of learning is emphasized just prior to the successful GSA meeting when Carlos looks in the mirror and thinks, "The image staring back surprised him: neither a hopeless loser nor a phony, made-over stud. He was simply Carlos Amoroso, a *pendejo* at times, but mostly just a typical teenage boy trying to become a man."[96] Instead of needing to create an overly stylized sense of self, Carlos realizes he can accept himself and accept others, but he cannot accept the exclusionary behavior of "bigoted homophobes" who may hurt friends like Sal.[97] By setting up the scenes this way, Sánchez suggests it is possible to grow beyond the antigay sentiment of the past, which has harmed too many youths. Conversely, the text overlooks several other injustices such as racism and gives all of its attention to matters of gender and sexuality. Sánchez's focus on gender is brought to the fore in a related way when Carlos becomes tired of a friend's sexist insults and cruel treatment toward one of his friends, thus setting up Carlos to be the hero.

One of the most homophobic figures in the text—Carlos's friend Playboy—reads as an unlikeable masculinist throughout much of *Getting It*. From what the novel shows, Playboy's friends are by no means immune to his policing of normative gender constructs. For instance, Playboy taunts one of his friends—Pulga—who is also Carlos's friend. Readers observe how Playboy harasses the boy by calling him "pussy-whipped" repeatedly and demeans the amative relationship that Pulga has established with his girlfriend.[98] When Carlos tires of Playboy's unrelenting harassment, Carlos stands up and retaliates by pushing this bully. This push leads to some physical fighting, causing Carlos to reflect that he "remained pissed at Playboy for the black eye, he also felt weirdly relieved. The fight had released something long-simmering in their relationship, though Carlos couldn't exactly describe what."[99] As these youths' tussle, the narrative tells that Carlos became aware of the problematic nature of such bullying. His self-development gave him the confidence and social power to challenge Playboy's authority. Notably the two youths' fight never is fully resolved by the story's denouement, but it leads to Carlos being defined as a socially conscious youth in the eyes of the school. Through these moments, he transforms into a heroic figure who challenges homophobia and ignorance that creates toxic atmospheres for myriad students. Carlos also learns that the presence of queer youth in schools is not as uncommon as many may assume. Aside of his new acquaintance Sal, Carlos learns that one of his close friends—Toro— also self-identifies himself as queer. This knowledge leads him to think about matters of sexuality in ways that go beyond the surface level, causing him to rethink what he knows. In this regard, Carlos exists in a kind of shifting ground where he is open to learning novel ideas and new possibilities. By way of Carlos's transformation, this narrative suggests there are multiple benefits to embracing our ideals such as friendship, enlightened social perspectives, and community opportunities that support our well-being.

CULMINATING IDEAS: ENHANCING SCHOOLS TO BENEFIT THE COMMUNITIES

According to recent studies, it is believed that there are more than 4,000 GSAs of varying forms existing in schools and universities across the United States, including Puerto Rico, and related kinds of US sites such as military bases.[100] Having positive spaces for queer and trans students is necessary because of the alarming rash of suicides that have taken place around these issues in the past decade. Although the narratives of González and Sánchez never clearly show suicide as an acceptable option, they allude to the idea and show other kinds of epistemic, psychological, and physical violence that LGBTQ students face including the feeling of being "displaced"—as the back cover of González's book says.[101] This emphasis on being "displaced" emphasizes the way that heterocentrism can drive queer Latinx peoples away from familiar peoples and places like local homes and schools. The question of sexuality in schools is by no means a new one, and in fact, critics such as the renowned French philosopher Michel Foucault has theorized this subject extensively in his pioneering volume titled *The History of Sexuality*. Foucault hypothesizes,

> Take the secondary schools of the eighteenth century, for example. On the whole, one can have the impression that sex was hardly spoken of at all in this institution. But one only has to glance over the architectural layout, the rules of discipline, and their whole international organization: the question of sex was a constant preoccupation. The builders considered it explicitly. The organizers took it permanently into account.[102]

Foucault's theory of architectural design lays bare what few administrators and teachers will discuss publicly, even as they make an intentional effort to prevent children from happening upon the taboo knowledges of sexuality. The negativity toward such personal expressions of the self has yet to be addressed substantively by the US government's agencies or the lion's share of communities. Most schools discuss a fraction of the broader spectrum of sexual knowledges in health classes, where matters of desire and queerness often are downplayed. Addressing these circumstances requires students, teachers, and administrators to do their homework, create new alliances, as well as recognize the challenges that come from negativizing sexuality in general. To address this more substantively, schools can benefit by observing how artists, intellectuals, and writers are addressing these matters.

By comparing *Getting It* and *The Mariposa Club*, we discern how these two texts provide a comment on the fashioning of the self and social spaces. These narratives make the comment that the self-fashioning of Carlos and Trini are youth experiences that show more than simply allowing for self-expression. These instances illustrate that personal transformations indeed can open up new ways of thinking, though the subsequent developments might not be what the youths first anticipated. What was imagined as the ideal often shifts when the youths' limitless imaginations give way to new configurations that challenge the school's prior notions of purity as well as other reductive standards that hinder students' expressions. Sánchez's narrative suggests to readers that blending ideas and circles of friendship at schools can lead to community benefits. On the other hand, his storyline tells that excluding potential allies and friends such as queers—to construct a hypermasculine and heterosexual identity—is an empty, isolating task. *The Mariposa Club* implies similarly insofar as the school's administration tries to maintain a veneer of heterosexuality that would deny students a chance to develop themselves as well as meaningful *alternative spaces* where they can live LGBTQ lives and build friendships.

Getting It and *The Mariposa Club* show students who reimagine school spaces, which are not physically changed but come to exhibit positive social intimacies and transformations. To develop this discussion of social intimacy further, the next chapter considers some departures from quotidian social reality by exploring the intersections of writing and social spaces on the Internet. Like many social spaces on the Web, schools can provide a provisional social blueprint for helping vulnerable students as well as beyond. These portrayals show that relatively few resources are needed to transform educational spaces into more inclusive sites. Multipurpose rooms, cafeterias, and libraries can be enhanced in subtle ways for the sake of creating queerly affirming spaces. As these novels tell, the signage, table spaces, and supportive faculty can begin the process of decolonizing schools, which filters out into the landscapes beyond schools.[103] Not only do schools become transformational spaces for youths, but they also hold the potential to be the town's locus of social change. Such efforts recreate the dynamic that Angeletta KM Gourdine envisions in her book *The Difference Place Makes*, where she contends places are "read and (re)constructed."[104] Gourdine reminds that youths and their allies *can write* the future rather than solely be subjected to it. Instead of sitting on the sidelines, these stories raise up brave students as key contributors, showing that they make a positive impact by creating alternatives that safeguard the well-being of vulnerable youth as well as fosters an egalitarian future.

NOTES

1. Marivel Danielson, *Homecoming Queers: Desire and Difference in Chicana Latina Cultural Production* (New Brunswick, NJ: Rutgers University Press, 2009), 2.
2. Rigoberto González, *The Mariposa Club* (Boston: Alyson Books, 2009), back cover.
3. González, *The Mariposa Club*, 5–6.
4. Jason Cianciotto and Sean Cahill, *LGBT Youth in America's Schools* (Ann Arbor: University of Michigan Press, 2012), 49.
5. Gloria E. Anzaldúa, "now let us shift . . . paths of conocimiento . . . inner work, public acts," in *This bridge we call home: radical visions for transformation*, eds. Gloria E. Anzaldúa and AnaLouise Keating (New York: Routledge, 2002), 541.
6. González, *The Mariposa Club*, back cover; Alex Sánchez, *Getting It* (New York: Simon & Schuster, 2006).
7. González, *The Mariposa Club*, 25.
8. González, *The Mariposa Club*, 6.
9. González, *The Mariposa Club*, 22.
10. González, *The Mariposa Club*, frontmatter.
11. Rigoberto González, *So Often the Pitcher Goes to Water until It Breaks* (Urbana: University of Illinois Press, 1999).
12. Karma R. Chávez, *Queer Migration Politics: Activist Rhetoric and Coalitional Possibilities* (Urbana: University of Illinois Press, 2013).
13. Janet Cooke, "Gays Coming Out on Campus, First Black Group at Howard," *The Washington Post*, April 24, 1980; Kevin Jennings, *One Teacher in 10: Gay and Lesbian Educators Tell their Stories* (Boston: Alyson Press, 2005).
14. The Gay and Straight Alliance Network estimates there are more than one thousand gay and straight alliances in US schools.
15. M. Jacqui Alexander, *Pedagogies of Crossing: Meditations on Feminism, Sexual Politics, Memory, and the Sacred* (Durham, NC: Duke University Press, 2005), 11.
16. Brian Arao and Kristi Clemens, "From Safe Spaces to Brave Spaces: A New Way to Frame Dialogue Around Diversity and Social Justice," in *The Art of Effective Facilitation: Reflections of Social Justice Educators*, ed. Lisa M. Landremen (Sterling, VA: Stylus Publishing, 2013), 140.
17. Ellen D. B. Riggle and Sharon S. Rostosky, *A Positive View of LGBTQ* (Lanham, MD: Rowman & Littlefield, 2012), 11.
18. Jessica Valenti, *The Purity Myth: How America's Obsession with Virginity Is Hurting Young Women* (Berkeley, CA: Seal Press, 2010), 109.
19. Henri Lefebvre, *The Production of Space*, trans. Donald Nicholson-Smith (Malden, MA: Blackwell, 1974), 88.
20. González, *The Mariposa Club*, 36.

21. Ralph E. Rodríguez, *Latinx Literature Unbound: Undoing Ethnic Expectation* (New York: Fordham University Press, 2018), 18.

22. See, for instance, David Parkin, *Kinship: An Introduction to Basic Concepts* (Malden, MA: Wiley-Blackwell, 1997); Robert Parkin and Linda Stone, eds. *Kinship and Family: An Anthropological Reader* (Malden, MA: Wiley-Blackwell, 2004).

23. The Gender and Sexualities Alliance Network was formerly known as the GSA Network.

24. Daniel Enrique Pérez, "Toward a Mariposa Consciousness: Reimagining Queer Chicano and Latino Identities," *The Chicano Studies Reader: Anthology of Aztlán, 1970–2015*, eds. Chon A. Noriega, Eric Avila, Karen Mary Davalos, Chela Sandoval and Rafael Pérez-Torres (Los Angeles: UCLA Chicano Studies Research Center, 2016), 570.

25. Yolanda Martínez-San Miguel, *Caribe Two Ways: Cultura de la migración en el Caribe insular hispánico* (San Juan: Ediciones Callejón, 2003), 355.

26. Lawrence La Fountain Stokes, "Queer Diasporas, Boricua Lives: A Meditation on Sexile," *Review: Literature and Arts of the Americas* 41, no. 2 (2008): 294–301.

27. Alexandra Rodríguez de Ruíz and Marcia Ochoa, "Translatina Is About the Journey: A Dialogue on Social Justice for Transgender Latinas in San Francisco," in *Trans Studies: The Challenge to Hetero/Homo Normativities*, eds. Yolanda Martínez-San Miguel and Sarah Tobias (New Brunswick, NJ: Rutgers University Press, 2016), 154–55.

28. Ross Collin, "Making Space: A Gay-Straight Alliance's Fight to Build Inclusive Environments," *Teachers College Record* 115, no. 8 (2013): 7; J. B. Mayo, Jr., "Critical Pedagogy Enacted in the Gay-Straight Alliance: New Possibilities for a Third Space in Teacher Development," *Educational Researcher* 42, no. 5 (June/July 2013): 267.

29. Lance Trevor McCready, "Some Challenges Facing Queer Youth Programs in Urban High Schools: Racial Segregation and Denormalizing Whiteness," in *Gay, Lesbian, and Transgender Issues in Education: Programs, Policies and Practices*, ed. James T. Sears (New York: Routledge, 2005), 190–92.

30. Russell B. Toomey, et al., "High School Gay-Straight Alliances (GSAs) and Young Adult Well-Being: An Examination of GSA Presence, Participation and Perceived Effectiveness," *Applied Developmental Science* 15, no. 4 (October 2011): 176.

31. Marci R. McMahon, "Self-Fashioning through Glamour and Punk in East Los Angeles: Patssi Valdez in *Asco's Instant Mural* and *A La Mode*," in *The Chicano Studies Reader: An Anthology of Aztlán, 1970–2015*, eds. Chon A. Noriega, Erica Avila, Karen Mary Davalos, Chela Sandoval, et al. (Los Angeles: UCLA Chicano Studies Research Center Press), 295.

32. González, *The Mariposa Club*, 22.

33. González, *The Mariposa Club*, 22.

34. González, *The Mariposa Club*, 35.

35. Jack Halberstam, *Female Masculinity* (Durham, NC: Duke University Press, 1998); Omise'Eke Natasha Tinsley, *Ezili's Mirrors: Imagining Black Queer Genders* (Durham, NC: Duke University Press, 2018); Susan Stryker, "(De)Subjugated Knowledges: An Introduction to Transgender Studies," in *The Transgender Studies Reader* (New York: Routledge, 2006).

36. Lawrence La Fountain-Stokes, "Translatinas/os," in *Transgender Studies Quarterly* 1–2 (2014): 237.

37. Russell Goldman, "Here's a List of 58 Gender Options for Facebook Users," *ABCNews.go.com*, 13 Feb. 2014, Web.

38. Jase Peeples, "RuPaul Further Responds to Transphobic Accusations," *The Advocate.com*, 26 May 2014, Web.

39. "Pilot," *Pose*, written by Steve Canals, Brad Falchuk, and Ryan Murphy, directed by Ryan Murphy, FX, 2018.

40. Tinsley, *Ezili's Mirrors*, 1.

41. Tinsley, *Ezili's Mirrors*, 4.

42. Yolanda Martínez-San Miguel and Sarah Tobias, "Introduction: Thinking beyond Hetero/Homo Normativities," *Trans Studies: The Challenge to the Hetero/Homo Normativities* (New Brunswick, NJ: Rutgers University Press, 2016), 14.
43. Mayra Santos-Febres, *Sirena Selena Vestida de Pena* (Doral, FL: Stockcero, 2008).
44. "Saturday Night Glee-ver." *Glee*, written by Matthew Hodgson, directed by Bradley Buecker, Fox, 17 April 2012.
45. See, for instance, Thomas R. Conway and Ruthann Crawford-Fisher, "The Need for Continued Research on Gay-Straight Alliances," *Journal of Curriculum and Pedagogy* 4, no. 2 (2007): 125–29.
46. Michelle Ann Abate and Kenneth Kid, *Over the Rainbow: Queer Children's and Youth Adult Literature*, eds. Michelle Ann Abate and Kenneth Kidd (Ann Arbor: University of Michigan Press, 2011), 1.
47. Daniel Enrique Pérez also hypothesizes that the location of Caliente Valley is meant to resemble the town of Coachella Valley in the US state of California, which is the place where González spent a portion of his youth.
48. González, *The Mariposa Club*, 52.
49. González, *The Mariposa Club*, 53.
50. This same trope of fear plays out in another popular text about the formation of a GSA: Brent Hartinger's youth novel *Geography Club* (2003). Despite its name, Hartinger's novel has nothing to do with geographical studies and the students use the name "Geography Club" as a cover because they view a GSA as being contentious.
51. González, *The Mariposa Club*, 3.
52. González, *The Mariposa Club*, 4.
53. González, *The Mariposa Club*, 3.
54. González, *The Mariposa Club*, 4.
55. Manuel Muñoz, *The Faith Healer of Olive Avenue* (Chapel Hill, NC: Algonquin Books, 2007); Rita Indiana, *La estrategia de Chochueca* (San Juan: Editorial Isla Negra, 2003).
56. González, *The Mariposa Club*, 6.
57. González, *The Mariposa Club*, 5.
58. González, *The Mariposa Club*, 4.
59. González, *The Mariposa Club*, 7.
60. González, *The Mariposa Club*, 8.
61. Ana M. Lara, "Uncovering Mirrors: Afro-Latina Lesbian Subjects," in *The Afro-Latin@ Reader: History and Culture in the United States*, eds. Miriam Jiménez Román and Juan Flores (Durham, NC: Duke University Press, 2010), 307.
62. González, *The Mariposa Club*, 3.
63. González, *The Mariposa Club*, 14.
64. González, *The Mariposa Club*, 3.
65. González, *The Mariposa Club*, 11.
66. Daisy Hernández, *A Cup of Water Under My Bed: A Memoir* (Boston: Beacon Press, 2014), 89–90.
67. Hernández, *A Cup of Water Under My Bed*, 90.
68. Hernández, *A Cup of Water Under My Bed*, 102–3.
69. González, *The Mariposa Club*, 27.
70. González, *The Mariposa Club*, 131.
71. González, *The Mariposa Club*, 132.
72. González, *The Mariposa Club*, 133.
73. González, *The Mariposa Club*, 148.
74. González, *The Mariposa Gown* (Maple Shade, NJ: Tincture Press, 2012).
75. González, *The Mariposa Club*, 216–17.
76. González, *The Mariposa Club*, 211.
77. Alex Sánchez, *Rainbow Boys* (New York: Simon & Schuster, 2001).
78. Thomas Crisp, "The Trouble with *Rainbow Boys*," in *Over the Rainbow: Queer Children's and Youth Adult Literature*, eds. Michelle Ann Abate and Kenneth Kidd (Ann Arbor: University of Michigan Press, 2011).

79. Karen Tongson, *Relocations: Queer Suburban Imaginaries* (New York: New York University Press), 11.
80. Sánchez, *Getting It*, 14.
81. Angela Valenzuela "Education," in *Keywords for Latina/o Studies*, eds. Deborah R. Vargas, Nancy Raquel Mirabal, and Lawrence La Fountain-Stokes (New York: New York University Press, 2017), 52.
82. Sánchez, *Getting It*, 24.
83. Sánchez, *Getting It*, 1.
84. Sánchez, *Getting It*, 48.
85. "Orgullo Latino," *In the Life*, PBS, June 1, 2012.
86. Sánchez, *Getting It*, 7.
87. Sánchez, *Getting It*, 17.
88. Sánchez, *Getting It*, 19.
89. Sánchez, *Getting It*, 58.
90. Sánchez, *Getting It*, 7.
91. Sánchez, *Getting It*, 22.
92. C. J. Pascoe, *Dude, You're A Fag: Masculinity and Sexuality in High School* (Berkeley: University of California Press, 2007), 55.
93. Sánchez, *Getting It*, 77.
94. Sánchez, *Getting It*, 69.
95. Sánchez, *Getting It*, 71.
96. Sánchez, *Getting It*, 207.
97. Sánchez, *Getting It*, 98.
98. Sánchez, *Getting It*, 180.
99. Sánchez, *Getting It*, 183.
100. Laura Finley, "Gay Straight Alliance (GSA)," 483.
101. González, *The Mariposa Club*, back cover.
102. Michel Foucault, *The History of Sexuality—An Introduction Volume 1: An Introduction*, trans. Robert Hurley (New York: Random House, 1978), 27–28.
103. González, *The Mariposa Club*, 141.
104. Angeletta KM Gourdine, *The Difference Place Makes: Gender, Sexuality, and Diaspora Identity* (Columbus: The Ohio State University Press, 2002), 18.

II

Far from Home: Alternative and Imaginary Spaces

THREE
Connecting and Performing Online

Interactive Experiences in Two Multimedia Texts by Queer Puerto Rican Artists

> The powers and the privileges technology offers are always inscribed by other circuits of power and privilege. Cyberspace is not the final frontier; it is not a space of liberation; it is not a decolonized zone where gender, nation, and the constraints of culture lose meaning.[1]
>
> —Juana María Rodríguez

The narratives discussed in the prior chapters spoke to the possibility of fostering more egalitarian spaces *close to home*, yet these pieces also showed glimmers of social belonging in alternative spaces beyond that of the US domestic sphere. This representation mirrors the realities near the start of the early 2000s where a great spectrum of Latinx queer peoples made alternative social spaces in ways that go beyond that of daily home-life.[2] Even with such moves, queer Latinx peoples have not done away with the home-space entirely; rather this third chapter illuminates how queer Puerto Ricans have adopted another set of approaches—what I call the *queerly inventive*—for enacting social spaces that cultivate positive and pleasurable intimacies that have commonalities with that of the home-space, while still allowing people to explore sides of themselves that extend beyond the common US notions of domestic life. Through this study, I examine several Latinx cultural contexts that display this queerly inventive phenomenon, which is explained as a socially engaged artistic tendency that integrates elements that resonate as highly imaginative, playful, and performative. In considering these artists' contexts, I understand their inventive creations to be powerful forms of sociopolitical resistance that resemble the ways that queer Latinx peoples are working to decolonize social spaces and pursue dreams.

In the multimedia pieces that I consider here, the queerly inventive can take the form of radical, striking, and unusual creative work that serves as a powerful and political counterpoint to the oppressive majority cultures that have cast aside and shamed Latinx queer lives. Such queer inventions consist of integrative (or hybrid) sites and scenes that reject the shortsightedness of dominant authorities that have attempted to put down non-normative genders and sexualities. This phenomenon is visible in the cultural production late in the twentieth and early in the twenty-first centuries, where a sizable number of queer Latinx artists found the World Wide Web to be one of more socially transformative spaces because they both led to new social connections with like-minded individuals as well as allowed for original modes of cultural production such as "web-conscious" storytelling that exhibited a integrative multimedia format. Although such developments were not perceived as surprising to experts in the field, some polling groups, such as Pew Research, hypothesized a so-called "digital divide" where Latinx peoples were perceived as being less oriented toward using digital media and technology. However, ample evidence exists that diverse Latinx communities have taken ownership over digital milieus, including a variety of smartphone apps, social media, and website production.[3] Queer Puerto Rican artists such as Rane Arroyo and Ángel Lozada captured these experiences in printed publications by fashioning innovative formulations that mirror cyberspaces. These pieces effectively generate bridges between materials from the early 2000s, including sound bites from the media, music, television, and Web forums. These integrative pieces are legible as creative sites of intersection where experiences and feelings of queer intimacies can be explored more openly, even if they are constrained at times by some limitations in digital technologies. In depicting these cyberspaces at the start of 2000s, queer Latinx artists challenge the common practices of storytelling as well as institutional systems that have threatened the well-being of these same communities.

A small coterie of scholars such as Juana María Rodríguez and Dara E. Goldman offer telling commentaries on the way that Latinx cyberspaces are constituted despite pervasive social forces that shape the imagined and real landscapes of the larger world. Despite such forces, the characters in these texts exemplify how a myriad of Latinx communities are creating, reshaping, and commenting on the online world in a wide array of contexts.[4] In an astute commentary on the connections between the Internet and Puerto Rican cultural contexts, Goldman explains that "The nature of cyberspace facilitates the construction of alternative communities," and thus, "the Internet disrupts conventional terrestrial space and constructs an alternative spatiality."[5] Like Goldman, I find that this alternative spatiality provides notable opportunities for queer Latinx community-building, self-expression, and resisting the oppressive phenomena occurring across the Americas and online. Even so, Rodríguez's epigraph reminds us that digital domains continue to be built within the preexisting contexts, languages, and systems of the dominant cultures, which are legible as limiting freedoms and slowing down social change. To attend to these dynamics, we must remain critically minded about the pervasive nature of colonizing forces as well as watch for opportunities to fashion alternative forms of queer Latinx spaces. Such initiatives can be explored by examining the creative work of two Puerto Rican writers who demonstrate a considerable savvy in these areas. In particular, this chapter looks to the multimedia creations of the poet-playwright Rane Arroyo and the author-activist Ángel Lozada—both of whom self-identify as Puerto Rican in their ancestry and published writings concerning the social lives of queer Latinx peoples on the Web. Their inventive writings recreate queer spaces from the Internet such as chatrooms and email accounts to craft a blueprint for resisting normative forms of sociality and storytelling. In the process, their texts put forth resistances to accepted styles and social mores of Anglophone dominant cultures.

In Arroyo's collection of writings, *How to Name a Hurricane*, and Lozada's novel, *No quiero quedarme sola y vacía* (*I Don't Want to End Up Alone and Empty*), several Latinx figures use the Internet to extend their friendships across vast distances and find amorous connections with new people. Specifically, Arroyo's "Cyber Conquistadores" consists of several short email messages that are exchanged between a main figure named Santo and his friends. Arroyo's short pieces of writing are included in a collection, many of which are integrative in composition. In these cases, Arroyo's email messages link poetic phrasing with elements of popular culture, which is visible when he writes "Eye candy tastes better with J-Lo feeding the ears."[6] This eclectic mix might be labeled as being short forms of free verse, however such taxonomy belies the textual complexity of Arroyo's creative project. These integrative pieces constitute a hybrid space where media and writing come together intimately, showing the ways that people socialize digitally. English and Spanish are mixed with words of the digital domain, including hybrid terms such as we find in Arroyo's text where a chatroom is titled "Str8menLook2," which brings to mind how heterosexuals might actually be more *heteroflexible* than they admit. This mixing of language and desire is certainly not uncommon. In fact, these connectivities were theorized by the poet and theorist Gloria Anzaldúa, who explained that "at the juncture of cultures, languages cross-pollinate and are revitalized."[7] This hybridizing and revitalization is an inventive form of play that has caught on and mirrors the communications of Instagram, Twitter, Grindr, Growlr, and other popular new media forms. These writings showcase figures that are connective in approach and aim to shorten the social distances created by systemic biases like homophobia, racism, and related social ills that arise in patriarchal cultures. Developing an understanding of these writings' portrayals allows a nuanced knowledge of the ways that interpersonal relations can shape the making of community spaces in Latinx communities.

As Arroyo and Lozada represent popular approaches for socializing in virtual spaces, they offer readers new formulations of more traditional genres of writing, including love poetry and epistolary fiction—writings that have played key roles in documenting remarkable personal events and feelings textually. To be more precise, instead of creating a monotextual narrative, their work embraces the multiplicity of feelings, identities, and spaces that make up the wide range of queer Latinx lives daily. This hybrid quality becomes further apparent as the textual characters play several social roles such as in the case of Lozada's main character la Loca, who performs for readers in the text in moments where they imagine they are a cyborg-like character named "Seven of Nine," a sexually charged figure from the 1990s television show *Star Trek: Voyager*.[8] Incorporating this cyborg figure near the very start of the text fittingly exemplifies the hybridizing of human and machine that manifests in the rest of Lozada's unorthodox narrative, where Lozada blends the story of la Loca with images of performance, performers, music, and text in diverse forms.[9] In these performative scenarios, the texts' speakers call attention to the physical spaces of their bodies, commenting on the ways bodies are mapped for several purposes like specifying the real dimensions of erotic intimacies and the fact that queer bodies become vulnerable to violent assailants when they communicate with unknown figures online.[10] These acts of body mapping and performance are legible as illuminating the ways that queer Latinx bodies and identities are linked to online spaces, yet face difficult questions such as—How does one negotiate the back-and-forth between online and offline world in a safe manner? How should queers reconcile the varying truths manifesting in *the digital* and *the real*?

During the 1990s and early 2000s, researchers in several academic fields pointed to the ways that bodies are imagined as having notable spatial dimensions and sexual qualities that play substantive roles in constituting quotidian life.[11] The physical spaces created by human bodies can be made tangible and tactile through grounding experiences like that of the five senses as well as charting perceptions like the notion of "personal space" that often feels crucial as we interact with myriad people socially in the real, material world. Although the Internet may be perceived as untactile at first glance, much of the Internet is concerned with corporeality like the explicit materials of pornography, dance performances, health websites, and sports. Among this plethora of physical imagery, the bodies of people of color repeatedly are eroticized and perceived as taking up public space—a peculiar, racist notion predicated on the idea that white bodies are the assumed norm in most public spaces. In the eyes of white observers, bodies of color are perceived as Other—

neither the norm, nor belonging in public spaces. Hence, instead of taking bodies for granted, this chapter develops an interpretation of how two queer Puerto Rican texts exhibit striking bodily intimacies and corporeal resistance that act against normative discourses of bodily propriety. Instead of showcasing so-called ideal white bodies engaged in normative heterosexual practices, these texts' bodies are presented in irreverent and sexually transgressive situations. These texts thus transgress normative practices on two levels. That is, while the authors are cross genres into a hybrid format, the characters also cross boundaries in response to the quotidian prohibition against queerness in heteronormative contexts. This queerly inventive approach of challenging restrictive norms and public spaces through transgression is a demonstration of the way that queer Latinx peoples are engaging in what Leticia Alvarado calls "abject performative strategies."[12] For Alvarado, such strategies provide a means of moving "beyond the entrenchment of respectability politics" that places constraints on our freedoms, our sense of self, and our social imaginary.[13] Such abject stratagems enable alternative ways of imagining Latinx lives and the world. By exploring such abject, irreverent experience within multimedia contexts, Arroyo and Lozada highlight how queer Latinx bodies are immersed in cultural scripts where non-normative social performances are deeply personal, political, and pleasurable. By exploring these intimate and integrative acts of digital sociality, the texts lead us to ponder what is "real" and how notions of reality shape our concepts of daily relationality.

As Arroyo and Lozada have been perceived as using personal experience in their writings, scholars would contend there are benefits to considering these authors' own real-life experiences. These light-skinned and gay Puerto Rican authors lived on the US mainland for many years yet have deep familial ties to the island cultures of Puerto Rico. These personal experiences are reflected in the storytelling, even as these works go beyond the genre of memoir and autobiographical writing. These authors capture the realism of online interactions, yet their writing also makes use of several key elements that play key roles in creating a playful and inventive sentiment. The social tensions, for instance, within these two authors' writings are depicted as driving the characters and performers to act in ways that are bound to be viewed as comical and unusual. Lozada's use of expletives and a lusty character fascinated by sex toys largely create a realistic and irreverent dimension in these scenes. These erotically inventive moments work against the staid sense of propriety pervading the US public sphere at the start of the twenty-first century. Showing the realities of sexuality more openly than the prior texts, these writings offer readers a space to reflect on what it means to be "oneself" and explore possibilities beyond normative place-making sanctioned by Anglophone dominant cultures. As such, Arroyo and Lozada effectively create artistic blends like those of Anzaldúa in her commentary and cultural theory. Like her, they show how the bridging of cultural elements leads to pioneering cultural forms that depart from the sort of work anticipated from mainstream Latinx artists.

Bringing together Latinx queers, these mixed-media productions draw in diverse audiences and allow for the building of new coalitions and community that challenge the status quo. As scholars like Richard T. Rodríguez has shown, LGBTQ communities have fostered a mixed "queer familia" by finding common cause in social spaces and movements.[14] In an extension of these ideas, this chapter explains how the Arroyo and Lozada use provocative approaches from the online world to create a queerly inventive form of writing that holds potential to activate critical thinking and reader consciousness beyond the physical confines of their local communities. To say it in another way, I contend this writing fosters deeper contemplation about what it means to live as an openly queer Puerto Rican person in the United States where the expectations for moral conduct and normative identity practices collude to create constraining circumstances. Wrestling with expectations and logics of capitalist cultures, the characters try to let off steam by pursuing the pleasures of online and face-to-face acts of sexual expression. In verbalizing desires, readers observe online performances that mix language and embrace online lingos, which results in a hybrid and queer form of composition. I theorize this hybrid occurrence as manifesting across the authors' texts, including in the contexts of the characters' identities and the antinormative qualities of the textual materials themselves. For instance, the authors instantiate these innovative hybrid texts by blending literary genres and languages, such as English and Spanish; moreover, this approach is perceivable in moments such as when Lozada's main character describes their attempts at connecting over the Internet by using the hybrid word "*clickea*"[15] (i.e., they click), which can be read as changing the English "click" into a Spanish verb, thereby creating verbal pathways that allow for greater freedom.

Across the narratives of Arroyo and Lozada, the characters' deviation from the textual norm ostensibly mirrors the way that the characters stray from the accepted national paradigms of gender and sexuality. Lozada's text explains this idea most clearly at the beginning of his text where his protagonist, who self-identifies as "la Loca" (or madwoman) describes their identity in a feminine and third-person manner, which enacts a multilayered persona. Yet the book also suggests this main character was born a male. This mixing of genders is also visible when the main character makes the following statement near the text's beginning: "*Lo combina todo*."[16] This phrase could be translated as "She combines it all," "He combines it all," and "They combine it all" because in this statement, no gendered pronoun is used. Hence to honor this character's fluid identity, I use "they" when speaking of la Loca so that they are neither misgendered, nor limited by a particular identifier. Further, this statement of "combine it all" fittingly encapsulates Lozada's overarching modus operandi in the book insofar as this text synthesizes varying materials, languages, and cultural experiences. *How to Survive a Hurricane* and *No quiero quedarme sola y vacía* resemble a queer performance of hybridity that resists the divisiveness of strict social structures, such as the homophobic and transphobic policy that is still found woven into many US national practices. Moving beyond the hostilities of daily life, these cyber-performances resist normativities as well as create opportunities for connection and social engagement with people who similarly value queer desires and sexual practices.

As researchers such as William V. Flores and Rina Benmayor have shown, Latinx populations craft a range of connectivity and community-building in multiple spaces, creating an experience that has been called "cultural citizenship."[17] Such theories of citizenship focus on the claiming of space, which offers a productive means for considering how queer Latinx figures such as la Loca inhabit digital spaces that resist dominant beliefs like the idea that queer sexualities are problematic and should remain hidden. Instead of hiding these lives, Lozada and Arroyo offer performative texts that bring the online realities (or truths) of queer sexualities into the open for readers to ponder. This resistance counters the dominant US culture's repressive ideals of moral and cultural purity, which shore up several discriminatory notions such as the fallacious idea that white and heterosexual lives are superior. These hybrid texts can be read as countering problematic sociopolitical imperatives, which have been found to have the effect of inhibiting individual expressions such as personal statements about who we love.[18]

APPROACHES FOR THE WEB-CONSCIOUS TEXTS OF PUERTO RICAN QUEERS

Both Arroyo's collection of writings *How to Name a Hurricane* and Lozada's experimental novel *No quiero quedarme sola y vacia* exhibit striking similarities that call on us to consider the significance of their unusual, parallel approaches. A cultural analysis of these texts' similarities provides a more nuanced understanding of the ways that queer Latinx peoples communicate, perform a range of identities in the online world, and respond to quotidian challenges such as a lack of spaces where they can perform their desires openly. This lack of spaces leads to the creation of diverse online platforms, and although these texts only capture a partial sense of what virtual intimacy can be, they illustrate the potentials of weaving textual spaces. However, these online spaces are predicated on a set of unwritten (or unspoken) rules that depart from conventional (and heteronormative) social expectations, thus creating certain challenges as well as opportunities for queer Latinx people like those shown in these texts. For instance, within Arroyo's writing, we observe a secondary character describe his own online identity as a "mask," thereby signaling that in the online world we create different versions of ourselves, some of which may appear untrue by USs dominant standards.[19] Although the idea of "masking" may resonate as disingenuous, I interpret this element as illustrating the ways that people indeed perform various senses of self that are hybrid and depend on several factors such as social contexts and other personal circumstances. Recently, Alice Marwick has documented how people use social media to create ideal (and alternative) versions of themselves outside of who they typically present themselves to be in the landscapes of the real material world.[20] This same idea is echoed in Lozada's experimental novel in several forms; therefore, I find that these layered social portrayals of the queer Puerto Rican body encourage us to move beyond simple heteropatriarchal notions of Latinx identity, as well as beckon us to consider the ways in which sexuality complicates views on color, ethnicity, and race.

My project does not attempt to assign any identity forcefully, but rather it critically examines how the subjects portrayed in the aforesaid texts negotiate the experience of creating queer Latinx cultural identities online. As I explain, the characters' personal identities appear multifaceted and at times partial, which suggests that these queer hybrid experiences are by no means easily generalizable or uniform. My use of the phrase *queer hybrid identities* allows me to hypothesize and unpack a portrayal of cyberspace experiences that comments on today's diverse queer Latinx life-paths in online spaces. To begin, I interpret these two texts' forms and their characters as being highly inventive composites of several disparate social and cultural elements such as poetry, popular music, and related mainstream forms of media. In this fashion, these creations resemble what Lawrence La Fountain-Stokes has identified as "ghetto bricolage."[21] La Fountain-Stokes understands a range of queer Puerto Rican artists as building on the ideas and materials available to them in their local neighborhoods and beyond. Hence, instead of thinking solely in terms of a class-based spatial formation, this volume ruminates on the manner in which these texts portray space as having a mix of cultural and linguistic ties. In portraying this mix, Arroyo and Lozada make the comment that embracing hybridity is a creative means of responding to the constraints and so-called *truths* that many antigay groups have tried to impose on queer Latinx people and the many diverse allies who take up queer causes. In this way, Arroyo and Lozada counter purity discourses that are used to mobilize unrealistic goals of achieving norms of respectability and maintaining "truths" that often have the effect of making hybrid identities be seen as "less-than" or problematic to the public sphere.

Although online spaces certainly cannot ameliorate all problems related to the discourses of purity and respectability, the mixed-media texts of

Arroyo and Lozada further the idea that in the contexts of online spaces, there are other ways of thinking about self-image and public image. Instead of seeing queer online spaces as having the same ideals and norms of the mainstream media's notion of the public sphere, there are other so-called expectations, rules, and views about how one should act and interact with others. In Lozada's case, for example, he illustrates how the main character la Loca stretches the truth about their physical being, and la Loca admits these fibs when they explain their actions in the third-person voice: "Neither is she looking for an LTR [long term relationship], that's a lie, she's looking for sex. But like almost all the queens on the Internet, she's dishonest" (*Tampoco busca LTR, eso es mentira, busca sexo. Pero como casi todas las locas en el Internet, es deshonesta*).[22] The online world enables la Loca to manipulate their public image and create a persona that is more physically appealing, thus enhancing their own respectability within the online world. Although some ethicists might see this behavior as deviating from the dominant ethical way of thinking, such behaviors have become the new norm because of how people wish to create the life they most desire. Indeed, significant time has been devoted to thinking about the potentials and shortcomings of technological landscapes, such as the potential for truth-stretching and the breakdown in amative encounters. Shaka McGlotten comments on such elements by exploring the ways that digital domains are perceived as utopian zones where dreams come true.[23] But as McGlotten explains, "Rather than a smooth space that flows, digital virtuality amplifies the inconstant stutter of desire. The technologies we hope will facilitate connection can instead block or confuse it."[24] Instead of seeing these realities as inherently problematic, I view these stutters—or *ruptures*—as speaking to the real experiences of queer hybridity instantiated in the overlaps of online and offline worlds.

In the writing of Arroyo and Lozada, the ruptures can be read as calling attention to the social performativity of queer Latinx online experiences insofar as they show these experiences are embedded in preestablished cultural scripts as well as go beyond such expectations. These ruptures and discontinuities arise both through the digital connections as well as through the other limitations of the textual format, hence illuminating the ways that some performances can have unintended outcomes and meanings. Juana María Rodríguez explains, "Digital discourses, those virtual exchanges we glimpse on the Net, are textual performances: fleeting, transient, ephemeral, already past. Like the text of a play, they leave a trace to which meaning can be assigned, but these traces are haunted by the absence that was the performance itself, its reception and its emotive power."[25] Similar to how Rodríguez suggests, the online performances in the aforementioned writings are shaped by the intangibility and unwieldy qualities of the Internet, which often prevents the very "touch" that is desired in such intimacies. Even as online worlds are seen as being hospitable, the lack of a foothold leads us to other views. However, instead of maintaining the melancholy that accompanies the disappointments of online ruptures, Arroyo and Lozada portray these dynamics as sources of humor and opportunities for a witty comment on the ways people become reliant on the Internet for various purposes, including erotic gratification and intimacy. Such humor and wit suggest a depth of affective experience and intelligence that moves beyond the fallacious notion that Latinx peoples are uninformed. In effect, these texts showcase the performativity and technological intelligence of Latinx lives by finessing the connectivities of the real and digital as well as the artistic and popular.

By bringing these texts together, this chapter speaks to a set of circumstances that Latinx queers experience in artistic expressions, the mainstream US media and the real world. In particular, the texts' protagonists challenge the idea that Latinx queers must adhere to the truths and knowledge of an Anglophone, heterocentric world, which largely commands native Spanish speakers (like the protagonist in Lozada's text) to "Learn English" ("*Aprenda Inglés*").[26] They carry out this challenge to the dominant powers by offering readers a queer form of knowledge—of themselves and their surrounding communities. Arroyo and Lozada proffer a pair of mosaics, which consist of a mixed set of the Latinx daily experiences. To understand these experiences, I interpret the protagonists' dialogues as being performative utterances that generate perspectives and questions about hybridity, spaces, and the expectations of truth. Rather than maintaining a fixed, monolithic notion of truth, these texts embrace *the performative*, which allow for a broader sense of human existence near the start of the twenty-first century. These authors suggest that it is possible to find alternative spaces for social experience, in which queer Latinx folks produce their own subjective, community-based versions of life, knowledge, and truth. In depicting these characters' social experiences as hybrid, the texts offer up a socio-spatial blueprint for living without the constraints of the dominant vision of legitimacy. Through their performances of queer hybridity, the characters cultivate knowledge and personal truths that empower readers to think in new ways and cannot be disciplined easily by the dominant powers that be.

CONNECTING THE CONTEXTS AND HISTORIES OF QUEER WEB TEXTS

Arroyo's prose and Lozada's text instantiate this queer hybridity by embedding online communications within conventionally printed books, creating multimedia texts that build on the narrative forms of epistolary fiction. Historically, the epistolary genre dates back to at least the eighteenth century when Samuel Richardson published the novel *Pamela*, a story about a servant who tries to avoid her master's seductive advances.²⁷ Since that time, the epistolary genre has evolved to include Web-based storytelling, hence suggesting the genre's long-lasting, yet malleable form. Like Richardson's text, the works of Arroyo and Lozada similarly explore the human issues of desire, though their texts take a fresh approach inasmuch as they merge the epistolary narrative with the Web and other genres, such as novelistic writing, personal essays, and poetry. Arroyo and Lozada are not alone in this respect as writers such as Tatiana de la Tierra have published notable Web-based stories, which suggest a larger pattern of mixing Web-based writing with US storytelling.²⁸ Concerning these developments, Debra Ann Castillo and Luis Correa-Díaz have hypothesized this kind of writing as reflecting the evolving desires and interests of the contemporary era.²⁹ Within her essay, Castillo analyzes two email-based narratives: Cristina Civale's short story "*Perra Virtual*" and Rosina Conde's novel *La Genera*, showing how these texts encourage readers to explore new kinds of writing, as well as generate new interpretative strategies.³⁰ In this crossroads of discussion, Castillo states, "Internationally, Internet and web-conscious narratives have begun to consolidate into an increasingly large and recognizable print subgenre."³¹ Castillo's exegesis of cybertexts offers a sophisticated and path-breaking analysis of cyber-writing that sets the stage for critiques in Latinx Web contexts, and although I agree there indeed has been a proliferation of Web-conscious texts, it may be challenging to prove that these works constitute a "recognizable print subgenre" because of how these cybertexts are composed in a variety of ways. In contrast, I contend that the unruly hybridity of these texts and characters can demonstrate a queer resonance because it frequently pushes the boundaries of aesthetic beauty and good form by connecting elements. As Néstor García Canclini argues, "Hybridity has a long trajectory in Latin American cultures. We remember formerly the syncretic forms created by Spanish and Portuguese matrices mixing with indigenous representation."³² Through the prism of Canclini's ideas, we can deduce that the work of Arroyo and Lozada is in keeping with larger cultural trends, yet Canclini never takes into account how the ephemerality and physicality of queerness factors into hybridity.

As Arroyo and Lozada tell their stories, they can be read as both extending the creative practices of Latin American traditions, even as they synthesize a motley set of elements such as knowledges and spaces from a range of queer Latinx communities. In the case of Arroyo's writing, his collection *How to Name a Hurricane* consists of a mixture of writings, but I will focus solely on one larger segment in his work, "Cyber Conquistadores."³³ Through this title, Arroyo suggests queers have *conquered* the online world by mastering the knowledge of the Web's geography. More specifically, this segment is a set of email texts that have been sent to a fictional man named "Santo." This character's name brings a quasi-religious undercurrent to a text that would otherwise appear as irreligious, or blasphemous, depending on one's spiritual values. Arroyo's work appears unconcerned with hagiography though and more interested in painting Santo as a good friend to the people, who send him email- and web-based messages. The character functions as a "saint" to the extent that he prevents his friends from being lonely; however, he never physically heals anyone in the traditional sense, nor does he ever signal that he has overcome loneliness himself. Much like the writing of Lozada, we observe a frustration with isolation, which is mitigated to some extent through the characters' online flirtations. Readers observe Santo's propensity to socializing in the e-text's socially coquettish and inventive messages. The readers never learn Santo's identity; however, these email pieces relay substantive characteristics that place a spotlight on who he is and prefers. At first glance, we learn he performs the role of a sociable, queer Latino man in the online sphere of chatting, and he enjoys eyeing the male physique for the sake of pleasure. Nevertheless, he demonstrates an interest in the subjects of Caribbean history and religion, suggesting his identity is irreducible to stereotypes like the hot-blooded "Latin lover" shown in much of the mainstream media.

Even as these queer Latinx characters convey a familiarity with the online world, the readers never gain a complete knowledge of who these characters are. They remain elusive and partial. In Lozada's text *No quiero quedarme sola y vacía*, the main character never reveals their full name, and they prefer to use a multitude of names within the text. This lack of information bespeaks their tendency to perform many identities instead of one singular identity. Mostly though, they self-identify as "la Loca"—a term that could be translated as either being an antigay pejorative (i.e., madwoman or faggot) or a moniker that reclaims Latinx queerness (i.e., queen), which in turn can be viewed as a form of resistance to homophobia.[34] In a similar manner, la Loca's identity appears difficult to simplify as this character comes across to readers as being gender-fluid and readers only receive fragments that describe their Puerto Rican heritage and time in the United States. But this fragmentary, patchwork-like self-mirrors what we see in Arroyo's text insofar as both are shown from a point of view (or knowledge) that resists generalization. Such portrayals offer a mosaic-like quality that multicultural identities themselves evince as they integrate several forms of cultural identity. In Arroyo's case, we can observe a set of Latinx identities that speak both English and Spanish as well as understand queer cultures. This mixing of language and personae reads as a repudiation of monolithic, pure forms. That is, in choosing to perform a variety of personae, the texts' authors proffer nontraditional representations that privilege syncretic approaches, while encouraging readers to celebrate our multidimensional selves.

Through this lens of performance, we may better comprehend how the texts contest the dominant culture's demand for a fixed and truthful sense of identity. Already, critics such as Andil Gosine and Lisa Nakamura have studied the performance of ethnicity and race in online spaces, demonstrating the manner in which cyberworlds create our experience, affect our socializing, and sometimes problematically shape perceptions of identity.[35] Moreover Carla Kaplan writes, "Performativity can be a subversive practice because it reveals that identities are not really 'our own' and that we are not really 'what we are'; rather, we are how we identify—a process that is mutable and changeable."[36] Like Kaplan's work, I argue we must remain attentive to the unstable and evolving ways in which people, such as my texts' queers, speak of themselves and others. Thus, it is imperative for us to consider the ways in which queer Latinx men perform the discontinuities of their lives online and deal with being viewed as having inappropriate and untruthful desires. These men perform their lives at the social fringe because, according to Arroyo's character, they shirk the majority's penchant for norms like the "missionary position," and they offer a more celebratory and positive way of looking at the intersections of gender, ethnicity, and sexuality.[37] An integrative framework of critical performance studies provides a means to examine how the characters' textual and online performances challenge the oppressive truth claims of ethnocentric and homophobic groups.

When we consider the sum of these textual performances, they add up to something more meaningful as well as something dissimilar from the majority of writings that publishers produce year after year. Unlike the preponderance of texts that pivot on the usual love story of heterosexuals, Arroyo's and Lozada's texts center on the comings and goings of many lovers in the life of a main figure, or character. The cultural critic Judith Roof addressed this subject in her book *Come as You Are* where she speaks to how the vast majority of published narratives rely on a heterosexual story formula or "heteroideology."[38] The immense numbers of texts that follow this well-worn path have created a standard that precludes queer people who aim to join together in loving or social ways. And although queer people have found the ability to read these straight stories against the grain, such as by looking at moments of homoeroticism, the fact remains that the lack of queer visibility in the 1970s and 1980s left many readers without hope, role models, or other kinds of guideposts. Yet recent texts from the past decade, including that of Arroyo and Lozada tell another story, in which heterosexual coupling is not the main focus or outcome of the plot. Within their work, we observe queer Latinx figures expressing countercultural desires for several men outside of committed relationships, and this approach does not lead them to the overidealized outcome of coupling. Instead, these lives lead us to see the challenges that can occur in the so-called true ideal of coupling and settling down in a traditional home.

RETHINKING THE LOVE STORY AND SOCIAL SPACES IN LOZADA'S QUEER TEXT

In his text, Lozada builds a Web-conscious narrative by departing from a dominant paradigm that is called the "Puerto Rican love story."[39] Lozada partially explains this idea by way of a set of notes that frames a major chapter. The chapter shows how the protagonist—la Loca—engages in a relationship, but ultimately loses their companion to another man. La Loca appears to write about these matters to understand them, giving their writing a journal-like quality. In this first section, Lozada's character also explains how they attempted to publish their writings about relationships, but these did not mirror the Puerto Rican love story. They say that after submitting their creative work to several critics, "they demanded of him, by emails that he deliver to them a novel with plot" (*le exigieron, por emails, que les entregara una novela con trama*).[40] Although this implies there are problematic limits created by publishing norms, Lozada's words also expose the way that some publishers subjugate unestablished writers and force them to offer a less radical, uniform text. At the close of his chapter, the text's narrator sarcastically says to his critics, "Oh Bitches, I am so sorry. I am so sorry that I could not give you a Puerto Rican love story. I am incapable of writing a good plot."[41] This irreverent comment evinces a campy, theatrical quality, even as the story maintains the protagonist's continued desire to find a sense of togetherness. The narrator's sarcasm is significant because it is a performance of something other than the truth: Lozada—and his main character la Loca—are well educated and capable of writing. Lozada effectively uses the critics' denunciation as a means of defying the dominant conventions associated with the so-called typical Puerto Rican love story. As a result, he dismantles a singular textual notion of reality by linking his text to others, such as the love story, creating a chain of textual realities. In the process, Lozada's narrative suggests to readers there is no single version of artistry that is entirely authentic, authoritative, or true.

Instead of performing the inculcated social standard, in which an author submits to a publisher, or a man finds long-lasting love with a woman, Lozada's text depicts a queer person who repeatedly defies convention in physical, social, and textual ways. Lozada's protagonist, for instance, aims to find multiple partners in online forums. This experience is shown through embedding online chat, which may be seen as rather lascivious, in a narrative that is mainly composed of the la Loca's observations, reflections, and storytelling. In the past, media scholars, such as Andoni Alonso, Jennifer Brinkerhoff, Anna Everett, and Pedro Oiarzabal have theorized the digital dimensions of diasporas, but it appears few researchers have considered the queer dynamics of digital-based art created by Latinx peoples.[42] One of the scholars who have studied this subject—Juana María Rodríguez—has documented the sometimes peculiar circumstances that hinder online amative encounters for Latinx peoples. She notes that she herself has been regarded with skepticism in lesbian or bisexual chatrooms because of how some Internet users misrepresent themselves to others, such as when some heterosexual men *perform* the role of a lesbian online.[43] As Rodriguez shows, this dissembling generates a problematic sense of mistrust and unease in online spaces. These anxieties associated with knowing the true identities of others are dramatized most clearly in Lozada's work, in which the main protagonist la Loca frequently worries that one of their online suitors may turn out to be a "serial killer."[44] This concern for safety underscores the stakes of online social spaces as well as reinforces Rodríguez's view that our cultures' imperatives to have a single sense of truth affects our online interactions.

Scholars of epistolary fiction, including Linda S. Kauffman, have investigated the amorous dimensions of letter-based narratives, asserting that desire and trust play substantive roles in animating many characters' actions. Kauffman's analysis of epistolary writing suggests that this genre is particularly well suited to nontraditional gender performance. She insists that "amorous epistolary discourse subverts so many conventional dichotomies and explores so many transgressions and transformations."[45] The transgressive quality of amorous epistolary writing provides fertile ground for the performance of queer Latinx lives, which often defy the propriety of Hispanic cultures in the United States. In this way, the epistolary pushes boundaries and calls attention to the meaningful social links between characters or a character and a reader. Kauffman's own observations also grant us a lens to theorize the performative aspects of Lozada's beginning, in which his epigraph speaks to the discontinuities of a queer Latinx person's social roles. Lozada's epigraph consists of this concise definition: "The being: that performance, a chaotic pastiche of displacements and clichés, always mutant, never fixed" (*el ser: ese performance, un pastiche caótico de desplazamientos y clichés, siempre mutante, jamás fijo*).[46] Lozada's telling epigraph calls attention to the chaos that results when people are compelled to perform certain roles, yet that performance must contend with numerous variables such as social forces, policies and views that exist beyond the control of the performer. Lozada's words *"desplazamientos," "mutante,"* and *"jamás fijo"* also intimate the experiences that Latinx queers feel when people exclude them: displacement and detachment. This idea is reinforced in the wording of *"el ser,"* which hints at an experience of difference or uniqueness that goes beyond normative processes of US-based identity construction. Instead of a unifying social experience, readers receive the idea of a solitary, isolated being, hence suggesting this individual's suffering is problematic.

These feelings appear to be the result of homophobic sentiment in the textual world, which is encountered by the main character while they visit in Puerto Rico, thus leading to their desire to remain on the US mainland. Lozada's epigraph mirrors some of his book's other paratextual materials that similarly set the stage for an unconventional narrative. Lozada's text provides descriptions on the back cover that speak to the book's focus. Although most texts offer something similar, these elements play an important role in readers' experiences because these fragments give a road map for understanding Lozada's dynamic work. Lozada's back cover reads, "It is a novel in Spanglish that shows a great ability in his capacity to manipulate texts of diverse origin (internet, popular music, advertising language and canonical literature among others" (*Es una novela en Spanglish que muestra una gran habilidad en su capacidad de manipular textos de diversa índole (internet, música popular, lenguaje publicitario, y literatura canónica, entre otros*). In much the same way, Arroyo's back cover alerts us that his text similarly transgresses boundaries: "There's no denying it, media culture has ushered in a new era of visibility for gays in America. Yet somehow the gay Latino doesn't fit into this sound-bite identity and usually isn't included in national media images. Arroyo offers a corrective." These paratexts are informative inasmuch as they offer a new knowledge about Latinx queers. Most notably, Lozada's wording about the "sound-bite identity" invites readers to think about the ways that people think about queer culture—usually the mainstream media has imagined queers as being either victims AIDS or affluent white English speakers. With this, we can appreciate the text as being an informative narrative that reveals the diversity of queer cultures, as well as challenges us to think of the ways in which the mainstream media misleads with half-truths.

Further, the title of Lozada's text, another key paratext, encourages us to take stock of another significant aspect of his narrative. The titular phrase—*No quiero quedarme sola y vacía*—is especially fitting after la Loca loses their long-term companion to another man. La Loca tries to avoid being lonely, yet they feel isolated, and this feeling is not limited to their own romantic experiences. They greatly miss their mother, and this maternal absence intensifies their desire to connect with others. Because of this, la Loca spends significant amounts of time searching online for a new partner, and in the process, we note that the process of finding a companion online is a performative one because when the characters go online in the works of Arroyo and Lozada, they create screen names, which have the effect of creating a social identity. When we observe la Loca going online in the text, they talk about themselves in the third person, using the identity of "*la Ansiosa*" (the Anxious Lady), which is one of the more feminine identities that they perform in the text's diegesis. Although la Ansiosa never self-identifies as transgender (or trans) per se, the text suggests that the spaces in the narrative as well as the online spaces that they frequent enable a considerable measure of gender fluidity. In their self-description, which they share online, this gender-fluid narrator explains their life by using the following Web-conscious lingo:

> The anxious lady puts personals on the web: Puerto Rican looking for LUV: In search of LTR: Spanish/Puerto Rican/Portuguese/ African: In this AOL Masquerade Ball, LoVe Vs.Lust, Lets See What Magic U Have 4 this boy. . . . that's a lie, she's looking for sex. But, like almost all queens on the Internet, she's dishonest. (*La Ansiosa pone personals en la red: Puerto Rican Looking for LUV: In search of LTR: Spanish/ Puerto Rican/ Portuguese/ African: In this AOL Masquerade Ball, LoVe Vs.Lust, Lets See What Magic U Have 4 this boy. . . . eso es mentira, busca sexo. Pero, como casi todas las locas en el Internet, es deshonesta*).[47]

In an echo of Arroyo's mask imagery, la Loca's statement about the "Masquerade Ball" speaks to the playful and performative dynamics created by online communications. In their masquerade, they bend the truth, creating personae that are fiction and fact. In this, we gain a new knowledge of la Loca's desires and their viewpoint on the truth: even though they deceive online, they also tell readers some truth about their life, thus making us complicit in the fictionalizing of their life. The fiction and reality of la Loca's life is further complicated by the fact that la Loca has much in common with Lozada himself, leading some informed readers to understand this text as an autobiographical story of struggle and thus be even more poignant. However, for readers the query remains: To what extent is this text true or actually a *hybrid* of truth and fiction? Many scholars today accept the perspective that autobiography is a fictionalization of one's life story, and while critics might characterize such blending as inauthentic or *impure*, there are several interesting questions and results to be considered in this exact dynamic. For through weaving an impure story that is the result of cobbling many identities and spaces together, Lozada illuminates the fact that people such as his readers engage in hybridized (and, thus, impure) dynamics more often than they think. With this approach, la Loca extends their story's impurity to the text's readers, bringing us into the fold and making us a part of this fictionalizing and masked identity.

By making readers complicit, Lozada creates a new social dynamic where the readers are led to question the repercussions and significance of their participation in such blending, masking, and truth-bending. Such phenomena are by no means new to be sure, yet the intersection of purity ideals within digital and new media contexts has become a frontier of cultural research today. Researchers like the anthropologist Mary Douglas have illuminated the implications of cultural contexts where people have transgressed purity norms and face negative forms of blowback and other kinds of social sanction.[48] As Douglas shows, the belief in purity ideals has been constituted and maintained in a range of physical, racial, and social dynamics, yet the question that Douglas was unable to contemplate in 1966 was the way that discourses of purity would be refracted in the social spheres created by Internet technologies. Ann Travers explores the drive for racial purity in the context of the Internet, showing how digital mediums are used to advance white supremacist vitriol.[49] Like Douglas, the work of Travers shows how such drives for purity rely on assumptions and racist presumptions that have the effect of denigrating people. In much the same way, efforts at maintaining sexual purity on the Internet often read as foolhardy and pernicious in the minds of many critics who remain wary of increasing efforts to censor and police online spaces. Such efforts to regulate online spaces have far-reaching implications that ultimately could lead to restrictive legislation that would inhibit the possibility of self-expression in public or semipublic contexts like chatrooms. Lozada's multimedia writing signals that Latinx queers must live the life they desire to have and not be limited by mores, which mandate adherence to limiting notions of purity and truth.

QUEER LANGUAGE AND STYLE IN THE MULTIMEDIA TEXTS OF ARROYO AND LOZADA

La Loca's resistance to normative processes is reinforced by the formatting and styling that are constituted in the way that the material is printed on the text's physical page. Lozada and Arroyo will position Web chat apart from the rest of the text's writing, suggesting both a distance and a link between these disparate materials. This brief break between the prose writing and the Web chat can be viewed as a sort of pause, which I view as resembling the pause that many performers use before they enter into a new voice or a section of their dramatic monologue. Although some readers might perceive this break as an inelegant or choppy moment between the textual pieces, we also can read this portion as a short symbolic silence—a silence representing the performance of the spoken word, which is reliant on the space created by breath, pause, and quiet. In effect, Lozada and Arroyo use spacing and forms of formatting to foster a sense of performativity in their work. These texts' performativity becomes clear as we observe the way that Arroyo rehearses his textual approaches in the introduction of his anthology. Arroyo writes,

> When I first read Jean Genet, Gertrude Stein, Federico García Lorca, Reinaldo Arenas, Jean Cocteau, James Baldwin and so many others, I learned from them that the marginalized writer must achieve at least three simultaneous goals: (1) shatter the restrictions of the genre, (2) work in multiple genres, and (3) cull the dislocations that only the exile, whether exterior or interior comes to know intimately.[50]

In his statement, Arroyo bespeaks a bold initiative of innovating and hybridizing ideas from his queer mentors, performing a kind of homage that mirrors the varied "voices" that Arroyo collects within his anthology.[51] These voices and sounds are made manifest in the textual spaces of the page, which parallel the real virtual rooms where these Latinx men chat in digital and imaged ways. These page spaces are crystalized versions of the ephemeral; however, these writers' texts are neither lifeless nor artless. Arroyo and Lozada use the spaces of the page and sounds of written word to create an inventive playfulness that resists commonplace approaches, while encouraging readers to engage with the intimacies that both writers hold up as alluring and generative. As Arroyo writes, "I was and continue to be intrigued by *intimacy*: that talk with the man on the barstool next to you before last call."[52] In this moment, Arroyo's italics spur readers to immerse themselves in the meaningful, yet transgressive experiences of socializing in spaces of desire—those sites where connections between people first begin to be formulated.

Arroyo's email texts further exhibit this nonconformist dynamic as the figures in his email messages speak about changing their usernames, as well as refer to one another with forenames such as "LocoCowboy" and "NinePiratas."[53] These half-Spanish, half-English usernames function as a move beyond earthly physiques and traditions that link these Latino writers to biological families; as a result, these users exhibit a hybrid status as part-virtual, part-human. In Lozada's work, we see the use of these screen names play out in a chat session between the protagonist la Loca and one of their suitors in a chatroom called "Latino M4M," which suggests that this space is meant for Latino men who are interested in other men. La Loca takes the screen name of "WasHts," and by taking on this role, they perform a local identity by living in Washington Heights, New York—a place known to have many Spanish speakers. Lozada's approach creates a sense of queer hybrid space where two places become one, or to say it another way, a bridge is made between the online world and the offline world of Washington Heights. This linking of spaces enables the participants to reimagine prior notions of space and identity, creating a performance space that is more hospitable to queer people. Yet as Lozada shows his readers, this digital space is not without certain problems. For example, during a flirtation between la Loca and one of the suitors, we see la Loca's online efforts begin to fall apart. In this moment, the author describes the character in a feminine way, writing:

> But in the moment the Internet falls apart. She tries to connect but he can't. She clicks. She clicks again. She clicks every 10 minutes over the icon that connects her to Verizon. . . . Upon the fall of the Internet this evening the edges of desire remain outside of her perimeter.
> (*Pero de momento se cae la red cibernética. Intenta connectarse pero no puede. Clickea. Clickea otra vez. Clickea cada 10 minutos over the icon that connects her to Verizon. . . . Al caerse el internet los límites del placer esta noche quedan fuera de su perímetro.*)[54]

Their repetitive clicking, which ultimately fails to reestablish the connection, both emphasizes the nonfunctional quality of his Internet connection as well as calls attention to the way we pin our hopes to online technologies and the spaces they promulgate. Their repeated attempts to connect over the Internet and the resulting frustrations signal their strong desire (or some might say, *urges*) for an intimate connection with another, thereby creating a witty comment on our digital reliance as well as the way that technology companies have played a role in shaping (or stunting) the private experiences of desire in Latinx communities. In a similar fashion, Lozada's use of *perimeter* speaks to the way that desire increasingly is being spatialized online (or experienced as being spatial) in the contexts of technology, making a substantive link between the human being and the machine where hybrid experience can take on many forms.

Once la Loca enters into this online space, they begin to chat with a user named "BoricuaBestial"—a man who becomes a suitor for a short time span. In this chat, the two Puerto Rican men use colloquial speech that is laden with abbreviations, typographical errors, and code-switching, among other unique online elements. The online name of la Loca's suitor, "BoricuaBestial," is challenging to translate because the word *Boricua* is used to describe a person indigenous to the island of Puerto Rico, yet many present-day Puerto Rican people self-identify as Boricua regardless of their birthplace, hence reifying the text's idea of cultural hybridity. This mixing is implied by the word *bestial*, which implies the man is beast-like, or half-human, half-animal. Lozada shows this beast-like man as being rather forward in the following chat:

BoricuaBestial: Muchacho

WasHts: dime

BoricuaBestial: Estoy abburido

WasHts: yo tambien

BoricuaBestial: hmm

BoricuaBestial: if U have any plans for tonight?

WasHts: I have plans for tonight, but I can cancel them.

BoricuaBestial: What are Ur stats?

WasHts: 160#, 5'10", 32w, black hair, brown eyes, Puerto Rican [55]

Their embrace of the online idiom, such as "Ur" (i.e., your), and their use of Spanglish further exemplifies their nontraditional, hybrid identities. In this mixed language, we see that one of chatters' goals is determining the so-called truth about the other. The men ask to see photographs of one another, and in this aim to assess appearance, they attempt to learn each other's physical truth. BoricuaBestial asks la Loca: "Do you have a self pic" (94) ("¿Tienes un self pic?").⁵⁶ After exchanging photographs, the men compliment each other and express a mutual attraction. They gain the knowledge that there is a chance for them to connect, though it is only when they meet in person that we see this suitor is not la Loca's "cybernetic macho of his dreams" (*macho cibernético de sus sueños*).⁵⁷ Though BoricuaBestial appears ideal to la Loca—in terms of his desirability—la Loca ultimately sees him as lacking because this suitor has no interest in using condoms, and in la Loca's eyes, this shows a form of ignorance. Through this, la Loca privileges the knowledge that condoms are a means to preserving one's health. Lozada reinforces the importance of knowledge when la Loca realizes he has incurred considerable financial debts and may become homeless due to all of his shopping. Lozada's conclusion is a sobering one because rather than maintaining the hackneyed story formula of a happy ending, it resembles more of a cautionary tale that warns of the perils of unsafe sex as well as neoliberalism's exploitative practices, which can lead to someone—like la Loca—being evicted from their home.

La Loca's domestic experience is imperiled by prior excessive spending at retail stores, creating the idea that they cannot pay the rent and thus may face eviction from their apartment. Interestingly, la Loca shows this threat through embedding the language and statements that debt collectors and businesses use, suggesting that one's life and home is under threat from a cold and hostile business world that solely cares about procuring money instead of real people's lives. In the latter part of *No quiero quedarme sola y vacia*, Lozada shows what la Loca is hearing: "this is Signet Bank. You need to call us at 1-800-343-4545 to discuss your account. Your payment is past due. . . . This is Apple credit. You need to call us at 1-800-443-4545 to discuss your account. Your payment is past due."⁵⁸ These statements take various forms, yet are repeated in a similar fashion, which is evocative of the ways that many companies use similar technological platforms to pursue people who are unable to pay their bills. This repetitive approach is followed by an eviction notice from his landlord, who leaves the following note on his apartment's door: "YOU HAVE NOT KEPT YOUR PROMISE OF PAYING YOUR RENT ON TIME. YOU HAVE FORCED US TO TAKE LEGAL ACTION AGAINST YOU. I MUST HEAR FROM YOU AT ONCE."⁵⁹ By using all capital letters and imbricating this language into his narrative, Lozada illustrates that the outside world threatens to make them homeless, and in the following chapters, readers see la Loca has in fact been cast out by the landlord. In this same regard, on being evicted, the narrative's writing becomes shorter and limited, connoting that being homeless has inhibit-ed the creative capacity of the storyteller and created additional dangers. Notably it is the transgression of the moral imperative to fulfill one's "promise" that largely initiates this eviction process, yet we can turn the tables on this viewpoint and ponder how the promise of America has failed to manifest itself for la Loca, who now faces the ultimate penalty of being homeless and endangered by a life on the streets.

In a comparable way, the inventive writing of Arroyo has been addressed by a small number of scholars such as Richard T. Rodríguez, who has theorized the "architectures of Latino sexuality" that Arroyo crafts within his work.[60] Rodríguez's work provides a helpful lens to begin making sense of Arroyo's unconventional assemblage of email texts, which allude to a man's personal history. Unlike Lozada's text, which depicts a character concerned with finding a suitor for the present and future, we see the characters in Arroyo's text as being concerned about the past: both the recent and distant past. His text calls attention to two kinds of history, or to be more precise, a historical knowledge of the characters' past and the colonial history of the New World. Despite looking back, Arroyo's text principally consists of Web-based communication, and these exchanges resemble performances, which are composed of playful banter between a queer Latino man named Santo and his friends, who converse about myriad matters, ranging from Web surfing to the history of the colonizer Cristóbal Colón (Christopher Columbus). In so doing, Arroyo's email texts lay bare the savvy and whimsy of Latinos' online socializing—an activity that continues today in present-day platforms like Facebook, Twitter, and Instagram, among others. As in these current formats, the men in Arroyo's online texts use ludic screen names to perform their social identities and connect with their friends across distances:

> E-mail:
> Dear Santo, sí, you, dude, the Internet is like gay heaven minus the Sundays! You were right! Gracias, ese for setting up my Pinta to explore new worlds. Didn't believe we'd still be friends when you moved to Houston. But here u are! We are. Wow, lots of links to studs and angels. Eye candy tastes better with J-Lo feeding the ears. What borders? Oh yeah, my new name is LocoCowboy. Amigo, gotta go. Will send pix soon! In birthday suit? . . . In cyber space, I'm a rope bridge over an abstract chasm. Columbus, each man is a world.[61]

In these cases, Arroyo's characters articulate their knowledge of Colón in a context far outside the fifteenth century, linking the explorer to the present, and more specifically, queer social life. A most intriguing aspect of this passage is the way in which this queer Latino man relates to a larger "world." The "Pinta" appears to be a computer connected to the World Wide Web, while an unnamed character interpolates Colón—making it appear that he and Colón are talking casually about their love lives. This approach brings Colón into a queer social circle, whereby the emailer alters our perception of him—effectively queering Colón. Through revisioning of history, the emailer makes striking parallels between exploring the New World and the online world, signaling the virtual world is ripe for exploration (yet not the exploitation that many have come to associate with the colonization of the New World). Although Arroyo's chapter of emails is labeled as "Cyber Conquistadores," there is neither a depiction of conquering, nor an effort to take spaces away from another. Rather, we see cyber-based exploration. Although this mix of Colón and playful sexual banter suggests a reimagining of history, it also creates a temporal hybridity that links the past and present, putting previous notions of truth and contemporary ideas of fiction on a kind of equal footing. Such a balancing act urges readers to consider the similarities of these two related notions of existence, leading readers to see realities that often are silenced. Latinx people continue to resist the silencing they have experienced in the contexts of online spaces by creating playful personae, Web accounts, and other digital presences that link Latinx people to diverse locales, encouraging people to go beyond their prior social limitations.

CELEBRATING ONLINE FLUIDITY AND PLAYFULNESS IN QUEER WEB NARRATIVES

Presently critics are witnessing a veritable efflorescence of Latinx social developments, in online venues, thereby illustrating the myriad interests and creative talents existing in today's communities. In the case of Instagram and Twitter, for instance, Latinx people have created numerous accounts (or online avatars) for connecting with Latinx individuals and groups; for example, organizations such as the relatively new Latino Outdoors organization exemplifies this hybridity that Arroyo and Lozada evidence within their own creative work. Through their online platforms on Instagram and Twitter, Latino Outdoors promotes engagement with both the natural world and other Latinx folks who are similarly interested in environmental activities, ideals, and interests such as taking trips into forests, mountains and other landscapes. On their website's "About Us" tab, the group explains their mission statement as being this: "We bring *cultura* into the outdoor narrative and connect Latinx communities and leadership with nature and outdoor experiences."[62] Their goal to "connect" the outdoors with the social sphere of human experience conveys the idea of making nature and human social life into a more cohesive configuration. In so doing, they encourage Latinx communities to join with nature, thus connoting the idea that a disconnect currently exists between a majority of Latinx populations and green landscapes.

To a similar degree, queer peoples of all colors are assumed to be urban denizens and generally not seen as capable of surviving the rugged outdoors. In contrast to this kind of limited thinking, readers learn that Santo and la Loca depart from several of the prevailing US assumptions concerning Latinx and queer communities. Arroyo's writing counters parochialisms by developing imagery of hybridity such as when Santo incorporates the traditional thematics of biblical texts with a queer-positive point of view. Readers observe this idea in an email from another Latinx email writer, who says to Santo: "I'm not jaded, amigo, just want a country of my own. I want to be president of Sodom & Gomorrah. . . . Ignore pictures of me naked under palm trees because I'm not wearing sun block and glow like an apple begging to be kidnapped to Eden. An impulse, these days, is similar to building a permanent statue in God's mind."[63] In this portion, the email writer chooses to side with the supposedly immoral cities of Sodom and Gomorrah; through this approach, he hybridizes a queer sensibility with religious knowledge, reconstituting the meanings associated with Sodom and Gomorrah. In stating his desire to be the "president" of these biblical scenes, he also empowers himself metaphorically, which results as significant when we acknowledge how many antigay people habitually use the Sodom and Gomorrah story to demonize LGBTQ people. The email writer thus plays a new role for his reader(s) in a queer way, allowing for a reinterpretation of the religious text. His performance of a queer Latinx leader in a religious scene leads his readership to see the potent possibilities that Web-conscious texts offer to readers and writers.

Arroyo's narrative additionally mirrors Lozada's text because his work speaks to the problems that are wrought by contracting HIV/AIDS. In one of the email messages, a writer implies that Santo has become very ill with the syndrome. Arroyo's text reads: "Santo, idiota, there are men in cyber space waiting for u2. Was the hospital terrible? No tacos there, I'm sure. I'm checking on flights. . . . Flesh comes with problems. . . . SIDA isn't a death sentence anymore."[64] This depiction of Santo's AIDS-related condition suggests that Santo now has a new hybrid existence. He is now host to a virus that changes not only people's health but also how others treat him socially. In refusing to dwell on this, the email writer looks for a travel itinerary so that he can spend time with his ill friend. Yet this time in the hospital cannot prevent Santo from passing. Before Santo dies, we see that the emailer creates a virtual connection to Santo, and as such, this email writer (and Santo) are made hybrid in cyberspace. One of the email writers says, "My homepage is dedicated to mi amigo, Santo. He is in Heaven for sure or else Satan does have a monopoly on the cosmos. I invite Santo to be the ghost in my machine, free rent."[65] By way of language, Santo's persona becomes embedded in the memory of cyberspace, creating a supernatural figure that persists. This electronic, hybrid ghost enables Santo's identity to endure and, thus, challenge the prohibition on queer Latinx lives in US public spaces. Accordingly, Arroyo's book makes an entreaty that readers use such digital contexts as a means of saving similar life knowledge. This form of online preservation also holds potential to foster a partial, reoccurring performance of such vulnerable identities, particularly as we the readers look on these texts with fresh eyes. In our reading of Arroyo's texts, we summon his ghost and become enmeshed in his personal story. Hence, we can infer that Arroyo is suggesting that we become hybrid with cybernetic elements whenever we participate in the online spaces created by Latinx queers. This hybrid ghostliness is furthered by the way that Santo's story is now preserved in libraries around the world in the real-life print-based text itself.

Arroyo's collection of texts, like Lozada's novel, concludes without a clear sense of finality. As we see, the socializing between his fellow Web surfers continues after Santo's death, implying these online performances of identity are perpetuated as they are stored on computers or in new cloud technologies. This is not to say that these identities are entirely coherent or duplicates of their more organic counterparts. Rather, these digital versions of the enable us to understand the concatenation of elements that constitute Latinx queer lives. The writings of Arroyo and Lozada indicate that online socializing can at times disrupt simplistic notions of identity, knowledge, and truth. Certainly, the Internet never recreates the characters' selves entirely, but through these Web-conscious texts, we are shown that there is no single, absolute sense of truth in matters of sexuality because digital elements of language and performance create ruptures in the social realities of queer Puerto Rican peoples. These online worlds may seem untouchable and nearly *dream-like*, but for a sizable number of participants, online worlds can be *everything* and a crucial component of resistance to ingrained normativity.

NOTES

1. Juana María Rodríguez, *Queer Latinidad: Identity Practices, Discursive Spaces* (New York: New York University Press, 2003), 117.
2. Horacio N. Roque Ramírez, "'That's My Place!': Negotiating Racial, Sexual and Gender Politics in San Francisco's Gay Latino Alliance," *Journal of the History of Sexuality* 12, no. 2 (Spring 2003): 224–58.
3. Ana Gonzalez-Barrera, Mark Hugo Lopez, and Eileen Patten, "Closing the Digital Divide: Latinos and Technology Adoption," 7 Mar. 2013. http://www.pewhispanic.org/2013/03/07/closing-the-digital-divide-latinos-and-technology-adoption/.
4. Dara Goldman, *Out of Bounds: Islands and the Demarcation of Identity in the Hispanic Caribbean* (Lewisburg, PA: Bucknell University Press, 2008), 195.
5. Goldman, *Out of Bounds*, 195.
6. Rane Arroyo, *How to Name a Hurricane* (Tucson: University Press of Arizona, 2005), 21.

7. Gloria E. Anzaldúa, "Preface to the First Edition," in *Borderlands/La Frontera: The New Mestiza*, 4th ed., eds. Norma Cantú and Aída Hurtado (San Francisco: Aunt Lute Books, 2012), 20.

8. Ángel Lozada, *No quiero quedarme sola y vacía* (San Juan, Puerto Rico: Isla Negra Editores, 2006), 12.

9. Lozada, *No quiero quedarme sola y vacía*, 71.

10. Lozada, *No quiero quedarme sola y vacía*, 74.

11. Radhika Mohanram, *Black Body: Women, Colonialism and Space* (Minneapolis: University of Minnesota Press, 1999); Susan Jeffords, *Hard Bodies: Hollywood Masculinity in the Reagan Era* (New Brunswick, NJ: Rutgers University Press, 1993).

12. Leticia Alvarado, *Abject Performances: Aesthetic Strategies in Latino Cultural Production* (Durham, NC: Duke University Press, 2018), 11.

13. Alvarado, *Abject Performances*, 11.

14. Richard T. Rodríguez, "Family," *Keywords for Latina/o Studies*, eds. Deborah R. Vargas, Nancy Raquel Mirabal, and Lawrence La Fountain-Stokes (New York: New York University Press, 2017), 63.

15. Lozada, *No quiero quedarme sola y vacía*, 131.

16. Lozada, *No quiero quedarme sola y vacía*, 2.

17. William V. Flores and Rina Benmayor, "Introduction: Constructing Cultural Citizenship," *Latino Cultural Citizenship: Claiming Identity, Space and Rights* (Boston: Beacon Press, 1997), 1.

18. Lorena Garcia, *Respect Yourself, Protect Yourself: Latina Girls and Sexual Identity* (New York: New York University Press, 2012), 84–85.

19. Arroyo, *How to Name a Hurricane*, 21.

20. Alice E. Marwick, *Status Update: Celebrity, Publicity, & Branding in the Social Media Age* (New Haven, CT: Yale University Press, 2013), 5.

21. Lawrence La Fountain-Stokes, *Queer Ricans: Cultures and Sexualities in the Diaspora* (Minneapolis: University of Minnesota Press, 2009), 141.

22. Lozada, *No quiero quedarme sola y vacía*, 60.

23. Shaka McGlotten, *Virtual Intimacies: Media, Affect and Queer Sociality* (Albany: State University of New York Press, 2013).

24. McGlotten, *Virtual Intimacies*, 2–3

25. Rodríguez, *Queer Latinidad*, 118.

26. Lozada, *No quiero quedarme sola y vacía*, 26.

27. Samuel Richardson, *Pamela or Virtue Rewarded* (New York: Penguin, 1981).

28. Tatiana de la Tierra, "Porcupine Love," in *Ambientes: New Queer Latino Writing*, eds. Lázaro Lima and Felice Picano (Madison: University of Wisconsin Press, 2011), 75–83.

29. Debra Ann Castillo, "http://www.LAlit.com," in *Latin American Literature and the Mass Media*, eds. Debra Ann Castillo and Edmundo Paz-Soldán (New York: Routledge, 2000), 232–48; Luis Correa-Díaz, "Literatura latinoamericana, española, portuguesa en la era digital (nuevas tecnologías y lo literario)." *Arizona Journal of Hispanic Cultural Studies* 14 (2010): 149–55.

30. Cristina Civale, *Perra Virtual* (Buenos Aires. Argentina: Planeta, 1998); Rosina Conde, *La Genera* (Mexico City: Universidad Autónoma de la Ciudad de México, 2006).

31. Castillo, *Latin American*, 234.

32. Néstor García Canclini, *Hybrid Cultures: Strategies Entering and Leaving Modernity*, trans. Christopher Chiappari and Sylvia L. Lopez (Minneapolis: University of Minnesota Press), 241.

33. Arroyo, *How to Name a Hurricane*, 21.

34. Lozada, *No quiero quedarme sola y vacía*, 11.

35. Andil Gosine, "Brown to Blonde at Gay.com: Passing White in Queer Cyberspace," in *Queer Online: Media Technology and Sexuality*, eds. Kate O'Riordan and David Phillips (New York: Peter Lang, 2007), 139–54; Lisa Nakamura, *Cybertypes: Race, Ethnicity and Identity on the Internet* (New York: Routledge, 2002).

36. Carla Kaplan, "Identity," in *Keywords for American Cultural Studies*, eds. Bruce Burgett and Glenn Hendler (New York: New York University Press, 2007), 126.
37. Arroyo, *How to Name a Hurricane*, 27.
38. Judith Roof, *Come as You Are: Sexuality and Narrative* (New York: Columbia University Press, 1996), xxii.
39. Lozada, *No quiero quedarme sola y vacía*, 48.
40. Lozada, *No quiero quedarme sola y vacía*, 31.
41. Lozada, *No quiero quedarme sola y vacía*, 48.
42. Jennifer Brinkerhoff, *Digital Diasporas: Identity and Transnational Engagement* (New York: Cambridge University Press, 2009); Anna Everett, *Digital Diaspora: A Race for Cyberspace* (Albany: State University of New York Press, 2009); Andoni Alonso and Pedro Oiarzabal, *Diasporas in the New Media Age: Identity, Politics and Community* (Reno: University of Nevada Press, 2010).
43. Rodríguez, *Queer Latinidad*, 130–33.
44. Lozada, *No quiero quedarme sola y vacía*, 74.
45. Linda S. Kaufman, *Discourses of Desire: Gender, Genre and Epistolary Fictions* (Ithaca, NY: Cornell University Press, 1986), 26–27.
46. Lozada, *No quiero quedarme sola y vacía*, 9.
47. Lozada, *No quiero quedarme sola y vacía*, 60.
48. Mary Douglas, *Purity and Danger: Concepts of Pollution and Taboo* (New York: Routledge, 2002).
49. Ann Travers, *Writing the Public in Cyberspace: Redefining Inclusion on the Net* (New York: Garland Publishing, 2000), 98.
50. Arroyo, *How to Name a Hurricane*, xii.
51. Arroyo, *How to Name a Hurricane*, xi.
52. Arroyo, *How to Name a Hurricane*, xii–xiii.
53. Arroyo, *How to Name a Hurricane*, 21.
54. Lozada, *No quiero quedarme sola y vacía*, 131–32.
55. Lozada, *No quiero quedarme sola y vacía*, 94.
56. Lozada, *No quiero quedarme sola y vacía*, 94.
57. Lozada, *No quiero quedarme sola y vacía*, 96.
58. Lozada, *No quiero quedarme sola y vacía*, 84–85.
59. Lozada, *No quiero quedarme sola y vacía*, 86.
60. Richard T. Rodríguez, "Architectures of Latino Sexuality," *Social Text* 33, no. 2 (June 2015): 83–84.
61. Arroyo, *How to Name a Hurricane*, 21.
62. Mission Statement, Latino Outdoors, 27 February 2016, http://latinooutdoors.org/about-us/.
63. Arroyo, *How to Name a Hurricane*, 23.
64. Arroyo, *How to Name a Hurricane*, 23–24.
65. Arroyo, *How to Name a Hurricane*, 25.

FOUR
Mapping Poetic Spaces

Subversive Intimacies of Humans and Nonhumans in the Scenes of Anzaldúa and Arroyo

> We evolved from a one-cell animal. It's all recorded in the cells of the body. We're part animal, but people just want to be divine and angelic. They disown part of the self. People made the serpent into the most vile, obnoxious, horrible of all creatures, so I've made it a symbol of the soul.[1]
>
> —Gloria Anzaldúa

As Latinx queer peoples took to creating new spaces beyond the domestic sphere including virtual sites and clubs, some creators from these same communities garnered attention for crafting scenes in poetry that involve landscapes and nature. Often explored by poets, the ideas of nature are a versatile discourse that poets use for commentary, discovery, and pleasure. The renowned writer Gloria Anzaldúa has received a number of accolades for imagining poetic scenes of nature and spaces that transformed how people understood identity and borderlands between the United States and Mexico. The transformative capacity of her poetry also can be discerned in several of her long-form writings as they weave together genres such as poetry and criticism as well as imagery departing from humdrum realism. Reflecting on her uniqueness, Bernadette Marie Calafell and Jorge Capetillo-Ponce have extolled Anzaldúa for her creative texts that resist simplistic categorization.[2] This poetry resists ingrained western thought by mixing indigenous religious beliefs with daily US contexts to raise up new artistic visions. In particular, Anzaldúa's texts often link human beings with less loved creatures like snakes and unsavory scenes such as earthquakes to create sophisticated commentary.

To explain this poetry, I elaborate on the ways that Anzaldúa destabilizes boundaries between humans and the nonhuman for the sake of challenging acts of othering and displacement that harm diverse beings. As Anzaldúa tells in the epigraph, a broad range of people try to maintain boundaries through acts that "disown" humanity's history of being related to animals. Such disowning can be traced to the anthropocentric belief that certain human beings (who are white) have believed themselves to be superior and should not be mixing with people or beings who are different from themselves. Nevertheless, Anzaldúa embraces such subversive mixing by integrating animals and the natural world into her poetic figures, creating hybrid scenes.[3] Her poems "Reincarnation" and "Encountering the Medusa," for example, depict humans who are combined with serpent-like creatures.[4] Although such depictions occur across indigenous stories in the Americas, for some it remains curious why Anzaldúa might highlight the bodily aspects of these hybrids who may appear simply monstrous to untrained eyes. To understand these mixed figures, we must look to the ways that Anzaldúa links together bodies, desires, and nature late in the twentieth century and early in the twenty-first century—a period in which people of color, people with disabilities, and people with HIV often were seen as nonhuman and monstrous.[5] Sadly, able-bodied and white heterosexuals put up physical boundaries as well as more symbolic ones to keep out so-called threatening figures that might "corrupt" the white order's purity. Hence, I interpret Anzaldúa's poetry as an endeavor in "loosening our borders" and building bridges like partnerships and coalitions.[6] Further, I recognize her mixing such as her linking of plants and women in the poem "*mujer cacto*" (cactus woman) as being an embrace of transgressive, queer intimacies that were seen as *unnatural* at the end of the twentieth century.[7] Understanding the historical and spatial implications of such poetry grants readers a blueprint for the cultivation of more egalitarian spaces and greater self-expression beyond existing societal constraints.

Remarkably, a similar kind of poetic writing strategy is employed by one of Anzaldúa's contemporaries, a queer Puerto Rican author named Rane Arroyo, who worked as a professor of English and creative writing before his death. As in the case of Anzaldúa, the topic of spatial experiences plays noteworthy roles in the scenes he creates in his collections of poetry. In an interview, he reflected on the subject of spatial experience and posed the question: "Who knows more about place than the displaced?"[8] Through this query, Arroyo urges the reader to see him and his poetic scenes in terms of displacement and spatial dynamics. Arroyo emphasizes this idea further when he identifies as "an interior exile"—someone who crosses borders and feels "that I don't fit easily anywhere." Arroyo was born in Chicago, Illinois, in the United States, and he also self-identified as Puerto Rican due to his parents' ancestry and connections to the island. Unsurprisingly, his writing often demonstrates feelings of being "in-between"—an idea that also shines through in much of Anzaldúa's own verse as she offers critical reflections on her experiences in the Mexico-US borderlands. Like Anzaldúa's poetry, Arroyo's verses allude to ideas of being betwixt and between through imagery of physical contact and encounters between the human and nonhuman including representations of hybrid figures like mermaids and a shark-man—creatures who are synthesized from distinctive landscapes like the land and the sea. In this chapter, I read these poetic scenes as metaphors for the blending of communities and landscapes that have been kept at a distance through policies like institutionalized segregation. This blending creates *queer bodily spaces* that reject the imperative to keep unlikely—or *queer*—pairings from coming into contact. Arroyo and Anzaldúa counter this ingrained drive to prevent queer encounters by presenting scenes that destabilize societal boundaries and contest the underlying societal anxiety about unorthodox forms of bodily contact like queer intimacy.

The longstanding anxieties and distaste for bodily contact between LGBTQ people are discernible in the landmark US Supreme Court cases *Bowers v Hardwick* (1986) and *Lawrence v Texas* (2003). In both, heterosexuals' anxieties about gay male sexuality were brought to light along with legal questions about the citizen's right to equal protection, freedom, and privacy. The court case raised queries such as: Should the private lives and sexual relations between consenting adults be subject to the legal scrutiny of the state and federal governments? In part, this chapter contends that Anzaldúa and Arroyo allegorize these anxieties and issues of the time through the creation of hybrid beings including Anzaldúa's serpent-like people and Arroyo's half-shark and half-man (or what some may label mermen, mermaids, or merpeople). In the case of Arroyo's shark-man for instance, he explains his own connection to a group called the Sharks—a street gang that is depicted in the award-winning US musical film *West Side Story*. Arroyo's shark-man can be read as allusion to the film, but this depiction also offers a humorous and playful reinvention that points to the miscegenation of human beings. In *West Side Story*, a white man named Tony (played by the white Richard Beymer) and a Puerto Rican woman named Maria (played by the white Natalie Wood) become intimate, suggesting copulation; however, the film never suggests a progeny is born—as we see in Rane Arroyo's text. His motivation for creating this mixed shark-human child is evident in his own statement "I like mixing things up—high culture and low culture, straight and gay."[9] Through this mixing, Arroyo fosters connectivity and creates bridges between nonhumans and human communities that have been separated and displaced by powerful US institutions and colonial forces. To explain the imagery of these unusual artistic formulations, I ruminate on the contexts and techniques employed by these two writers. Looking to their stylistic approaches, which are integrative and varied in composition, leads me to interpret these poems' scenes as imaginative art forms that exhibit a *queerly inventive* writing strategy, which bridges art with desire.

As I explain in a prior chapter, the *queerly inventive* is a concept for identifying the artists' creative writing styles and innovative approaches that allude to matters of sexuality and identity. This artistic tendency is discernible as we piece together a selection of pieces. Likewise, this pattern is observable in visual artwork such as that of the photographer Laura Aguilar and the painter Tino Rodríguez, who create scenes that share the merging of humanity, intimacy, and natural contexts. To a similar extent, this framework is a fruitful approach for imagining new alternative approaches that bridge the gap between real and imaginary worlds—the spaces that many queers look to for inspiration and hope amid the toxic homophobia, racism, and related kinds of Othering that permeate much of the landscapes in the United States in subtle and overt forms. This queerly inventive approach comes through in scenes of figures who feel frustrated, powerless, and Othered. As difficult as such dynamics can be, these figures are shown as persevering to make visible their feelings of being ostracized by dominant US cultures. These exceptional poetic scenes bespeak desires for change and a means of fashioning a better life that may strike observers as uncanny at first, though they also resonate as familiar to the extent that they exhibit parallels with the myths and legends that we often tell across a great range of contexts.

Although the hybrid figures in these poetic projects are not always shown to be queer or Latinx in blatant terms, I contend the texts' depictions of monstrous beings should be read as allegories of queer Latinx experiences. To provide some context here, we must recognize that being queer and Latinx in the 1980s, 1990s, and early 2000s was a challenging and stressful experience because of the many prejudices of the time. LGBTQ people were seen as criminals and *breaking the rules* such as the traditional gender binary that only permits two public forms of self-identification: heterosexual man and heterosexual woman. Thus, allegory allows Anzaldúa, Arroyo, and many more writers to speak about what it means to be perceived as a monstrous rule-breaker. While such approaches may appear cryptic, such breaking of binaries could not be more relevant when we consider the debates and experiences of LGBTQ and genderqueer people who still are seen as defying such binarisms. Anzaldúa points to these cultural dynamics in *Borderlands / La Frontera: The New Mestiza*, a collection that addresses both hybrid cultural experiences as well as geopolitical dynamics of borders. She says that our world "claims that human nature is limited and cannot evolve into something better. But I, like other queer people, am two in one body, both male and female."[10] Anzaldúa speaks to similar transgressions in this collection, reflecting on one of the identities she considers in several ways: a figure

Figure 4.1. The oil painting "Eternal Lovers" by the Mexican-American artist Tino Rodríguez (2010).

known as "the mestiza." She explains mestizas are a "new hybrid race" by explaining "*En 1501 nació una nueva raza, el mestizo, el mexicano* (people of mixed Indian and Spanish ancestry), a race that had never existed before."[11] In the United States and many more countries, miscegenation (or the mixing of races) has been demonized as a crime or impropriety that goes against the cultural and state-based ideologies of purity and respectability. Looking back, multiple state legislatures in the United States enacted anti-miscegenation laws that attempted to prevent the intermarriage (or sexual relations) of ostensibly distinct races by criminalizing them.[12] Although, the plethora of US court cases about these relations clearly show that they were part of the cultural landscape. This subject comes through Anzaldúa's writing as she celebrates *mestizaje*—the mixing of races. Anzaldúa articulates this sociocultural hybridity despite potential objections of purists and supremacists, positing this in the contexts of "Aztlán"—a real and imagined space that has been seen by critics and intellectuals as bridging the lands of the Aztecs, México, and the United States. Through her words, Anzaldúa critiques the powers that demonize hybridity, and in so doing, she resists prevailing colonial systems that impose segregation and divisiveness.

Situating these spatial discourses in the contexts of Anzaldúa and Arroyo grants us a means of theorizing how imaginative forms of resistance such as queerly inventive spaces are a part of a broader landscape of Latinx creativity and intellectual poetry. Rafael Pérez-Torres proffers an illuminating critical history of Aztlán by explaining how Anzaldúa's poetry exemplifies such concepts, showing how she suggested Aztlán is a mixed landscape that extends beyond limiting spatial taxonomies like public and private and limited cultural ideals such as the American Dream, which frequently neglects the inner hopes and lives of Chicanx and Latinx peoples.[13] Pérez-Torres's assessment of the concept and related ideas speaks to how Chicanx and Latinx artists have refigured this notion to create a sense of home and belonging because many queer Latinos feel like they are outsiders that have had to *create a new roadmap* for living in authentic, real forms.[14] The scenes in Arroyo's *The Singing Shark* and Anzaldúa's poetry constitute a spatial formation that I view as "ethical geography" in light of the way that their thoughtful depictions of hybrid lives, bodies, and social experiences lead us to rethink how ethics and morals are maintained in a range of social spaces. Julie Urbanik notes, "Ethical geographies are concerned with examining how notions of right and wrong not only differ spatially, but are also place-dependent (i.e., it is considered ethically right to experiment on animals in a laboratory, but not in a home)."[15] It is this intersection of place, ethics, and justice that serves as a focal point for this chapter. Through this lens, I interpret the aforesaid poets' writing as urging us to (re)consider how spatial experience can influence our views of past and present sociopolitical problems like displacement and social marginalization; these encoded contexts inspire ways of resisting sociopolitical injustices like homophobic and racist acts.

Although the poetry of Anzaldúa and Arroyo may foster this resistance in several forms, readers observe hybrid beings speaking out about social tensions and immobility, or what might be called feelings of being socially and physically *liminal* or *stuck in place* due to the dominant US normativities entrenched across diverse landscapes. Though disheartening at times, these two poets' scenes notably depict these tensions and sentiments of immobility by exhibiting an inspiring and sophisticated stylistic that offers another way of looking queerly at the world as well as means of engaging with it. Conveyed in carefully crafted verses that integrate elements of nature, popular culture, and human reality, the poets' artistic pieces invite a broad audience beyond intellectuals and scholars. By way of these depictions, the poets urge readers to take stock of their own landscapes' socio-spatial tensions and immobility such as: What is holding us back from creating socially positive formations of change in the contexts of queer Latinx lives and environments? To develop this critical lens further, let us consider the poets' writing by thinking through the ethnic and sexual dimensions of Latinx lives and poetic traditions.

POSITIONING POETICS: HYBRID BODIES AND NATURAL SPACES IN ART AND CRITICISM

The scholarly frameworks developed by environmentalists and researchers in ethnic studies encourage critics to be mindful of the manner in which context, space, and place inform diverse projects of cultural production. Such forms of scholarship identify a move away from the "metronormativity" that Jack Halberstam has theorized in response to the myth that all queer subjects will (or should) migrate from the so-called homophobic countryside to the supposedly liberated urban centers.[16] As Mary L. Gray, Colin R. Johnson, and Brian J. Gilley suggest, the experiences and theories of queerness extend far beyond the urban spaces thought to be most hospitable for LGBTQ peoples.[17] The poems considered here offer a contrast to the normative by resituating queer bodies in imaginary and everyday spaces, which paves the way for fostering alternative epistemologies and spaces for rethinking prior social structures that regularly enervate and hinder queer world-making. In blazing this trail, these poems also make manifest a space to explore the sociopolitical links between daily human life and animals as well as the following question: What possibilities exist for Latinx queers *to belong* in US contexts when their social worlds privilege Anglophone and heterosexual family-making as the proper pursuit?

Following the thought of Kristen Ross and Joseph Harrington, I hypothesize poetry like that of Anzaldúa and Arroyo can be read as instantiating more hospitable spatial scenes that are dialogic, relational, and social in composition.[18] With such thought in mind, the scenes of Anzaldúa and Arroyo represent communicative and social intimacies — that is, sites of thought and relationality — that encourage us to embrace our more authentic and playful selves across a wide spectrum of places, while doing away with the unethical violence that is directed toward queer Latinx peoples. Critics and scholars also are realizing the benefits of honoring and studying the ethical relations between Latinx groups and spatial formations such as public parks where people exchange ideas and socialize. Agencies such as the US National Parks Service embraced this path by reaching out to Latinx groups through using social-media campaigns like "the *Encuentra Tu Parque*" (Find Your Park) campaign to build social awareness and inclusiveness.[19] In a comparable way, Arroyo himself embraced the socially conscious principles of Buddhism that call for a greater respect for nature and all living creatures. Many Buddhists like Arroyo have long practiced a vegetarian or vegan way of life, aligning with the environmentally conscious aesthetics that are put forth in poetic form. Anzaldúa's writing likewise shows how her creative process and theory were in dialogue with religious belief systems of indigenous cultures such as the ancient Aztec civilization, which held animals in high regard and integrated these figures into daily practices and traditions. This relation of nature and writing is theorized by AnaLouise Keating, who interprets Anzaldúa's writing about an ancient Aztec deity named Coatlicue—a woman who wore a skirt of snakes.[20] For Anzaldúa then, mixing the bodies of serpents and humans is legible as a means to reject the toxic negativity that is directed toward social and physical difference; that is to say, this embrace of bodily difference allows her to dignify radical bodily otherness and mixing that have played positive roles in varied lives.

As Anzaldúa showcases snakes, Arroyo focuses on creatures from waterways who demonstrate an ethical mind-set and intelligence that mirror the acumen of everyday people in our world today. In contrast, many Anglophone cultures continue to cite their so-called higher-level intellectual capacity as a way of justifying the abuse of the environment and reaping of myriad animal populations. Such activities have not only harmed the ecology and food chain across our global landscapes but also have caused mass extinctions of creatures that have evolved on the Earth for millions of years. The renowned theorist Donna J. Haraway explores the ways that animal species have been imperiled as well as shaped by human activities in myriad locales in her book *When Species Meet*, showing the constructedness of so-called human superiority and the power that humans wield over animals again and again.[21] This ideation is captured by her concept of "human exceptionalism," which partially mirrors the theoretical concept of American exceptionalism, though in this case the term speaks to how humans are envisioned as meriting power over so-called *lower animals*. In contrast to such a vision, Anzaldúa and Arroyo turn the tables irreverently on people in positions of power and authority by aligning themselves with animals and natural landscapes. Through such mixing, the poems' figures channel the animals' fierceness, strength, resiliency, and prowess. Moreover, these approaches of mixing animals and human forms is not unheard of in Mexican and Mexican American cultural contexts, especially when we consider how numerous groups in Mexico and the United States have embraced the thought-provoking craft of building *alebrijes*, which are artistic representations of fanciful and unreal creatures that are multicolored and involve a physical synthesis of bodily attributes from assorted animals. Though such artwork may be regarded negatively at times as primitivism, these cultural formations also offer opportunities for resisting, and accordingly, experts in several fields have begun to publish more broadly about the relations of queerness and natural formations.[22]

Although the field of queer nature studies is still burgeoning, queer poets have been writing about nature for thousands of years. US poets, including Emily Dickinson, Walt Whitman, and Audre Lorde (among others) have written verse portraying animalistic and earthly imagery, which evoke feelings relating to societal forces and ideas far beyond the confines of the natural world. While ostensibly radical in their composition and style, these writers build on a larger cultural tradition where authors have brought nature and humanity into contact as well as blended *the animal* and *the human* for thousands of years. Indeed, this tradition of mixing the creature and the human is also legible in the ancient belief systems of Greece and Egypt where deities encapsulated such blending. In Ancient Egypt, the god associated with death and the afterlife, Anpu (also known as Anubis) evinced the head of a jackal and the body of a man. Similarly in modern writing, readers observe the mixing of human intelligence with an animal physique such as in the case of Franz Kafka's novella *The Metamorphosis*, where Gregor Samsa takes the shape of an insect and possesses the mind of a man.[23] This same idea is implied in H. G. Wells's science fiction narrative *The Island of Dr. Moreau* (1896), in which animals and humans are sutured together.[24] Wells's novel anticipates the sociopolitical problems created by eugenics and the science of mixing animals with humans genetically. Interestingly, Anzaldúa and Arroyo appear less concerned with the fallout of depicting such animal-human hybrids in the context of poetry. Historically, the scenes created within poetry have provided a space for radical creative thought, and as a prior chapter suggests, Mexican American artists (as well as many more) have shown an openness to connecting lived experiences to nonhuman creatures like *mariposas* (butterflies). Daniel Enrique Pérez speaks to this pattern where "Chicano and Latino identities are reconfigured in cultural production using butterflies as metaphors."[25] These acts of metaphorizing in time point to a pattern that merits greater critical consideration because of a preponderance of queer artists and thinkers have taken to pattern of syncretism.

In the past decade, scholars across several fields have advanced impressive research by opening pathways in the discussion of the ways that animal imagery has been imbricated with the ideas and lived experiences of Latinx peoples.[26] Relatedly, the writer of natural history Dan Flores for instance, posits insights on the way that the US government has played certain roles in perpetuating the divide between human beings and animals through his own writing about relations between Anglo Americans and the much demonized Western coyote.[27] As Flores discusses the way that human history parallels that of coyotes, his writing illustrates that we have much in common with this animal that he calls an "American original." For while humans like to think of themselves as being civilized, good-natured, and refined—*everything that the coyote supposedly is not*—Flores calls attention to the fact that humans repeatedly have attempted to eradicate vast numbers of coyotes and other humans. In his popular book *Coyote America*, Flores provides a history of how early white Americans aimed to kill off the indigenous coyote and wolf populations in hopes of "protecting" their land, livelihood, and local communities:

So with the goal of blanketing river valleys and mountain ranges with poison bait stations that aimed to kill every predator of every species in a region, with its new funding the bureau now proceeded to build a plant in Albuquerque New Mexico, to produce strychnine tablets in volume. Chillingly and unsentimentally dubbed the Eradication Methods Laboratory, this federal killing facility moved to Denver in 1921, where it would go on to perfect an amazing witch's brew of ever more efficient, ever deadlier predacides. Chemists and researchers in the Eradication Laboratory, with government jobs and benefits, presumably realized the American Dream in the 1920s, buying houses, automobiles, radios, and washing machines, all the latest technologies of the decade.[28]

Alongside the devastation, Flores's invocation of the American Dream stands out in a noticeable way. Although Flores ruminates only sparingly on this aspect of the dream, such commentary lays bare the implications of what was happening under the aegis of US government. Flores creates a stark contrast by illuminating how the gleaming success of early Americans came at the cost of destroying an ancient and integral set of species across a large swath of the ecosystem. This pairing of the American Dream with death and destruction largely leads readers to reconcile the ghastly moments that went into the (un)making of US cultures and landscapes. For many early Americans and even today's world, creating the ideal nation meant purging natural landscapes of unruly elements that challenged white populations. As an example, throughout US history, people across the LGBTQ spectrum have been depicted in film and media as being like many animal predators—seeking out people to prey on. This idea was dramatically depicted in the 1961 educational film *Boys Beware*.[29] In contrast to such negativity, Anzaldúa and Arroyo take an alternative approach that embraces animality and the naturalness of people as a central component. Through bringing together peculiar characters and readers, these poets cultivate a subversive space where queerly hybrid figures connect with humans in a less stratified and more egalitarian sociality, thus turning marginality into transformative coalitions.

ALIGNING WITH NATURE: ANZALDÚA'S POETRY OF SLITHERING, SPINNING, AND QUAKING

In 2009, Keating published a superb collection titled *The Gloria Anzaldúa Reader*. In this compendium of never-before-seen and prior-printed pieces, a number of poems, essays and writings from Anzaldúa's extensive archive were made available for the public. Among the many fine pieces, readers will find poems featuring hybrid beings and voices that go beyond several American social standards. To understand these poetic scenes, I turn to the ideas of scholars in cultural studies and ethnic studies, which advance critiques of the way that people of color, people with disabilities, and queer peoples have been dehumanized through institutionalized forms of violence that aim to keep people "in their place." The systemic efforts to keep down minority groups such as people of color can be observed throughout the history of the United States. In the 1800s for instance, the ingrained US customs and policies allowed slaveholders to treat enslaved African Americans as if they were animals, though in many cases, the animals of Southern plantations reportedly received kinder treatment than the slave populations.[30] Researchers such as Mel Y. Chen also have theorized a similar set of social phenomena in the contexts of art and quotidian experiences, questioning how cultural production and phenomena link racialized thought processes to experiences of animality and intimate matters like sexuality.[31] Chen's lucid research delves into the spatial orientations of animalistic cultural production, showing how westerners' ideas of "animal spaces" have been constituted in multilayered forms like the maintenance of entrenched norms, laws, and societal structures, which diminish and disempower so-called nonhuman spatial experiences.

Frequently relegated to peripheries, nonhuman spaces such as the historical habitats of animals are cast by human beings as being part of larger economic systems and industries that fall under the purview of the wealthy and corporations—groups that have accrued authority and repeatedly overpower discussions of equal protection and freedom. To counter this depersonalization of the nonhuman, Anzaldúa has made the animal experience into a personal matter where spatial experience like context plays key roles. During an interview in the late 1990s, an interviewer asked Anzaldúa to share a comment about her personal and spiritual beliefs, though her commentary went far beyond the anticipated western viewpoint. In her reply to the interviewer, she expounds on our ideas of animality and nature by saying that these beings shape her worldview, saying: "I'm concerned with why people differentiate animals from humans. To me, we're all related, even to the grass. . . . People aren't even aware that animals have consciousness or souls or anything. Human is everything, and everything that's not human is a servant of mankind."[32] Anzaldúa's sagacious explanation exemplifies a closeness to animals and natural contexts, while showing how these entities are perceived as Other or "different" by much of the dominant Anglophone culture and corporate world. In this way, Anzaldúa enacts solidarity with animality and the ecological—a point that she reifies when she states, "We're part animal."[33] Her words reveal her embrace of this animal and natural otherness, urging readers to become mindful of the deep personal connections that *all people* share with the natural world. By laying bare our more natural side, Anzaldúa reveals Other sides of the social sphere and invites readers to be conscious of the power dynamics and hierarchies existing in these overlaps between all living beings. Such acts of consciousness-raising can lead readers to reflect on deleterious assumptions and practices like the depredation of vulnerable animal life for profits.

In taking this approach, Anzaldúa resists the stultifying and ubiquitous forces of US capitalism and conformity that routinely threaten the environment. To personalize the animal, she crafts poetic imagery in her autobiographical essay *"La Prieta,"* which connects her humanity to that of an arachnid, creating a hybrid—a human spider.[34] In this portion, she self-identifies as being a "sort of spider-woman" who mirrors the Hindu religious deity named Shiva. Anzaldúa invokes this image of Shiva as she distinguishes herself as having a dynamic sense of selfhood with many ties of affinity across diverse communities. In her words, she explains how personal experience resembles a "many-armed and many-legged body with one foot on brown soil, one on white, one in straight society, one in the gay world, the man's world, the women's, one limb in the literary world, another in the working class."[35] While symbolizing the multifacetedness of her individuality, Anzaldúa's spider-self also reads as a way of honoring her connectivity and intimacies with a wide-ranging mix of communities across the landscape. Thus, although the figure of the spider often is perceived as a cold, solitary, and predatory creature, here Anzaldúa has constructed the spider in a countercultural (queer) way, transforming the spider into a positive emblem. This unique spider-self can be read as being a socially active bridge-builder who builds new kinds of relations as well as novel perspectives that can inform those around her.

As Anzaldúa's spider figure symbolizes the human being's constructive impulse and intimacy with diverse communities, she also imbues the arachnid with the capacity to be a creator of new knowledges. This idea becomes visible in her poem "Like a spider in her web" where a spider-woman manifests as the purveyor of artistic creation. Situating this spider figure in the comfort of bed, Anzaldúa writes about a spidery figure who will "spin images and words."[36] Though commonly seen as a site of sexual intimacy, this bed provides a locale for the spider-woman to *create* artistic production including verses and stories. Instead of being a creator of conventional intimacy, Anzaldúa's spidery bed is legible as creating an emotional and intellectual intimacy with the reader, resisting imperatives of compulsory heterosexuality. Unlike heteronormative relations in which the social paradigm relies on a dominant masculinity and a submissive femininity, this spider-woman poeticizes her personal experience, highlighting an intimacy that is created with her body as well as the reader that is drawn into witnessing these poetic scenes. While such imagery does not connote acts of masturbation, the poem shows an intimate self-reliance, implying that this animal-human hybrid possesses the agency to foster another world with oneself (and readers) in a meaningful manner. Notably this ability to create new worlds ostensibly is granted through the spider's acts of spinning, thus bringing to mind the ideas of

Peter Anthony Mena and An Yountae, who contend that the animal element functions as "the decentering point of rupture towards a new consciousness."[37] By engaging a new kind of consciousness, another set of beliefs are upheld, which allows for an alternative form of ethical geography where the honoring of queer Latinx individuality is supported. And by way of the spider-woman's hybridity, new understandings of the self are attainable and valued. Instead of showing difference negatively, Anzaldúa shows how such forms of difference provide meaningful pathways to creative intimacy, knowledge and Other social possibilities that are defiant of the societal models that have given rise to civic and underlying inequalities.

Eco-critical scholars like Timothy Clark posit that the perceived differences or distinctions that are often said to exist between animals and humans are in fact arbitrary and socially constructed through the normalizing and repetition of daily practices.[38] Considering this notion in more depth may lead readers to perceive the possibility of an equivalence or homology between animals and humans. Accordingly, researchers such as Timothy Clark encourage us to place animals and humans on equal footing, which exhibits a kind of reverence and mindfulness similar to that of Anzaldúa. Notably, this reflective and mindful capacity comes through within Anzaldúa's short poem "Reincarnation" as it depicts a snake (or serpent) that exhibits some of the same qualities that humans are capable of possessing. In her poem, readers learn a snake has shed its skin, and afterward this creature ponders which part "I had discarded."[39] Anzaldúa uses synecdoche here to show the creature's molted skin emblematic of the self that continues to evolve and grow. Through this poetic strategy, Anzaldúa leads us to ponder how *our own past* is often disowned in the process of creating our present and future selves in the public world. This poem's plurality of the self—the discarded self and the present self—speaks to how queer people often undergo processes of coming out, self-fashioning, and personal change while they reckon with the onslaught of a homophobic public sphere that demands conformity. In a similar way, this same idea of change comes through in the poem's title "Reincarnation," which suggests the cyclical and changing nature of life's processes—a vision that attests to the great extent of human diversity beyond one cultural ideal. This cyclical quality is further emphasized by the unique way in which Anzaldúa positions her poem's verses on the real printed page.

Unlike many poems that rely on repetition and symmetry, Anzaldúa's "Reincarnation" unfurls a set of curvaceous lines across the page, leading readers to experience these lines as one might observe a snake slithering upon the ground. In creating this serpentine space, Anzaldúa invites readers to consider their own movements and relationality within the spaces they inhabit. Such relationality remains ongoing and unfinalized in much the same form as the poem's verses, which never finish with any conclusive punctuation, can be read as intimating how nature continues across time and space. This visualization allows readers to understand the experiences of living creatures who are, like some Chicana queers, kept at a distance from the mainstream society. Instead of maintaining such distances, scholars such as Catrióna Rueda Esquibel have brought Chicana lesbian writings to the forefront by proffering explorations that "map out the terrain of Chicana lesbian fiction" and highlight texts that imbricate nature with corporeality.[40] As Catrióna Rueda Esquibel shows, there has long been a pattern of linking natural environs with queer Chicana artistry. This inventive mixing of nature and humanity is visible in Anzaldúa's "Yemayá." According to Keating, the poem is named after the "Yoruban orisha (goddess) associated with oceans and other waters."[41] The poem envisions the ocean as corporeal and sentient. In the verses, Anzaldúa says that Yemayá is the "ocean mother, sister of the fishes." This human-like seascape gives readers a means of understanding our commonalities with nature, which changes with the ebb and flow of the tides. To a similar degree, Anzaldúa has employed the language of landscapes to instantiate a disruptive and irreverent impact that pushes us beyond our comfort zone. Her poem "I Want to Be Shocked Shitless" (1974) provides a partial explanation of her sense of taste and artistry in poetic writing. On this poem, Keating affords us the insight that this poem was read by Anzaldúa at poetry readings as a way of fostering and praising thought-provoking creativities.[42] In her poem, Anzaldúa encourages her listeners to move her *emotionally* with words. She speaks to the audience by encouraging them to "Be an earthquake" that will move her body and mind in a substantive manner.[43] Through these words, Anzaldúa effectively merges her readers (or listeners) with the forces of natural Earth movements. Using several commanding words like *thunder* and *quake*, Anzaldúa implores listeners to become a hybrid and stalwart figure who is capable of fostering change.

Shocking approaches may be less desirable for sensitive readers, though Anzaldúa's poem also can be read as proposing the idea that a poem is successful when it stimulates people into action and transforms our understanding. In this sense, Anzaldúa's *thunder* and *quake* represent more than the destructive, frightening aspects that are commonly associated with natural phenomena. That is to say, her poem's discourse connotes the great value of having a generative intellectual stimulation that arises through intimacies such as poetry readings and deep knowledges of a poet's writing. Anzaldúa's representations of hybridity are by no means an isolated case in the broader spectrum of Latinx creativities. The Mexican painter Frida Kahlo and the Mexican American painter Tino Rodríguez similarly have been lauded for producing highly inventive pieces that merge human beings with the nonhuman. Kahlo's dream-like paintings *El venado herido* (*The Wounded Deer*) and *Raíces* (*Roots*) are vibrant visual portrayals of hybrid figures that are injured or immobile, connoting the thought that there is sometimes a cost to being *different*. As in the case of Kahlo's work, Rodriguez's paintings depict imagery that also shocks because of the way it bridges nature with human forms. His painting *Eternal Lovers* blends leaves and flowers to create skeletons that are embracing one another and kissing in a decidedly intimate manner. The realistic beauty of the colorful flowers contrasts with the deathly imagery of skulls, creating a surprising mix akin to that of Anzaldúa's work. In bringing us close to their kiss, Rodriguez suggests we are a part of this imaginary and natural intimacy. A comparable sort of intimacy is imagined in the work of the Chicana queer photographer Laura Aguilar, whose creative self-portraits in nature have drawn the attention of numerous scholars including Macarena Gómez-Barris, who sees a link between Aguilar's creativity and that of Anzaldúa's work.[44] In studying Aguilar's nude self-portraits in nature, Gómez-Barris points to a bridge-like scene that brings to mind the ideas of *This Bridge Called My Back: Writings by Radical Women of Color*, which was edited by Cherríe Moraga and Anzaldúa in the early 1980s. Much as we see in the poetry of Anzaldúa, the nude portraits of Aguilar create connectivities between Aguilar's body and nature as well as between viewers and nature. In these intimacies, Aguilar's substantial body stands out as well as blends into the scenes, implying humanity is linked to nature as well as central to its future. These hybrid scenes may feel astonishing at first, yet they *move* observers to think in much the same way that Anzaldúa and Arroyo have done with their verses. Like these poets, Aguilar's photography has graphically shown how people desire to be free from ingrained social ideals and bodily norms that regularly lead to pain and shame.

Anzaldúa and Arroyo have transformed such ideals and norms into more creative and positive cultural phenomena that foster intellectual dialogue. Anzaldúa's poem "Encountering the Medusa" evidences this pattern insofar as the mythical being of Medusa and its corporeal space can be read as an effort to spur dialogue about the experiences of queer intimacies and creativity. As the Medusa figure regularly is regarded as a fearful killer, queer peoples likewise have been likened to frightening monsters. Anzaldúa's portrayal of the mythical Medusa is spatial and transgressive in its content insofar as the speaker feels confined and haunted by the monster that seemingly looms in the mirror. Historically this monster has been understood as having snakes emanating from its hair and having the ability to turn people to stone. In the case of the poem, the speaker explains that after being haunted by this stultifying Medusa figure, they become caught in its stare. Anzaldúa's poetic scene instantiates a speaker who has "snakes in my hair," which suggests the speaker has become Medusa and thus embodied the merging of animal and human.[45] Feeling boxed into the scene's space, the speaker watches this scene unfold in the glass of a mirror, becoming trapped. This poem's mirror-world is shown to be a space of Otherness where a part of the

Figure 4.2. The photograph "Nature Self-Portrait #5" by the Chicana artist Laura Aguilar (1996).

speaker dwells in thought, inhabiting more than one space simultaneously: the real and the unreal. As a result, this scene's nightmarish mirror world comes to create a form of social intimacy with the speaker (as well as readers). Threatened at first, Anzaldúa's speaker appears to realize the creative powers of the Medusa figure, seeing her ability to transform a menacing enemy into something innocuous. While an outsider at first, this "daemon" figure in the poem merges with the speaker, henceforth hybridizing and unifying. This approach brings to mind the process whereby queers come to terms with their Other desires and accept their social reality—rather than hating and rejecting themselves for being queer. To be sure, accepting one's queer sense of self can be a challenge when families and society imagine expectations for us including conventional marriage and carrying on the family's legacy by having children. In this case, Anzaldúa's poetic scene transforms our lens on the once-monstrous Medusa. Rather than maintaining the monster as being a figure of evil, her poem encourages us to move beyond the superficial and reconsider the sense of self that is relegated to Otherness. This Otherness may resonate as a space of strife originally, but it ultimately becomes a means of inviting readers to reconcile their various selves and be creative in their own daring ways.

TEXTUAL INNOVATIONS: ARROYO'S POETRY OF SHARKS, HOLLYWOOD, AND LANDSCAPES

In a manner akin to that of Anzaldúa, the Puerto Rican poet Rane Arroyo conveys the cultural and physical experiences of living a life in-between by crafting unusual poems about imaginary creatures and landscapes. Rising to prominence in the 1990s and 2000s, Arroyo achieved great heights as a poet and academic, who published ten books of poetry and became a prominent, well-respected figure in academia and beyond. However, in 2010, this productive and award-winning writer passed away at the age of fifty-five. Even after Arroyo's early death, his inventive and heartfelt work lives on because of how his writing speaks to the life experiences of queer Latinx peoples in the twenty-first century. His poetry depicts queer figures in a variety of scenes and spaces, which serves to suggest the widespread spectrum of Latinx experience in the United States and beyond. In this writing, Arroyo draws on his personal experiences as a queer Puerto Rican man who exists within the languages of both English and Spanish. Just as writers observe in Anzaldúa's work, Arroyo repeatedly blends Spanish and English in a stylized format that resembles code-switching—the hybridization of languages that continues as cultures come into contact. Though others have employed this technique before, Arroyo's work also offers remarkable and telling portrayals of the natural world. In so doing, he elevates the experience of the living—both the human and the animal—in a memorable way that invites readers to reconsider the social significance of "the natural" within queer Latinx writings.

The natural and poetic imagery of Arroyo's work can be traced back hundreds—if not thousands—of years to eras where poets produced pastoral forms, which place human figures in a variety of rustic and serene landscapes. In such writing, shepherds would tend to their flock and travelers would visit distant lands, commenting on the spaces and waters they explore. Late during the twentieth century and more recently, certain natural images have gained prominence. For example, the image of the shark manifested in a sizable number of contexts ranging from major motion pictures (consider the popular *Jaws* movies) to more television movies like the B-movie series that began with cable television's *Sharknado* series. In these exemplars, the figure of the shark demonstrates intelligence and prowess that rivals that of human beings, suggesting a sort of parallel. This same logic of rivalry takes on numerous forms in many other storytelling forms such as fairytales where villains like the Big Bad Wolf are shown as being a threatening intelligence on par with the supposedly innocent protagonist Little Red Riding Hood. This same cunning of wolves can be discerned in a very broad range of cultural products such as stories of lycanthropy and werewolves, which manifest in diverse ways such as the television program *Teen Wolf* and the *Twilight* film series. These TV products advance the idea that humans have a more animalistic side to them, yet they are repeatedly vilified by those afraid of difference. In the cases of Anzaldúa and Arroyo, however, the texts present the idea that these unique creatures should be granted greater reverence, space, and sovereignty despite their misfit status.

Already the field of queer indigenous studies has begun to theorize the manner in which queer and sexual experience has substantive ties to the land and the ways in which American Indian peoples have been disenfranchised and dislocated from their spaces.[46] These critical studies have set the stage for understanding how nonconforming beings (such as the figures of Arroyo's work) experience a sense of unbelonging, displacement, and lack of connection to the space around them. Moreover, in the case of Arroyo's collection of poems, *The Singing Shark*, readers are treated to a range of poems that also provide a comment on matters of art, ethnicity, gender, sexuality, and social problems that are perpetuated in the mainstream media such as stereotypes. Several of his poems allude to, or suggest, queer hybridity, but the one that most interests me in this chapter is "The Singing Shark Dream, or Toto, I Don't Think We're in Tegucigalpa Anymore," in which the hybrid figure conveys a self-explanation and reflection. This poem's title mirrors lines from another queer fan favorite—*The Wizard of Oz*—thereby suggesting this poem to be a mix of old media favorites as well as inventive thinking.

To explain this poem's new thinking, the first pages of Arroyo's lengthy poem provides a backstory for the shark-man, illuminating how he came to exist against all odds. Arroyo sets up one of the poem's main ideas that resonates queerly: the poem's figures depart from naturalized processes of heterosexual reproduction. The shark-man is born from his mother's memories, yet he is treated as a freak of nature by the human world. This mother María is the same protagonist from the popular US musical *West Side Story*, which largely presents a story of New York's Puerto Rican community. This shark-man elaborates on Maria's character as a means of commentary about his own identity and (dis)connection to surroundings, which is shown to be decidedly unfriendly environs. From what Arroyo's poem suggests, the mother's mere social connection with a local street gang—called The Sharks—brings him into existence. This inventive story of creation appears nonsensical at first because of its highly imaginative nature, yet it provides Arroyo with a means to explore the social and spatial relations that are experienced by immigrants and migrants. In this case, Arroyo uses the shark-man's struggle in the human world to query other struggles. As a commonwealth of the United States, Puerto Rico peoples have been kept at a far distance from the United States, and this positioning has made Puerto Rican people feel like outsiders. This same idea is mirrored in this poem's protagonist where the young shark boy at first falls outside the doctors' preestablished standards of physical and linguistic normality. This shark boy hopes to be placed in a "big aquarium" instead of just a water cooler, thus showing his human ability to think.[47] Because of his shark-like body and his ability to reason, he exists in-between two worlds—that of the human and that of the animal. Although this poem might be read as a sad story about being stuck in an unsympathetic human world, the poem uses references from popular culture to create a fairly humorous commentary on his hybrid experience. Toward the middle of the poem, the shark states his motto is "have teeth, will travel."[48] In these words, the shark-man reconfigures the language of the human world for his own purposes, creating both a witty commentary and a telling statement about existing at interstices. While some disregard the poem for being silly, I interpret this inventive approach as being a means to address subjects of exclusion, exploitation, and prejudice that pervade the social landscapes of the United States.

Similarly, in Arroyo's collection *The Buried Sea*, another speaker continues this same phenomenon of mixing and hybrid space insofar as this collection delivers scenes that enmesh the language of the sea, oceanic history, and marine life. For instance, in Arroyo's collection *The Buried Sea*, he includes a poem "My First Novel," which portrays a set of scenes that are united in their relation to the sea waters.[49] Yet this poem goes beyond the commonplace imagery of seafaring as Arroyo's speaker also ruminates on the actions of nonconformists such as a drag queen who *"extinguishes the sky with glasses of ice and blue gin."* The poem speaks to readers in a direct way, encouraging them to recognize the multiplicity and change happening around them. However, even as these figures remain defiant, the poem alludes to the finality of death and mortality by including other brief images of a cemetery, a burning moon, a drowning moon, and gravestones. But this gloomy imagery never overwhelms the scene, suggesting that death can never destroy all of humanity's creativity absolutely. Arroyo's poem sends the message that at times we can break free from cultural scripts by moving beyond the spaces of the ordinary and constructing our own sense of ethics and geographies. Such spaces may exist in the interstices, but these locales provide advantageous perspectives on the broader social landscape.

As Arroyo's shark-man attempts to dispatch binaristic thinking of the civilized and the wilderness, "The Singing Shark" also calls into question the way that certain racial groups such as whites are granted greater sociopolitical privilege through ingrained systems. Historically across the US justice system, political arenas, the business world, and a wide array of other sites, the people who are granted greater status and are perceived as being morally upstanding figures are white Americans. A version of this set of circumstances plays out in Arroyo's *The Singing Shark* poem where the nameless shark-man explains how he was kept in an aquarium despite being partially human.[50] The shark-man's wording about white kids in "children carriages" draws attention to the way that white youth are encouraged to be themselves and seemingly have little hardship. In contrast, this shark-man is encaged, put on display for whites' entertainment, and has no self-determination. This disturbing scene conjures to mind the way that some Latinx people have been jailed in detention centers for simply traveling across land to enter the United States. Such sequestering and Othering is also eerily similar to the manner in which disabled people have been institutionalized and locked away because they departed from the norms of their family's preconceived ideas. This idea is reinforced when he says he had to "stumble," revealing the challenges of existing in a world constructed for able-bodied humans. This Othering likewise comes through in his words "freak son," which pulls at the readers' heartstrings due to how they signal the feeling that this shark-man is pushed beyond the limits of human normality. Much as the scholars of contemporary Freak Theory suggest, the unjust circumstances of inaccessibility can be identified in a bevy of contexts during history and that of cultural production.[51] Such representation comments on the prevailing systems that hinder equitable access as well as the processes through which non-normative bodies are hidden away from the social sphere.

Arroyo's "The Singing Shark" reinforces this idea of social absence when the shark-man speaks of his family and life through the cultural lens of Hollywood and mainstream storytelling. Through calling attention to media production, the shark-man's actions mirror that of Anzaldúa's poem about Medusa inasmuch as his comments on storytelling exhibit a reflective, metatextual dimension. This metatextuality, which comes through the shark-man's voice, shows him to be critical about the way that the media function and repeat stories in less investigative and nuanced ways. This approach contrasts with the critical discourses of scholars like Chris Philo and Chris Wilbert who explain, "A 'new' animal geography has emerged to explore the dimensions of space and place which cannot but sit at the heart of these relations."[52] Their collection explores the "agency of animals, and the extent to which we can say that animals destabilize, transgress or even resist our human orderings, including spatial ones."[53] These reconfigurings are evident in the work of Arroyo as his poem's speaker talks back to the media. Toward the middle of the poem, Arroyo's shark-man reconfigures normal orderings by mocking the media's formats including "MTV."[54] In taking a jab at the VJs of the 1990s, Arroyo's shark-man acts like a TV personality, but this moment of televisual performativity is also characterized by what is missing from his family's life—the continued love of his parents, which can never be regained fully, only reenacted. To a similar extent, the shark-man's identity, while partially explored, is never fully developed. Like children with disabilities who were hidden away from their relatives in the past, we never hear the name of this figure, which makes him appear anonymous. Yet he has a strong sense of self nonetheless. This sense of self is made in the anaphora of "I'm not" that is repeated at the end of the stanza. Intriguingly, these verses allude to who he cannot be: the understood and respected hero who is moral, conventionally beautiful and, thus, saves the day. But as an outsider, he can bring attention how our world shores up conventions of development and storytelling.

Arroyo's poem resists normative poetics by leading readers to ponder what it means to be regarded as *different* and be confined to the "Central Park Zoo."[55] Although zoos are often praised for preserving the lives of endangered animals, more often than not the animals' cages are considerably smaller than the terrain that the animals claim in their habitat. Hence in Arroyo's case, his shark-man's spatial experiences doubly convey a symbolism in that it speaks for both the animals and the people who have been dispossessed of their spaces and unfairly detained by the polity and other nation-states. While some may disapprove of identifying the existence of such sociopolitical connections between animals and humans, we must recognize that that line of thinking fails to see how animals, land, and humans have rather deep ties of affinity. Such connections suggest that animals and humans should be seen as having greater parity, yet their differences are highlighted more often than their commonalities and relations with humans. In a similar manner, our world casts aside the substantive relations between humanity and landscapes such as the relations we have to comforting verdant meadows or trees that improve our air.

Julian Olivares speaks to the relations of Latinx peoples and complex landscapes in his research on poetic writing, showing how Latina writers have crafted an artistic and meaningful poetics of space.[56] As Olivares shows us, these spaces are laden with anxieties and emotional elements that are intertwined with our intimacies. Such inner tensions emanate from Arroyo's poem "The Field," in which Arroyo imagines a speaker who provides commentary on a field of snow and the extent to which this snowy field both appears beautiful as well as brings to mind ideas of a cold disturbing scene.[57] The poem's speaker characterizes the snowy field as being a place of perfection, yet as the poem progresses, the nameless speaker implies this snowy place is also a site of turmoil where displacement and violence threaten the mental state of the speaker, who self-identifies as a "dreamer" and "dark."[58] Through these descriptors, readers gather that this figure has felt out of place because of his physical and cultural standing. To begin to decode this dynamic, I interpret this snowy field as an extended metaphor where the field and the snow stand in for noninclusive US realities, in which various marginalized groups such as queer people of color are struggling against the challenges of a world that is mediated as ideal—*a place of opportunity*—in the mainstream media and innumerable other contexts. But as Arroyo and others attest, such idealistic discourse belies the reality of attacks and aggressions that permeate the lives of migrants, who work in forbidding conditions on a daily basis.

The idea of place and space takes on a notable importance in Arroyo's poem "The Field," which presents a snowy landscape as being both a beautiful scene as well as a powerful and uncontrollable mass. This large snowy mass arguably mirrors another kind of enormous mass—the dominant white public across innumerable US landscapes. For instance, while the snow could be said to have a kind of angelic beauty in the poem, that beauty's goodness is only superficial. In the poem, this snow overwhelms and dominates the field where the speaker offers a remembrance of finding charming flowers for decorating their home. Throughout this scene, the snow inhibits the speaker's connection to the land, preventing the connection to the land that they desire. In this way, the snowy "whiteness" engulfing the speaker haunts them, causing them to dwell on these difficulties as well as try to make sense of the resulting aggravations.[59] Yet through sharing this scene, the speaker connects both to the field's potential—the flowers—as well as readers, uniting through the experience of this landscape. Bringing his readers into close proximity with this natural space allows Arroyo to challenge the factors and forces that create enervating feelings of alienation and loneliness. To accomplish this, both Anzaldúa and Arroyo employ free verse form that eschews tidy patterns, creating an approach that partially mirrors the changing realities of Latinx queer lives. This weaving of elements resembles an assemblage where components are linked and tessellated, suggesting a multifaceted stream of creativity. But these pieces also go far beyond reality. As in the magical realism of Isabel Allende and Gabriel García Márquez, human reality is transmuted through the innovation of fanciful ideas and styles that allow us to dream anew. While curious in composition, these pieces provide imaginative approaches and insights into the lives and experiences of the 1980s, 1990s, and early 2000s. In this time, sociopolitical forces colluded against vulnerable groups such as queers and Latinx people, but the work of Anzaldúa and Arroyo functioned as commentaries and lifeboats that lent a means to reimagine what the future might have in store for their communities.

RESISTING SIMPLE ENDINGS: DEVELOPING INVENTIVE FUTURES IN QUEERLY HYBRID POETRY

In the writings of Anzaldúa and Arroyo, the lived experience of Latinx queers and the natural world become intertwined, and as a result, these developments have made the fields of ethics and social justice studies more interdisciplinary and multidimensional. These fields are no longer just for scholars and theoreticians, but rather they are a space for artists and advocates. Such groups empower us to think critically about the ways that beliefs, ethics, and moral values continue to be embedded in a wide range of contexts, places, and spaces. The poetry of Anzaldúa and Arroyo suggest that ostensibly unconventional bodies, identities, and spaces generate a blueprint for social change. These blueprints speak to the power of forming imaginative alliances that might seem impossible at first glance but grant new options. In the writing of Anzaldúa and Arroyo for instance, queer figures join with natural entities to become stronger, move beyond prior problems, and contest the actions of unsympathetic oppressors.

As Anzaldúa and Arroyo suggest, social alliances may arise in a myriad of cultural expressions and, therefore, create the conditions of possibility for contesting the unjust realities in which we live. These poems offer the beginnings of bridge-building, which must be expanded if we are to safeguard vulnerable populations. Latinx and queer communities have much to gain by dialoguing with animal rights groups and environmentalists across the Americas. These groups work passionately and intentionally to prevent the extirpation of endangered animals such as Fender's blue butterfly, the gray wolf, the leatherback sea turtle, and the North Atlantic right whale, among others. These majestic creatures are being endangered by human actions both direct and more oblique, yet coalitions are making strides in protecting these populations. In a comparable, yet distinctive manner, many minority groups have struggled to gain protections and taken the debates of civil rights to the courts and streets. But there remains a key distinction here insofar as many real entities of the natural world lack the personal voice that lends a remarkable and powerful element in dialogues, courtrooms, and US Congress where decisions are made about these groups' futures. In these circumstances, poets can lend their creative and powerful voices to bring attention to the challenges and injustices that these groups are facing continually. Although these pieces may resonate with radical messages, it is often the case that radical forms have the potential to grab the attention of listeners. As Anzaldúa suggests, good poetry should "shock" and move us like earthquakes, enabling us to move beyond social immobility.[60]

The social tensions of being in-between, immobile, and not belonging appear to be omnipresent in the writings of Anzaldúa and Arroyo, but alongside these feelings, there are moments of change and connectivity between figures that might not be seen as allies at first glance. This set of relations and evolution could be understood in the terms of "queer ecology," which has been theorized by scholars such as Nicole Seymour.[61] Although such ecologies certainly prove to be rather different from those studied by the researchers in the natural sciences, they hold the potential to provide new insights for varying disciplines. Nonetheless, these poets' figures enable us to rethink the nature of the possible or who we can become in the future. In other words, both Arroyo and Anzaldúa empower readers to contest authority through blends of animals, humans, and landscapes, which make possible a glimmer of alternative ways of life. In effect, their poems foster an eco-consciousness as well as lead us to empathize with those bodies and identities that are cast out from the center of mainstream societal circles and groups. As this chapter has suggested, the poets' messages are by no means unrelated as both poets are speaking to the manner in which so-called normal white subjects — that is, those who are perceived as being Anglophone, heterosexual, and able-bodied — are held up as the social ideals. Meanwhile, animals, hybrids, groups, and natural formations are forced into a secondary status, being deprioritized and placed in a peripheral standing. Using an integrative and queerly inventive approach, Anzaldúa and Arroyo foster a consciousness that moves beyond the boundaries that have kept people "in place" and stultified the creative thought process for which the United States was once celebrated. Phenomenal Latinx innovators like Victor Leaton Ochoa and Ellen Ochoa show the value of pursuing inventive approaches, yet creative and pathbreaking thought seldom is given the same value among artistic communities because of the way that patents for inventions and similar intellectual property accrues greater pecuniary benefits in the long haul. Dynamics like these have inculcated the belief that science, technology, engineering, and mathematics (or STEM) are more necessary or financially rewarding fields of thought. Even so, the intellectual creativities of Anzaldúa and Arroyo help us to see the world in new ways, enabling people to raise their consciousness and accordingly move beyond bias that inhibits growth.

NOTES

1. Gloria E. Anzaldúa and Linda Smuckler, "Spirituality, Sexuality and the Body: An Interview with Linda Smuckler," in *The Gloria Anzaldúa Reader*, ed. AnaLouise Keating (Durham, NC: Duke University Press, 2009), 94.

2. Bernadette Marie Calafell, *Monstrosity, Performance, and Race in Contemporary Culture* (New York: Palgrave Macmillan, 2015), 55; Jorge Capetillo-Ponce, "Exploring Gloria Anzaldúa's Methodology in *Borderlands/La Frontera — The New Mestiza*," *Human Architecture: Journal of the Sociology of Self-Knowledge* 4, no. 3 (2006): 87–94.

3. Gloria Anzaldúa, *Borderlands/La Frontera: The New Mestiza* (San Francisco: Aunt Lute Press, 1999), 48–49.

4. Gloria E. Anzaldúa, *The Gloria Anzaldúa Reader*, ed. AnaLouise Keating (Durham, NC: Duke University Press, 2009), 21, 101.

5. Paulina Palmer, *The Queer Uncanny: New Perspectives on the Gothic* (Cardiff: University of Wales Press, 2012), 154.

6. Gloria Anzaldúa, "Preface: (Un)natural Bridge, (Un)safe Spaces," in *This Bridge We Call Home*, eds. AnaLouise Keating and Gloria Anzaldúa (New York: Routledge, 2002), 3.

7. Anzaldúa, *Borderlands/La Frontera*, 202.

8. Michael Nelson, "An Interview: Rane Arroyo, Author of *The Portable Famine*," BKMK Press, 2007. https://www.newletters.org/bkmk-books/portable-famine. Web.

9. Nelson, "An Interview."

10. Anzaldúa, *Borderlands/La Frontera*, 41.

11. Anzaldúa, *Borderlands/La Frontera*, 27.

12. Peggy Pascoe, "Race, Gender, and The Privileges of Property," in *American Studies: An Anthology*, eds. Janice A. Radway, Kevin K. Gaines, et al. (Malden, MA: Wiley Blackwell, 2009), 89–98.
13. Rafael Pérez-Torres, "Refiguring Aztlán," in *The Chicano Studies Reader, an Anthology of Aztlán, 1970–2015*, eds. Chon A. Noriega, Eric Avila, Karen Mary Davalos, Chela Sandoval, and Rafael Pérez-Torres, 3rd ed. (Los Angeles: University of California Los Angeles Press, 2016), 185.
14. Horacio N. Roque Ramírez, "'That's My Place!': Negotiating Racial, Sexual, and Gender Politics in San Francisco's Gay Latino Alliance, 1975–1983," *Journal of the History of Sexuality* 12, no. 2 (April 2003): 232–36.
15. Julie Urbanik, *Placing Animals: An Introduction to the Geography of Human-Animal Relations* (Lanham, MD: Rowman & Littlefield Publishers, 2012), 12.
16. Jack Halberstam, *In a Queer Time and Place: Transgender Bodies, Subcultural Lives* (New York: New York University Press, 2005), 36.
17. Mary L. Gray, Colin R. Johnson, and Brian J. Gilley, "Introduction," in *Queering the Countryside: New Frontiers in Rural Queer Studies*, eds. Mary L. Gray, Colin R. Johnson, and Brian J. Gilley (New York: New York University Press, 2016).
18. Joseph Harrington, "Poetry and the Public: The Social Form of Modern U.S. Poetics," in *Poetry and Cultural Studies: A Reader*, eds. Maria Damon and Ira Livingston (Chicago: University of Illinois Press, 2009), 266; Kristen Ross, "Rimbaud and the Transformation of Social Space," *Yale French Studies* 73 (1987): 104–20.
19. Keith Lombardo, "Encuentra Tu Parque: Cabrillo National Monument," NPS.gov, 8 August 2016. https://www.nps.gov/media/video/view.htm?id=6C9B8D80-FA90-B6A9-5C1333B6294DFAC2. Web.
20. Anzaldúa, *The Gloria Anzaldúa Reader*, 94.
21. Donna J. Haraway, *When Species Meet* (Minneapolis: University of Minnesota Press, 2007).
22. Catriona Mortimer-Sandilands and Bruce Erickson, eds., *Queer Ecologies: Sex, Nature, Politics, Desire* (Bloomington: Indiana University Press, 2010).
23. Franz Kafka, *The Metamorphosis and Other Stories*, trans. Michael Hofmann (New York: Penguin Books, 2007).
24. H. G. Wells, *The Island of Dr. Moreau* (New York: Bantam Classics, 1994).
25. Daniel Enrique Pérez, "Toward a Mariposa Consciousness: Reimaging Queer Chicano and Latino Identities," in *The Chicano Studies Reader, an Anthology of Aztlán, 1970–2015*, eds. Chon A. Noriega, Eric Avila, Karen Mary Davalos, Chela Sandoval, and Rafael Pérez-Torres, 3rd ed. (Los Angeles: University of California Los Angeles Press, 2016), 564.
26. Priscilla Solis Ybarra. "Borderlands as Bioregion: Jovita Gonzalez, Gloria Anzaldúa and the Twentieth Century Ecological Revolution in the Rio Grande Valley," *MELUS: Multi-Ethnic Literature of the U.S.* 34, no. 2 (2009): 175–89; An Yountae and Peter Anthony Mena, "Anzaldúa's Animal Abyss: Mestizaje and the Late Ancient Imagination," in *Divinanimality: Animal Theory, Creaturely Theology*, eds. Stephen Moore and Laurel Kearns (New York: Fordham University Press, 2014), 161–81.
27. Dan Flores, *Coyote America: A Natural and Supernatural History* (New York: Basic Books, 2016).
28. Flores, *Coyote America*, 98.
29. Sid Davis, dir., *Boys Beware*, Sid Davis Productions, 1961.
30. Frederick Douglass, *Narrative of the Life of Frederick Douglass*, eds. John W. Blassingame, John R. McKivigan, and Peter Hinks (New Haven, CT: Yale University Press, 2001).
31. Mel Y. Chen, *Animacies: Biopolitics, Racial Mattering and Queer Affect* (Durham, NC: Duke University Press, 2012), 14–15.
32. Anzaldúa, *The Gloria Anzaldúa Reader*, 94.
33. Anzaldúa, *The Gloria Anzaldúa Reader*, 94.

34. Gloria Anzaldúa, "La Prieta," *This Bridge Called My Back: Writings by Radical Women of Color*, 4th ed., eds. Cherríe Moraga and Gloria Anzaldúa (Albany: State University of New York Press, 2014), 209.

35. Anzaldúa, "La Prieta," 205.

36. Anzaldúa, *The Gloria Anzaldúa Reader*, 276.

37. Yountae and Mena, "Anzaldúa's Animal Abyss," 171–72.

38. Timothy Clark, *The Cambridge Introduction to Literature and the Environment* (New York: Cambridge University Press, 2011).

39. Anzaldúa, *The Gloria Anzaldúa Reader*, 21.

40. Catrióna Rueda Esquibel, *With Her Machete in Her Hand: Reading Chicana Lesbians* (Austin: University of Texas Press, 2006), 42–65.

41. Anzaldúa, *The Gloria Anzaldúa Reader*, 242.

42. Anzaldúa, *The Gloria Anzaldúa Reader*, 23.

43. Anzaldúa, *The Gloria Anzaldúa Reader*, 23.

44. Macarena Gómez-Barris, "Mestiza Cultural Memory: The Self-Ecologies of Laura Aguilar," in *Laura Aguilar: Show and Tell*, ed. Rebecca Epstein (Los Angeles: University of California Press, 2017), 83.

45. Anzaldúa, *The Gloria Anzaldúa Reader*, 102.

46. Qwo-Li Driskill, Chris Finley, Brian Joseph Gilley, eds., "Introduction," in *Queer Indigenous Studies: Critical Interventions in Theory, Politics and Literature* (Tucson: University of Arizona Press, 2011).

47. Rane Arroyo, *The Singing Shark* (Tempe, AZ: Bilingual Press, 1996), 79.

48. Arroyo, *The Singing Shark*, 80–81.

49. Arroyo, *The Buried Sea: New and Collected Poems* (Tucson: University of Arizona Press, 2008), 63.

50. Arroyo, *The Singing Shark*, 79.

51. Rosemarie Garland Thomson, "Introduction: From Wonder to Error—A Genealogy of Freak Discourse in Modernity," in *Freakery: Cultural Spectacles of the Extraordinary Body* (New York: New York University Press, 1996), 1

52. Chris Philo and Chris Wilbert, "Animal Spaces, Beastly Places: Introduction," in *Animal Spaces, Beastly Places: New Geographies of Human-Animal Relations* (New York: Routledge, 2000), 4.

53. Philo and Wilbert, *Animal Spaces, Beastly Places*, 5.

54. Arroyo, *The Singing Shark*, 81.

55. Arroyo, *The Singing Shark*, 78.

56. Julian Olivares, "Sandra Cisneros: *The House on Mango Street* and the Poetics of Space," in *Charting New Frontiers in American Literature: Chicana Creativity and Criticism*, eds. María Herrera-Sobek and Helena María Viramontes (Albuquerque: University of New Mexico Press, 1996).

57. Arroyo, *The Singing Shark*, 74.

58. Arroyo, *The Singing Shark*, 76.

59. Arroyo, *The Singing Shark*, 76.

60. Anzaldúa, *The Gloria Anzaldúa Reader*, 23.

61. Nicole Seymour, *Strange Natures: Futurity, Empathy and the Queer Ecological Imagination* (Chicago: University of Illinois Press, 2013).

FIVE

Navigating Spectacular Spaces

Regarding Bodies and Chilean American Lives in Reyes's
Madre and I: A Memoir of Our Immigrant Lives

> I treated my mother to the spectacle of tears welling up in my eyes as I boarded the back of her friend's car, and she witnessed me sobbing all the way until we reached the seaside resort in Delaware. We unloaded the car, accommodated ourselves in the rented cabin, and then I insisted on staying inside instead of going to the beach. "That's not normal," Mother claimed.[1]
>
> —Guillermo Reyes

Origins and their significance have remained a longstanding source of discussion for researchers who work in the interdisciplinary field of Latinx studies. The *place* that a writer originated from often is a subject examined in relation to preexisting norms and perspectives. In the dialogues about the writing of the playwright Guillermo Reyes, who was born in Chile and immigrated to the United States, it has been debated whether his life story and writing fits within the purview of the field of Latinx studies because Chilean Americans are less frequently seen as a part of the larger Latinx population, even though some scholars include them.[2] For instance, in preparing the present study, a scholar inquired: Why are you including a Chilean American in your manuscript? In response, I offer the growing belief that the field of Latinx studies is still evolving, hybridizing, and making space for more people at the table. Like Frances R. Aparicio explains, today's researchers are not solely interested in maintaining one notion of Latinidad (or Latino-ness), but rather there exists a growing movement toward the concept of "Latinidades," a pluralistic term that "has been open to transformations and rewritings."[3]

It is through this lens that we can best begin our consideration of Reyes's artistry.

For scholars who research diverse Latinidades, the question of why Reyes would be *included* is a query that evokes several social issues such as belonging, identification, and normativity. Intriguingly, Reyes brings some of these same subjects to the fore in his 2010 book *Madre and I: A Memoir of Our Immigrants Lives*, which was published in the respected series titled "Writing in Latinidad: Autobiographical Voices of U.S. Latinos/as." Despite the title, Reyes at times has reflected on whether *Latino* (and *gay*) are the terms that best fit his own circumstances and history.[4] Repeatedly over the course of his memoir, Reyes expresses a self-reflective sensibility and states that he is still unwilling to "embrace the idea of belonging somewhere."[5] Reyes's unsettled positionality in his memoir creates a nonconforming sensibility that resonates as queerly inventive because although he has ties to Latino and queer communities, he nonetheless leads readers to reflect on the fixity created by societal labels and systems that serve to maintain rigid taxonomies. Carving out a unique positionality, Reyes highlights how his personal history and the national history of Chile has instantiated his identity and self-perception in a complex fashion. As readers observe, Reyes's own personal history as young gay man who immigrated to the United States in the early 1970s is one of the contexts that shapes his life and memoir. Reyes immigrated to the United States after his own mother immigrated through an official initiative in Chile, which facilitated a process made possible by the US Immigration and Nationality Act of 1965. Also known as the Hart-Cellar Act, this legislation was made into law and signed by President Lyndon B. Johnson at the Statue of Liberty. This significant moment enabled a broader range of people to immigrate to the United States, including many groups who were displaced by violence. Such opportunities were of interest to diverse Chilean people who felt threatened by political violence that consumed the government and citizenry in the 1970s.

Following the 1973 military coup d'état in the nation of Chile, where President Salvador Allende's government was overthrown, the world bore witness to the rise of a cruel dictatorship headed by Augusto Pinochet. The US Central Intelligence Agency supported the overthrow of the democratically elected president and the installment of a right-leaning dictator that played a role in the intimidation, torture, and killing of thousands of people seen as opposition.[6] It comes as no surprise that people would wish to escape such violence, but the fact that US officials—people who supposedly value democracy—would help the Chilean military to oust a legally elected president, continues to astound some Americans who are less aware of the long history of US interventionism in various parts of the Americas. In regarding this time, Rody Oñate, Julie Shayne, and Thomas Wright have studied this political phenomenon and have suggested that the exiles and immigrants from Chile indeed wanted freedom from the threat of persecution, militarism, and violence. This is not to say that these migrants' moves to the United States should be considered as a singular and straightforward means of attaining a better life experience, but rather scholars interpret this mass migration and its results as reflecting a meaningful set of desires, history, and urgency. To theorize the motives, roles, and triumphs of Chile's history, a great spread of interdisciplinary scholars, including Macarena Gómez-Barris and Lessie Jo Frazier, has taken to studying the artwork, testimonies, and writings of people who witnessed and remember the past.[7] However, there is still a noteworthy segment of this larger population, which mostly remains undertheorized. This understudied enclave consists of Chilean people that have migrated to the United States and identify themselves as being LGBTQ. In particular, Reyes eloquently speaks to these subjects in *Madre and I*, which weaves an exquisite tale of his settling into the United States with his Chilean mother María. This insightful and revealing memoir offers an urbane social commentary on the sociopolitical challenges that queer and Chilean migrant peoples face in their journeys both to and from the United States.

Although Reyes's memoir addresses many of the same issues that other exile narratives discuss, his work goes further by focusing intensely on the interplay and social implications of unusual bodies and landscapes that exhibit a spectacular quality. Just as this chapter's epigraph suggests, the spectacle can occur in minor as well as large-scale scenes that evince arresting dynamics. This set of spectacular imagery comes about through Reyes's highly imaginative writing, which reflects on the ways that he experiences paralyzing sensations of shame and embarrassment. Although *Madre and I* narrates a family's move to the United States, the text also explores Reyes's inner strife of having a body that—in his eyes—looks "different" from what he and friends perceived as the norm.[8] In *Madre and I*, Reyes reveals his personal strife of having a rather hairy body that he perceives as resembling a "hairy ape," who was part man and part beast.[9] From a young age, his body begins to grow a considerable amount of hair, which leads him to shave with his "mother's Lady Razor," but the hair "returned overnight like kudzu weeds that take over a southern landscape."[10] To address his personal challenges, Reyes uses his seemingly hybrid body as a way of calling attention to the anxieties, ideals, and pressures that are embedded in US landscapes where conventional beauty dominates. Reyes thus transforms his hairy body into a spectacular sight (and site) that effectively makes a poignant commentary on the struggles of immigrants. In these ways, Reyes urges readers to ponder what it means to be both Chilean and American who struggles with conflicting perspectives on sexuality and bodily beauty. In this way, Reyes comes to resemble a hybrid figure because of his bicultural experiences as well as his belief that he is a "half-human creature like the Sasquatch."[11] To gain a more refined understanding of his text and its social implications, this chapter builds on the criticism of cultural researchers and offers an examination of sociopolitical dynamics that have led to painful forms of othering that constitute the experiences of Reyes and similar LGBTQ migrants.

In particular, this chapter builds on the groundbreaking work of social critics that have examined the ways that daily experience is influenced by spatial dynamics and the attendant sentiments of those milieus. That is to say, my research is informed by the insights of scholars that have examined the lived experience of intersectionality and the roles that spectacular social phenomena play in shaping the lives of US and Chilean peoples. The thoughtful research of luminaries, such as Kimberlé Crenshaw and Guy Debord, provide a foundation for explicating the interlocking experiences and spectacular forces that create the social challenges and triumphs that are depicted in Reyes's memoir *Madre and I*. These perspectives provide a means to speak to the ways that queer immigrants and migrants feel the constraining social dynamics of Chile and the United States, which frequently lead to the othering of unconventional bodies and sexualities. In writing about his ethnicity, hirsute body, and sexuality, Reyes reveals the manner in which the spaces of public spectacle and intersectionality lead to a set of pernicious social struggles. However, rather than accepting these conditions with passivity, Reyes's narrative interestingly uses the social dynamics of the spectacle as a means of calling attention to (and subverting) these spaces' ingrained cultural ideals of beauty. Through showing the heightened scrutiny and the uncomfortable self-consciousness that is created by bodily spectacles, Reyes's text makes the comment that spectacles can hold significant potentials for danger and pleasure. In taking this approach, his writing leads readers to think more analytically about the ethics, implications, and outcomes of migration, queer social behaviors, and personal writings.

CONFIGURING THE CRITICAL LENS, ILLUMINATING THE CULTURAL CONNECTIONS

A critical analysis of Reyes's memoir *Madre and I* requires readers to examine how the phenomena of human migration and self-identifying oneself can be conceptualized in terms of spectacular relations that are shaped by myriad intertwining elements, including the inculcated attitudes of spaces that include classism, ethnocentrism, and homophobia. To theorize these elements, my project considers *the spectacular* from several angles, which means that this book considers how scholars have elucidated the spectacular in terms of commodification, sociality, and theatricality. The poet and theorist Gloria Anzaldúa employs her own experience in her integrative personal essay "*La Prieta*," in which she explains how she felt gazed on by family. Under a heading titled "Images that Haunt Me," Anzaldúa describes a rather sobering moment with her own mother, where her body and identity are highlighted: "In her eyes and in the eyes of others I saw myself reflected as 'strange,' 'abnormal' 'QUEER.' I saw no other reflection. Helpless to change that image, I retreated into books, solitude, and kept away from others. . . . The whole time growing up I felt that I was not of this earth."[12] In the same manner of Reyes, Anzaldúa uses her own bodily experience as evidence and creates a mirror that reflects the homophobia of her society. She illuminates how the human gaze has been used as a means of othering Latinx queers and making these figures into inhuman outsiders. Instead of accepting this negativity as an insoluble pejorative, Anzaldúa uses her spectacular moment to lead readers to question the impact and underlying bias systemic to her society. Written as a bridge to a better future, Anzaldúa's critical commentary opens a path to consider necessary alternatives.

In a similar, albeit different context, the French theorist Guy Debord offers a rather focused and relevant study in his influential monograph *The Society of the Spectacle*, which provides a productive starting point for analyzing Reyes's depicted connections among human embodiment, the human image, and social power. Debord's perspectives on the spectacle proffer a means for explaining both the hope and the oppression that Reyes experiences. In the case of the latter, Debord speaks to the spectacle's oppressive powers by arguing that the spectacle "subjugates living men to itself" and leads to "alienation."[13] This work grants a lens for studying the inequalities of power that Reyes feels, yet Debord's influential research never speaks directly to the challenges that queer people of color face. At the same time, Debord and his fellow Situationists are highly critical of the spectacle and its various effects, while Reyes finds a means to rework the dynamics of the spectacle in his narrative for the sake of subverting some of the conditions that frequently cause consternation for queer migrants of color. Thus, like the cultural studies scholar Daphne A. Brooks, who has analyzed the performative and spectacular elements of black popular performance culture, Reyes ostensibly adheres to the viewpoint that embracing the spectacle in more critical terms can provide the world with a unique opportunity to create some more positive possibilities for the egalitarian future on the horizon.[14]

Although Reyes's text implies that there are positive and rewarding results that may come from engaging in the creation of spectacle, he is also attentive to the fact that spectacles may causes certain problems, such as commodification and exoticizing. On the problematic side, the perceived "difference" of migrants' bodies and unconventional sexualities may be seen as being diminished when they are constrained by spectacles, such as protracted public debates in the news media. One need only examine the story and public spectacle of the young Cuban migrant Elián González. In González's case, a media firestorm in 1999 turned a young boy's migration to the United States into a heated public debate and spectacle, which led to the diminishment and criticism of González and his family. While not all migrants face this heightened level of public scrutiny, the González incident is consistent with a larger set of social dynamics, in which the stories of so-called "ethnic others" are transformed by the white dominant culture—that is, the mainstream media—into sensational, top stories that many news companies use to increase their ratings and thus make money. This same kind of dynamic plays out within the contexts of "sexual others," whereby the so-called peculiarity of unconventional sexuality becomes the fodder for news companies that seek to increase their viewing audience and commercial revenue. This dynamic becomes visible in cases where sexual identities become commoditized and exoticized. We may consider case of the British pop singer George Michael, who was "outed" as gay in 1998 after being arrested for committing a so-called lewd act in a public bathroom in Beverly Hills in the US state of California. As in the case of González, Michael's perceived difference—his sexuality—arguably stoked the fire of public debate insofar as his perceived immoral conduct became tied to an aspect of his identity—his queerness—as well as his professional life. These two cases of spectacularization exemplify a larger problematic social phenomenon in which the dominant culture envisions the ethnic and sexual other as being linked to impropriety, and thus, they are made into a spectacle as a punishment for their putative misdeeds. Yet, rather than accepting this ingrained, negative dynamic, Reyes employs his unique life experience as a means to make the potentials of the spectacle serve him and those that he cares for in life.

In the cases of Reyes's *Madre and I*, the author uses his personal experience as a gay migrant to offer a commentary on the ways in which embodied experiences, such as ethnicity and sexuality intersect in daily, public circumstances. To understand these intersections, this chapter makes use of the critical frameworks that are used to elucidate the human experiences of intersectionality, which have been theorized by critics such as Kimberlé Crenshaw (1993), Patricia Hill Collins (1998), and Candice M. Jenkins (2007), among others.[15] In these studies, the authors construct a means to understanding what Jenkins calls "double vulnerability," which comes about as two forms of identity, such as gender identity and ethnic identity, are devalued or targeted by a group or individual that supposedly holds greater authority or privilege. Although Crenshaw, Hill Collins, and Jenkins address the intersectionality of women of color, we can apply their critical frameworks to make sense of Reyes's case. Through considering the ways that Reyes's ethnicity and sexuality interlock in the circumstances of the public spectacle, we can ascertain the larger social implications of Reyes's memoir. More specifically, by considering how ethnocentrism, homophobia, and racism collude, we gain a more accurate understanding of the sociopolitical forces that are at work within the lived contexts of Reyes and those of Other migrants. Likewise, through studying the interlocking experiences of ethnicity and sexuality that are shown within Reyes's spectacles, we obtain a richer understanding of how queer migrants like Reyes finds an inspiring sense of hope and mount a resistance against the powerful entities that attempt to disempower vulnerable people and discriminate against queer migrants.

To explicate the intersectionality shown in Reyes's text effectively, we must recognize the diversity and polysemy that is bound up with these identitarian characteristics and categories. For example, in using the term *queer*, I remain mindful of its multiplicity of meaning because the term conjures to mind a slew of ideas that resonate in negative and positive ways—depending on the speaker and audience. I use the term *queer* as a means of referring to the experiences of bisexual, gay, lesbian, transgender, and other unconventional sexualities. In this way, I follow the lead of other cultural critics and researchers that envision the term *queer* as an umbrella term, and hence, I concur with other scholars that see this idiom as being a means to speak to a set of similar circumstances and conflicts that millions of people face daily in this predominantly cisgender and heterocentric world. However, I remain attentive of the fact that this terminology also can present some drawbacks because at times it can be viewed as erasing or generalizing the particularity of humanity's diverse sexual experiences. Being mindful of these perils requires scholars to be aware of the social attitudes and unique vocabularies that inform the artistic expression and cultural circumstances of migrants like Reyes. Certainly, a similar kind of multiplicity can be located within the concepts of ethnicity and race, yet the feelings, history, and politics that give shape to these ideas tend to be subjective and unique, which thus requires researchers to be cognizant of multiplicity and avoid universalisms that generalize.

Reyes's personal narrative delivers a perceptive commentary about the physical hardships and inner anxieties that are caused by the experience of intersectionality that queer migrants face in both their country of origin and after arriving in the United States. Reyes's work expounds on the wearisome circumstances that he encounters in several natural and human-made spaces that ultimately are shown to be perilous insofar as these spaces are constraining, uncongenial, and traumatic. These spaces, including his private home in Chile, schools, and public beaches are shown as being neither hospitable nor inclusive inasmuch as they rigorously demand the migrant—Reyes—to conform to several dominant and mainstream cultural ideals, which include the aims of being beautiful, fair-skinned, heterosexual, and masculine. To speak to these matters, Reyes's *Madre and I* depicts how these ideals and the resulting intersectionality are imbricated with the spaces that Reyes inhabits. As his memoir shows, these spaces and their inhabitants directly and obliquely discipline his queer migrant body. This disciplining takes place because the dominant cultures of Chile and the United States largely regard Reyes's body, desires, and behaviors as being Other. He is viewed by those around him as being effeminate, overly hirsute, racially indistinct, and a "bastard" because he was conceived out of wedlock.[16] Through highlighting this alterity in his book, Reyes brings attention to the intense forms of public scrutiny that queer migrants routinely encounter in the United States and beyond. As such, Reyes sheds light on problematic aspects of physical and social ideals by showing how his body becomes a veritable spectacle in these moments of disciplining. By putting a spotlight on the spectacularization of these behavioral, physical, and sexual experiences, Reyes turns his body into a site that invites reflection. In showcasing his body as such, Reyes's text urges his readers to examine the ways in which US ideals of beauty, gender, and sexuality create unwelcome social repercussions; likewise, he invites readers to consider the nettlesome social effects of living in a cultural landscape that is obsessed with performing a kind of ideal self-image that is narrow in scope.

A YOUNG CHILEAN AMERICAN'S EXPERIENCE WITH SOCIAL ALTERITY

Reyes's memoir leads his readers to understand his unique position of otherness by beginning with the challenges that he experiences as a youth in both Chile and the United States. After Reyes's mother María migrates to the United States from Chile, she decides to bring her son for the sake of providing a better life and preventing him from being "an orphan."[17] This mother-son relationship is vital for both parent and child, especially because Reyes's father (who is María's lover) has removed himself from them. Because of this somewhat non-normative family dynamic, the young Reyes invents stories about his father to prevent others from seeing him as a so-called "bastard." This misrepresentation of his life mirrors other forms of dissembling and hiding that the young Reyes engages in over the course of his narrative. Readers observe this trope of hiding in various instances, but one of the most significant manifestations of this phenomenon is the way in which Reyes reflects on his experiences of being a hirsute youth.

During the years of his adolescence, he notices that his body is beginning to change, but instead of becoming like that of most adult men, his body becomes ostensibly "monstrous" because, as he explains, "Hair did eventually envelop and over-power my entire body."[18] In this instance and elsewhere, Reyes's excess hair is explained as being a constraint and a source of "*Nausea, panic, trauma.*"[19] He experiences these paralyzing sensations in his gym classes and public showers, where he feels his body is scrutinized. As such, he frames his body's hair as being an affliction and creating a spectacle. Although Reyes never suggests his excess of follicles is pathological, it appears that he does come to have an affliction known as body dysmorphic disorder (BDD), which results from his own anxieties about his physique as well as his belief that his body deviates from conventional notions of beauty.[20] Like many people, he self-diagnoses himself as having this disorder after searching for answers about why he feels so embarrassed about these physical matters. This becomes clear when he explains that as a youth, he wears "long pants and long sleeve shirts . . . and 'long sleeve pajamas' to cover the hair that began to take over his physique."[21] In describing his hair's growth as being a kind of "take over," Reyes demonstrates the way that the human body is a site (or space) that cannot be controlled, and without the power to control himself, he experiences pain, shame, and stigma. His only recourse is to hide his body to evade the pain created by the dominant culture's ideals. In doing so, his portrayals of these social events and feelings craft a strong exposé, showing how US culture perpetuates privileges for those that embody dominant physical and social ideals.

In his memoir, Reyes uses several significant metaphors to speak to these ideals and signal the disquieting idea that his body feels inhuman to him. In particular, Reyes describes his body as being that of a "beast."[22] For instance, Reyes explains that one of his US schoolmates insults him by calling him a "hairy ape" after he has been seen naked in the showers at school.[23] This comment about his body is lobbed at him in a public setting—"a ninth grade drama class"—and through these circumstances, he suffers with from a kind of shame because he is made to feel different.[24] Paradoxically, this description suggests that instead of being a place of learning, this school harbors ignorance: a lack of understanding and empathy for Reyes's situation. This ignorance and shaming effectively creates a disciplining of Reyes's body and identity, hence enforcing mainstream notion of beauty and normality. This comment and school space create social and psychological stresses for Reyes insofar as he must negotiate with bullies and the way that they cast him as being a strange spectacle. And although Reyes himself expresses distaste for this public scrutiny and the spectacles that result from heightened attention, he nevertheless shows a love for other forms of spectacle, namely the artistic kind. In this way, Reyes's memoir creates a textual contradiction in this way because he shows both a love and dislike for the sociality of spectacles. In doing so, he leads us to think more critically about why he harbors these feelings, and hence we are encouraged to consider our own stance on the subject.

Throughout his memoir, Reyes highlights his love of multiple dramatic performances and films, including *The Sound of Music* (1965) and *El Cid* (1961), which he reflects on and enjoys thoroughly.[25] It is through these moments that Reyes comes to see the productive possibilities created by artistic forms of spectacular productions, and arguably, this enjoyment contributes to his own self-development as an artist and playwright later in life. Most interestingly, as Reyes witnesses these spectacles, we see that he finds a means to suspend the rules of his humdrum daily life and thereby experience a pleasing form of spectacular otherness that is created through the escapism of mainstream filmmaking. During his youth, the theatrical spaces of performance and puppet shows enable Reyes to sidestep the lack and drudgery that he faces daily.[26] For instance, as a young boy in school, Reyes and his classmates worked with a teacher to perform a series of songs about the fight for Chilean independence, and this team effort reveals to him that there is more to life than being known as the fatherless child. Reyes tells his readers, "The fact that we created a spectacle, did it in an organizer manner, rehearsed it meticulously, and then presented it to the rest of the school, which applauded us, seemed miraculous to me."[27] Here, his descriptor of "miraculous" speaks to the way that this performance functions as a formative and powerful guidepost, in which he finds hope for a more artistic and creative future; similarly, this moment resonates with Reyes because a kind teacher named Mr. Mendoza arguably acts as a father figure to Reyes.[28] In effect, this father figure teaches him that the friendly social relations and bonds of this production's teamwork actually can create a means to a positive form of inclusion and togetherness. That is, through creating our own spectacles—on our own terms and in critical ways—we may find a more satisfying collectivity in spectacles, hence avoiding the unethical dynamic created by those aiming to make a spectacle of cultural and sexual difference.

EMBRACING THE SPECTACLE IN THE EVERYDAY, NARRATING THE SPECTACLE'S POTENTIALS

As Reyes's early engagements with spectacular dynamics showed him both the pains and the pleasures of spectacles, there is a common element of affect or as some say—feeling—that runs throughout these experiences. In considering these feelings, Reyes's memoir suggests that certain public spectacles—like that of the aforesaid scene involving his class's collective work and the feelings that result—reveal the considerable impact of sociality in spectacular sites. At the same time, as we consider the moments where Reyes feels Othered by the spectacle, we can discern ethical dynamics. In other words, through observing the negative feelings that result from humiliating spectacles, we may discern the ethics, or lack thereof, within particular spaces. This matter of affect and feeling has been examined closely by psychologists such as Sarah Grogan (1999), Michael S. Boroughs (2010), Ross Krawcsyk (2010), and J. Kevin Thompson (2010).[29] These scholars have critiqued and researched the norms, pressures, and resulting feelings that allow for social situations such as spectacles to take place. Grogan's work illustrates how Americans live in a cultural landscape that repeatedly and complexly reinforces limiting images of human embodiment, which resemble a kind of aesthetic that has ties to particular feelings of belonging, goodness, and normality. As Grogan shows, gay men are expected to be handsome and thin, regardless of their ancestry or culture. Being unable to meet these social expectations and norms can lead to troubling emotional experiences, hence pointing to an unethical dynamic in the public sphere. With these expectations come greater inner pressures to conform, meaning that these ideals can be socially and physically destructive as well as lead to more Othering that is formed in unethical ways.

Nonetheless, although some employ the dynamics of spectacle as a means of creating a negative emotion in others, Reyes arguably builds up a positive set of feelings by reclaiming the scene of the spectacular and using it to challenge negative forms of affect, such as panic, trauma, and unbelonging, which are constituted in spectacular social dynamics. In the narrative, he takes ownership over these dynamics and leads his readers to see that coming out—whether as a gay person or as a certain ethnicity—is an illuminating and productive path to take because it leads to a greater openness and understanding among people. For example, through Reyes's narration of his physical experiences, he educates others about these matters; in the process, he uses the notion of the spectacle in a creative and critical way, thereby challenging the cultural ideology that maintains that human bodies should look a certain way or engage in solely heterosexual behaviors. Reyes's use of the spectacular as a strategy is by no means a novel practice because activists have been creating spectacles intentionally for centuries; that is, myriad people have employed spectacles as a means of commenting on social and cultural problems. In particular, we see this approach in governmental and public spaces from the 1960s to 1970s when activists staged public spectacles, such as marches, riots, and sit-ins to raise awareness about inequality.

Reyes's approach of using the spectacular also arguably aligns with the strategies used by multiple gay liberation movements, which came into existence during the eras of the 1960s and 1970s as well as more recently. As critics, such as Art Hendricks, Rob Tielman, and Evert van der Veen have shown, there is constellation of visible queer events, such as the Compton's Cafeteria Riot and Stonewall Riots, whereby queers sought recognition and rights in greater numbers.[30] Through these forms of protest, queer people called attention to the way that the majority culture was treating queers in an unethical and unfair way. At the same time, this is not to say that Reyes's text is wholly a product of the same energies that arose after the famous queer rebellions in the United States. But during this time period, there was energy and momentum for social change and openness. In part, that energy appears to have carried Reyes's story forward. Similarly, many critics today, including myself, believe that we must perform the activism of addressing the lacunae in existing scholarship about the writing of women and queer people of color from the 1990s and 2000s. To address this silence, we must be mindful of how women and queers of color, such as Reyes, have been muted or made out to be the Other in the public sphere, including spaces such as publishing houses and organizations, which historically had been led by a mostly Anglophone white citizenry throughout much of the twentieth century. We can draw from the critical theory of scholars such as Macarena Gómez-Barris, who develops a queer standpoint—or as many Latinx studies scholars say, a *cuir* view—through working with the insightful artistry of queer and trans poets such as Pedro Lemebel.[31] Raising up Lemebel's concept of *"los sótanos sexuales"* (the sexual undergrounds), Gómez-Barris puts emphasis on those spaces and cultural materials that "are not easily absorbed by the nation-state."[32] In a comparable manner, Reyes resists the seemingly ubiquitous process by which bodies and sexualities are often folded into preestablished paradigms that frequently further the goals of larger organizations, nations, and systems such as capitalism. In this way, by saying he "had problems with both Latino and gay identities" and evading this nomenclature, Reyes short-circuits the simple identifications that authorities, organizations, state powers, and other groups have used as a classificatory technology that would reduce people to a simple containable idea.

Reyes's text challenges the heteronormative, white ideologies that inform the categories and cultural ideals of embodiment and sexuality in Chile and the United States.[33] Notably, Reyes mounts this challenge to the dominant ideology by building on the coming-out genre that arose during the 1980s and 1990s. During this time, editors such as Susan J. Wolfe and Penelope Stanley published the first major collection of works that addressed the experience of disclosing one's sexual identity. Their collection *The Coming Out Stories* paved the way for many more people to write and publish their personal experiences.[34] In several ways, the story of Reyes's memoir *Madre and I* mirrors the formula of the coming-out genre because Reyes uses the self-disclosure process as a means of breaking the silence about his own emotionally difficult experiences with physical shame and bodily difference. As in most coming-out stories, Reyes reflects on what the disclosure of his secrets would accomplish and involve. His narrative implies that despite the challenges of coming out, there could be some benefits to doing so. Reyes's situation is an example that reflects some of the longstanding debates and critiques of scholars working in the field of queer studies. Critics such as Eve Kosofsky Sedgwick have shown the way in which coming out—or leaving the closet—may not be quite as simple as it seems, and there may be limitations to, and problems associated with coming out.[35] By and large, I interpret Reyes's coming out—as a hirsute, gay migrant—as being a means to spur further conversation that can effect change.[36] This idea parallels the acti-

Figure 5.1. The Stonewall Inn in New York, New York, from the photographer Erwin Osuna.

vist work of another famous public figure, the activist and politician Harvey Milk. In one of his speeches, Milk explains: "I will never forget what is known as coming out. I will never forget what it was like coming out and having nobody to look up toward. I remember the lack of hope."[37] Milk's comment about the importance of role models and hope reminds us of the challenges that stifle the young Reyes. His text also reminds us that many young queer people today lack mentors and face uncertainty about who they can become.

We need only recall the suicides of the US youths: Justin Aaberg, Billy Lucas, and Tyler Clementi, all of whom are believed to have killed themselves in the year 2010 because of the unendurable humiliation and pain of gay-bashing.[38] To a similar extent, the people of Chile witnessed the extreme emotional and physical difficulties that queer men often face through the lens of a young man's beating and death. For example, a young gay Chilean man named Daniel Zamudio was attacked by several antigay men for no reason, and this unfair attack ultimately led to his demise several days later. This attack became a spectacle unto itself in both Chile and other parts of the world, thereby leading readers and viewers to reflect on the unethical and unjust actions of the attackers. Numerous stories of Zamudio's attack circulated on various blogs and websites, thus raising awareness of the perils that queer people face within the nation of Chile. In studying these events, I find that these narratives suggest that in the United States, Chile, and beyond, there often exists a lack of alternative and positive narratives (or possible futures) for young people to consider and follow. In the same way, with there being relatively few inspiring narratives in the mainstream media or libraries, it remains difficult for many youths to imagine how one's present life of struggle could develop into a more robust future experience.

Reyes's *Madre and I* offers inspiration to young people by showing how the young Reyes comes to terms with his unique situation and comes out to people as gay and hirsute. The text intimates that these coming out experiences lead to social openness and stronger social bonds. For instance, as he becomes more comfortable in discussing the difficulties experienced in connection with his hairy physique with his Korean American friend Eugene, he also becomes more comfortable with himself: "I explained to him the entire history of how and when this habit [of hiding himself] had started. . . . Something worked."[39] His observation that this coming out "worked" tells us that communication is vital for queer youth of color who experience numerous forms of stresses. This depiction reinforces the idea that young people need to have a greater understanding of what coming out can lead to, or means. In studying this, it becomes clear that the coming out experiences and spaces of queer youth of color require further theorizing. Reyes's memoir gives an inspiring portrayal and unique dynamics that also counter the rather reductive idea the coming out narrative is "finished" or "old news." Reyes's text offers proof of Esther Saxey's belief that the coming-out process takes place in a variety of dynamic ways such as in the case of disclosing one's inner, physical image to others.[40] In her study of autobiography and fiction, Saxey shows how the real-life stories of queer people convey a range of messages that cannot be easily generalized or dismissed. For instance, queer youth of color experience the coming out process in unique ways because of how their cultures often hold views on sexuality that are distinct from that of the mainstream, heterocentric majority culture. This difference thus leads to sui generis forms of coming-out stories that have yet to be fully theorized. Nevertheless, the potential benefits that queer youth of color can gain in coming out (and finding friends who fully appreciate them) are suggested in the research of psychology scholars such as Michael S. Boroughs, Ross Krawcsyk, and J. Kevin Thompson (2010). In their research, these scholars show that sexual minorities, such as gay and bisexual men, experience a disproportionately high incidence of BDD. As these researchers show, people who are diagnosed with BDD typically experience excessive anxiety or concern about their bodily appearance and fixate on some perceived defect, such as body weight, blemishes, or looks. In Reyes's youth, his experience of BDD both prevents him from socializing in public spaces as well as engaging in intimate, sexual behavior. To a surprising extent, Reyes makes a spectacle of the fact that he cannot feel comfortable in having sex, but when he ultimately overcomes this hurdle later on, his sexual intimacy is shown to be a rather meaningful and legitimizing social experience for him; therefore, providing a sense of hope that enables him to continue.

Although Reyes's physique causes him to hide his body and embrace a rather ascetic philosophy of "sexual repression," he breaks outside of his self-imposed limitations by exploring his sexual identity in simple verbal terms.[41] When he attends high school in the United States, he begins to develop feelings for his friend Eugene and is compelled to come out to him in hopes that Eugene might return his affection. Reyes does not use the term *come out* in this context, but the idea remains the same. His desires drive him to approach his friend, even though he risks making a spectacle of himself and his feelings. When the two of them speak in private, Reyes says:

"By any chance," I asked him, "are you gay?"

The denial was immediate, loud, and unmistakably panicky. "No! Absolutely not! No Way!"

That was clear.

"Why are you asking?"

"Because I think I'm in love with you."

I give him credit for not running away.[42]

As we see here, not only does Reyes come out to Eugene as gay, but we also see Eugene come out to Reyes as heterosexual—to firmly establish his identity as a heterosexual—and in the process, Eugene's actions speak to the ways that personal desires are bound up with concerns about how the public sphere perceives a person. Although Eugene could have rejected Reyes, we instead see a kind of understanding. Instead of this moment being a traumatizing spectacle, Reyes explains that it was much more affirming: "As an only child, it was crucial to develop this type of bond as well, and for a teenager who spoke of suicide, it became a lifesaver."[43] Coming out to Eugene and befriending him gives Reyes an emotional boost. He can be honest without having to live in shame, and this gives him the comfort and confidence that he needs. This scene, which I read as representative of some queer people's coming-out experiences, but certainly not all, demonstrates the manner in which the feeling of social acceptance often has the effect of empowering and legitimizing queer people who have been diminished on numerous occasions because of their sexual difference. The friendship that Eugene offers to Reyes continues and this continuation hints at the possibility of a better future, where he could live a life that is almost free from some the seemingly ubiquitous and enervating social problems of alienation, homophobia, intimidation, and xenophobia, which many queer migrants regularly face.

To understand how Reyes lives in fear of social rejection in the United States, it is necessary to recognize how the public punishment for being a "queer other" starts at an early age in Chile. When Reyes is approximately five years old and living in Chile with his family, he experiences two events that show him how Chilean culture equates effeminate behavior and homosexuality with abjection and wrongdoing. At this early age, Reyes expresses a desire for a doll that he admires when his family goes out for the town's feria, a regional holiday. However, when he asks for the doll, his family members express shock and concern, thus casting him as the family's Other. Because of Reyes's young age, he had never thought of playing with dolls as inappropriate behavior for a boy like himself. When he pouts and cries for the doll, his grandmother gives in, purchasing it for him. When he wakes up from his nap and receives the doll, she tells him, "If boys make fun of you, just don't come crying to me."[44] His grandmother's statement bespeaks how the Chilean majority culture views boys who play with dolls as queer or improper. Even so, while Reyes does not respond to his grandmother's comment, he does react with happiness on receiving the toy: "Overjoyed, I hugged the doll lovingly, then held it in my arms, rocked her, and turned her sideways to burp her and calm her down, and prevent her from crying."[45] Moreover, the young boy's actions do more than simply show a child playing. Rather than implying wrongdoing, Reyes's text shows that the young boy cares for the doll in the way that a parent cares for a child. Interestingly, the young Reyes fulfills the role of the caring, ethical parent while his own mother and grandmother were not empathetic caretakers to him in this moment. In Reyes's *Madre and I*, the home-space that people typically understand as being a safe sanctuary actually presents the threat of discrimination, shaming, and unjust parenting. Reyes's exuberance for the doll reads as a spectacular coming out scene in the sense that although his home-space rejects and scrutinizes his want for the doll, Reyes fashions a more queer-positive image by demonstrating a clear rejection of the dominant gender norms. Instead of hiding this spectacle, Reyes uses it to teach his readers about the great need to accept and welcome gender diversity in our world.

In the years following these events, Reyes explains that he turns inward, implying that he feels unable to express himself during his teen years. Reyes begins to feel sexually frustrated until he finally finds an outlet for his energy during a study abroad in his college years. Reyes travels to Padua, Italy, for "almost a year" to study the art of creative writing, and in the process, he makes new friends who open his eyes to the positive aspects of sexuality.[46] In this ostensibly more international space, which reads as being a positive form of spatial otherness for Reyes, he allows himself to explore his physical desires. In a way that appears contradictory, Reyes becomes more comfortable and happier outside of the traditional home-space and homeland. In particular, at a fellow student's party, he experiences his first public male-to-male kiss with a bisexual man who is Mexican American and also named Guillermo. Reyes writes: "The Other Guillermo was drinking with his buddies, both male and female, all laid out on the bed. He drew me to him and locked lips with me and everybody there laughed. It was essentially my first male-to-male kiss."[47] Although the space of the party proffers an awakening for him, it also functions symbolically as a spectacular space of coming out for Reyes insofar as the kiss is a public performance of his desires. By not rejecting this man's kiss, Reyes and the others present there legitimate the act as being an acceptable, pleasurable, and ultimately worthwhile way of life.

This "Other Guillermo," who is akin to a queer mentor to our narrator, symbolically frees our narrator from his own constraints by introducing him to the gay nightclubs of Milan. One evening, for instance, our narrator becomes intoxicated from a single beer and finds himself kissing another man in public. This moment is powerful for Reyes because it creates a kind of euphoria—the extent of which becomes clear when he says he "walked on air on our way back to the hotel."[48] This moment and space allows for another kind of coming out that leads him to become a regular at the club scene, which offers a kind of intimacy and social belonging that he is unable to find in his own family in the United States or Chile. However, on returning to his home in the United States, we see his previous social patterns of self-othering and repression surface again, which suggests that the United States cannot claim a civic or moral superiority—that is, by rising above antigay attitudes or homophobia—because perceptions of beauty and homophobia continue to remain culturally and geographically specific. For Reyes, his hometown in the United States still appears to be a place where he cannot be himself. In other words, the memoir *Madre and I* tells us that, despite its vaunted status as a multicultural site of inclusion, where everyone supposedly can pursue the American Dream, many US spaces continue to appear, feel, or seem intolerant of LGBTQ life.

In the United States, Reyes is unable to come out to his mother, María, let alone discuss the subject of sex, and this inability to come out of the closet perpetuates a boundary between them. Reyes explains his situation by describing his mother: "She could make crude jokes about sex. . . . But she could never seriously discuss with me any issues of desire."[49] Reyes's mother María is emotionally close to Reyes throughout the book, yet despite their familial intimacy, they can never discuss the human experience of sexuality. This idea is made clear when Reyes explains: "It mattered little that, in Hollywood, we lived in an environment of open sexuality. . . . My mother and I were innocents in a sea of decadence."[50] Reyes leads us to consider the limitations that are created when people cannot come out to one another about their feelings. Further, by situating himself and his mother in their place of residence—Hollywood, California—Reyes shows us that he lives a rather paradoxical life, which deviates from the norms of a very liberal town. In showcasing this contradiction, Reyes signals the ways that physical and social ideals of normality create affective boundaries that are exceedingly deleterious to social relationships. In this light, Reyes invites his readers to see the consequences of remaining in the closet; it is a silence that haunts Reyes and many others.

PERCEPTIONS OF ETHNICITY, RACE, AND IDENTITY IN REYES'S MEMOIR

Within several portions of Reyes's memoir *Madre and I*, the subjects of ethnicity and race are explored and linked to matters of sexual identity in meaningful ways. Reyes begins this discussion of ethnicity and race by speaking about his own family's unique identities and history. While his mother self-identifies herself as being white, Reyes largely views his absent father as being "non-white" because of the so-called darker color of his complexion; consequently, this mixing of ethnic identities leads Reyes to reflect on the subject.[51] The exact makeup of his father's ancestry remains unclear since his father only visits with the young Reyes on a few occasions, and in these conversations, they largely avoid discussions of race. Reyes explains, "Chileans have a peculiar attitude about race. . . . They consider themselves white if they are only partly white."[52] Reyes's statement about the "peculiar attitude" connotes a disconnect in views—that while certain people may see themselves as white, others may actually hold different or opposite viewpoint. In categorizing the Chilean attitude in this way, Reyes begins to raise questions about what ethnicity and race means for his culture and his own family. Although Reyes never arrives at a so-called definite understanding of his ethnic or racial identity, we see that these moments still lead him to question his identity. This idea becomes clearer as he visits various locations, and these spaces each lead to situations that offer another take on how ethnicity intersects with sexuality.

On several occasions, *Madre and I* shows how Reyes's body becomes a locus of desire for various people. In these moments, his suitors envision his body in ethnic terms and, thus, exoticize him. For instance, when Reyes first meets a possible suitor in Italy—who will later become his friend and sexual partner—the man asks Reyes: "'Where are you boys from? China?' . . . 'Well, you're exotic looking, whatever you are.'"[53] The Italian man's interpellation of Reyes's ancestry has the effect of making a spectacle of Reyes's body, hence valorizing his so-called difference, while also objectifying him in a reductive way. To categorize a person as being a particular ethnic or racial identity can have the effect of omitting other elements of a person such as their sexual identity. Such reductions can cause irritations or other undesirable feelings because human beings self-identify themselves in a variety of ways that often cannot be perceived at first glance. This same phenomenon occurs in another part of Reyes's life when he visits Mexico. Upon meeting a young man in Mexico, Reyes learns that the young man actually desires him in a similar way. This young man, named Armando, regards Reyes and says to him: "I like men who are whiter than I am."[54] In this moment, Reyes's ethnicity is read as being white and thus more desirable in sexual terms. Through Armando's words, whiteness is eroticized, and dark skin is devalued, which reveals the way in which ethnicity and sexuality are bound up with one another and ultimately lead to the exclusion of people of color. These moments are evocative of the complex ways in which people of color are routinely "outed" publicly as having certain ethnic or racial identities, and in many cases like Reyes's, these "outings" are often erroneous because ethnic and racial identity are actually difficult (if not impossible) to read in a way that accords with people's understandings of themselves. Reyes's experience thus reveals how a person's preconceived ideas and the interpretation of physical image may skew the way in which people think about the relationships of beauty, ethnicity, race, and sexuality.

Like many people who are born into blended families, Reyes ostensibly has a more multilayered experience in constructing a vision of his own identity because of how his father's ancestry and ethnicity remains indefinite. When he meets his father at a young age, he sees his father as, "much darker than I expected, with a brown tinge on his skin that appeared Polynesian. I could live with illegitimacy, but at the time, it seemed a greater shock to me that my father turned out to be non-white."[55] In this case, his word *shock* speaks to way in which he views himself and his ancestry. When he puts his father's body under greater scrutiny in this scene, he begins to examine his own body and identity once more. Reyes's text thus raises the question: Is Reyes himself actually non-white because of his father's skin color? Similarly, this moment alludes to Reyes's own complicity and preconceived ideas about ethnicity—from which no one is exempt. Although some critics envision the color line in hypodescent ideology, this same way of thinking is not always operative in other parts of the world. Reyes must consequently negotiate several socially constructed ways of discussing ethnicity and race both at home and while he travels abroad. By highlighting these matters, the text points to the way that people exert pressures on the sexual other to fit into culturally specific categories of identity that match the expectations of some cultural group or majority. And when the other's identity category deviates from preestablished standards, some closed-minded people either expect the ethnic (or sexual) other to depart from the space, or the other routinely is forced out. In such situations, category indeterminism in relation to ethnicity and sexuality can lead to denigration and humiliation.

What Reyes's *Madre and I* shows is both the challenges of coming out as a hirsute, queer immigrant, as well as the importance of providing mentorship to those who struggle with the hardships of coming out in a world that frequently has little empathy for the grim circumstances that young, queer people of color encounter. Rather than showing support, many parts of the world habitually make a spectacle of difference in numerous ways. It is this disconcerting and quotidian social practice that requires a thorough consideration and greater theorizing. Further, what this research reveals is that we cannot assume that the challenges of coming out will always be the same or easily reconcilable. Reyes's memoir bespeaks that we must remain cognizant of the social realities that young queer people of color face: difficult social struggles and demeaning insults such as when Reyes is called "*maricón*" (i.e., faggot) by his classmates.[56] *Madre and I* asks us to think about how we care for each other, urging us to confront the bigotry that denies people their dignity. Reyes's memoir intimates that we must think critically and be thoughtful as we explore these experiences with Otherness, which can be contradictory. In effect, Reyes's text indeed relays the idea that we must to come out *in support* of each other in public and private spaces where there are greater social risks. *Madre and I* ultimately makes the statement we must contest those restrictive and diminishing societal structures that threaten to belittle us as well as embrace our differences instead of fearing their marginality.

Correspondingly, Reyes's narrative suggests that we must be vigilant of the way in which we engage in spectacles because they have the potential to hold great power and significance in the socialities of the public sphere. In this same arena, Reyes's memoir urges us to reflect on the ethics of our daily actions and approaches to public life; hence, his writing could be read as initiating a discussion about the norms and beliefs that guide our continually evolving societies. Moreover, this writing connotes that if we wish to create a more egalitarian world where all people are valued, we must be empathetic and mindful of our actions' implications. One of the leading scholars of human rights Lynn Hunt contends that "Empathy only develops through social interaction," and she goes on to show that this social interaction is not limited to the real world.[57] As Hunt suggests, people can "extend their purview of empathy" through reading novels, and in the process, readers like those that study Reyes's text, may gain a stronger ability to understand the challenges that queer migrants encounter. Through this empathy and reading pieces of writing, such as memoirs, we find bridges that lead us to be more attuned to the ethics of our social interactions with queer migrants and youth. Reyes's memoir therefore provides a supportive, integrative space to bring people together and explore the ethics of everyday life including the spectacular, which has been shown to have a profound impact on the manner in which we see the bodies and identities of ourselves, our families, and communities around the world.

NOTES

1. Guillermo Reyes, *Madre and I: A Memoir of Our Immigrant Lives* (Madison: University of Wisconsin Press, 2010), 101.
2. Ignacio López-Calvo, *Latino Los Angeles in Film and Fiction: The Cultural Production of Social Anxiety* (Tucson: University of Arizona Press, 2014).
3. Frances R. Aparicio, "Latinidad/es," in *Keywords for Latina/o Studies*, eds. Deborah R. Vargas, Nancy Raquel Mirabal, and Lawrence La Fountain-Stokes (New York: New York University Press, 2018), 116.
4. Reyes, *Madre and I*, 199.
5. Reyes, *Madre and I*, 277.
6. Pascale Bonnefoy, "Documenting U.S. Role in Democracy's Fall and Dictator's Rise in Chile," *The New York Times*, April 14, 2017, A7.
7. Macarena Gómez-Barris, *Beyond the Pink Tide: Art and Political Undercurrents in the Americas* (Berkeley: University of California Press, 2018); Lessie Jo Frazier, *Salt in the Sand: Memory, Violence, and the Nation-State in Chile, 1890 to the Present* (Durham, NC: Duke University Press, 2007).
8. Reyes, *Madre and I*, 163.
9. Reyes, *Madre and I*, 104.
10. Reyes, *Madre and I*, 104.
11. Reyes, *Madre and I*, 104.
12. Gloria E. Anzaldúa, "La Prieta," in *This Bridge Called My Back: Writings by Radical Women of Color*, 4th ed., eds. Cherríe Moraga and Gloria Anzaldúa (Albany: State University of New York Press, 2015), 199.
13. Guy Debord, *The Society of the Spectacle* (Detroit: Black & Red, 2000), 16–32.
14. Daphne A. Brooks, *Bodies in Dissent: Spectacular Performances of Race and Freedom, 1850–1910* (Durham, NC: Duke University Press), 32.
15. Kimberlé Crenshaw, "Mapping the Margins: Intersectionality, Identity Politics and Violence Against Women of Color," *Stanford Law Review* 43 (1993): 1241–99; Patricia Hill Collins, "It's All In the Family: Intersections of Gender, Race and Nation," *Hypatia* 13, no. 3 (1998): 62–82; Candace M. Jenkins, *Private Lives, Proper Relations: Regulating Black Intimacy* (Minneapolis: University of Minnesota Press, 2007).
16. Reyes, *Madre and I*, 18
17. Reyes, *Madre and I*, 78.

18. Reyes, *Madre and I*, 107.
19. Reyes, *Madre and I*, 100.
20. Reyes, *Madre and I*, 106.
21. Reyes, *Madre and I*, 112–16.
22. Reyes, *Madre and I*, 103.
23. Reyes, *Madre and I*, 108.
24. Reyes, *Madre and I*, 108.
25. Reyes, *Madre and I*, 37.
26. Reyes, *Madre and I*, 65–66.
27. Reyes, *Madre and I*, 74.
28. Reyes, *Madre and I*, 74.
29. Michael S. Boroughs, Ross Krawcsyk, and J. Kevin Thompson, "Body Dysmorphic Disorder among Diverse Racial/Ethnic and Sexual Orientation Groups: Prevalence Estimates and Associated Factors," *Sex Roles* 63, nos. 9/10 (2010): 725–37.
30. Aart Hendriks, Rob Tielman, and Evert can der Veen, eds., *The Third Pink Book: A Global View of Lesbian and Gay Liberation and Oppression* (Buffalo, NY: Prometheus Books, 1993).
31. Gómez-Barris, *Beyond the Pink Tide*, 50.
32. Gómez-Barris, *Beyond the Pink Tide*, 50.
33. Lisa Leff, "Effort to Repeal Gay History Law Prompts Complaint," *San Diego Union Tribune*, October 3. Accessed March 19, 2014, http://www.utsandiego.com/news/2011/Oct/03/effort-to-repeal-gay-history-law-prompts-complaint/, 2011.
34. Penelope Stanley and Susan Wolfe, *The Coming Out Stories* (Watertown, MA: Persephone Press, 1980).
35. Eve Kosofsky Sedgwick, *The Epistemology of the Closet* (Berkeley: University of California Press, 1990), 70.
36. Ann Rees-Turyn, "Coming Out and Being Out as Activism: Challenges and Opportunities for Mental Health Professionals in Red and Blue States," *Journal of Gay and Lesbian Psychotherapy* 11, nos. 3/4 (2007): 155–72.
37. Harvey Milk, "The Hope Speech," in *The Mayor of Castro Street: The Life and Times of Harvey Milk*, ed. Randy Shilts (New York: St. Martin's Press, 1982), 362.
38. Dan Savage and Terry Miller, "Timeline," *It Gets Better Project*, October 2011, Accessed March 2014, http://www.itgetsbetter.org/timeline.
39. Reyes, *Madre and I*, 113–14.
40. Esther Saxey, *Homoplot* (New York: Peter Lang Publishing, 2008).
41. Reyes, *Madre and I*, 153.
42. Reyes, *Madre and I*, 111.
43. Reyes, *Madre and I*, 111.
44. Reyes, *Madre and I*, 13.
45. Reyes, *Madre and I*, 13.
46. Reyes, *Madre and I*, 154.
47. Reyes, *Madre and I*, 156.
48. Reyes, *Madre and I*, 159.
49. Reyes, *Madre and I*, 228.
50. Reyes, *Madre and I*, 229.
51. Reyes, *Madre and I*, 44.
52. Reyes, *Madre and I*, 44.
53. Reyes, *Madre and I*, 163.
54. Reyes, *Madre and I*, 251.
55. Reyes, *Madre and I*, 44.
56. Reyes, *Madre and I*, 51.
57. Lynn Hunt, *Inventing Human Rights* (New York: W. W. Norton and Company, 2007), 39–40.

Afterword

Looking to the Future: Remembering Spatial Creativities and Confronting Violence across Latinx Queer Contexts

> I remember one night on the walk to the Stud in San Francisco, a man took me in with disgust—my hairy legs, my painted lips—and called me "faggot," in that quiet direct way that always seems particularly menacing, looking straight into my eyes. I remember dancing particularly hard that night.
>
> —Justin Torres[1]

In the months following the massacre at the Pulse nightclub on June 12, 2016, there emerged a myriad of debates and questions concerning the shooter's motivations, the media's coverage of the tragedy, and the social repercussions of such violence. Researchers in Latinx Studies likewise theorized the shootings' alarming sociopolitical dimensions including its link to similar crimes and oppressions.[2] In reality, shootings like the Pulse massacre in Orlando, Florida, continue to be an enervating and perennial problem in the United States in the twenty-first century. These mass shootings miserably have become nearly normalized. Following the murders in Orlando, *The New York Times* labeled the event a "national traumatic injury" because of how the carnage devastated people's lives on a national level as well as more locally in two socially marginalized, interlaced groups: the Latinx and LGBTQ communities in the US state of Florida.[3] Simultaneously, there was a significant outpouring of emotion and support extending from places around the world, connecting people in an untold number of debates, discussions, and reflections. News coverage of the shootings and aftermath not only conveyed flows of heartbreak and horror but also spoke to the ways that people imagined the roles of intimate spaces and safety in daily lives.

In the aforesaid *New York Times* article, journalist Dan Barry contextualized the eeriness of the Pulse shooting by using the gloomy headline, "Realizing It's A Small, Terrifying World After All," which references the famous ride "It's A Small World" at Walt Disney World. The Disney parks and Orlando area are seen as spaces of pleasure and vacation for millions around the world, including queer Latinx peoples who transform the Disney parks into LGBTQ spaces on "Gay Days." *The New York Times* headline called attention to the way that ostensibly safe spaces for

Latinx queers continue to be vulnerable. This article's association of Disney World with the Pulse Nightclub also brings to mind a shared dynamic of perceived safety. As David R. Coon explains in his study of gay tourism advertising, many seemingly queer-friendly destinations like Disney's Gay Days and the Pulse Nightclub have stood in contrast to places that Latinx queers often feel the need to leave: those places with intense homophobia and racism.[4] However, as the Pulse shootings suggest, there is no queer Shangri-la. Justin Torres speaks to that dismaying reality in the epigraph, which calls attention to the way that a seemingly queer cityscape like San Francisco continues to have homophobia. Although *The New York Times* article headline connotes there has been "realization" that the violence is ongoing, the question remains: Who was not aware of this ever-present dangerous dynamic? As *The New York Times* speaks to a large global audience, the realization here appears to refer to the dominant culture—heterosexual white people—who thought the United States and the world had changed. Yet as Latinx queers will attest, there continues to be widespread homophobic, racist, and xenophobic violence.

As this book has endeavored to show, the problems of bias, harassment, and violence still contribute to our outlook, sense of self, and sentiments, including those of personal comfort and safety. Some speakers perceive the threats of racism and homophobia as being a *figment* of one's imagination, though the Pulse shooting (as well as the conversations that resulted) suggest myriad forms of homophobia and racism persist. In contrast, the scholar of Caribbean studies Rosamond S. King contends that our inner capacities for imagination provide a means of both addressing violent behaviors as well as ways of theorizing them.[5] Like King, I believe that our capacity for imagining and inventing enables us to begin making sense of the challenges we encounter in familiar and violent scenes, especially when the logics of public spaces feel rather constraining, heartless, lacking, and contrary to the social justice that many queer Latinx groups are seeking. As I have aimed to show, the spatial dimensions of our imagination can open up avenues for advancing dialogues about the conditions and events that create extreme turmoil for Latinx and queer groups. Tellingly, the physical space outside of the Pulse Nightclub became a space for imagining and remembering lost loved ones, which took the form of people paying their respects, leaving flowers, looking inward, making statements, and saying prayers. Notable officials and politicians traveled to this site as well, bringing attention to the space's significant social place in the national imaginary, suggesting this site has begun to serve as a key location in the imagining of queer Latinx lives. High-ranking governmental leaders such as former President Barack Obama and President Bill Clinton visited the location in the months following the attack, demonstrating grief and reverence publicly. Their presence enabled the larger public to rethink the realities that queer

Afterword 147

Figure 5.2. A memorial outside of the Pulse nightclub in Orlando, Florida, from the photographer J. D. Casto.

Latinx people are facing. More recently, there has been a movement that is aiming to transform the site of the Pulse Nightclub into a US national memorial and museum, which would permanently protect the space from being erased or forgotten over time.⁶ Yet, many questions remain concerning the logistics and a questionable potential profit from the site.

As we consider the Pulse shooting further, additional social and political questions have arisen, which merit further consideration and point to some peculiar patterns in US cultural experience. In particular, a rather unusual dynamic known as "pinkwashing" took place in the news coverage of the event, whereby the massacre had been codified largely as an antigay attack, which in turn has occluded the fact that most of the murdered people at the site were actually of Latinx ancestry or had significant ties to Latinx lives.⁷ Many cultural groups beyond Latinx people attended this club, but the one male shooter opened fire on the nightclub's "Latino Night," a night when many Latinx people were present. Imagining the Pulse Nightclub as solely a queer space indeed limits our ability to redress the many problems that undergird various US scenes. Though some uninformed observers may see a Latino night at Pulse as being an insignificant moment generally, the social dimensions of such an evening are regarded as meaningful to an array of critics and scholars. In examining this Latino night's social dynamic, the researcher Juana María Rodríguez has written that "Dancing is often the first way we learn how to conform to the culturally defined rules around heterosexuality, to move our bodies in appropriately gendered ways. So there is a special significance to being able to dance to Latin music in a queer nightclub, *pecho a pecho* (chest to chest), *corazón a corazón* (heart to heart), with whomever you want."⁸ As her commentary suggests, that moment of connecting with a potential partner, shimmying with your spouse, or dancing with an old flame involves a great amount of emotional and intellectual sentiment. As previous chapters suggest, intimate and social closeness between two bodies is generative of an energy *or heat* that can build a future. Correspondingly, to address the underlying problems that pushed queer Latinx people in the space of Pulse (including racism and homophobia), there is a need to build additional closeness or coalitions between Latinx and queer communities. Building strong bridges between these groups is vital if we are to foster progress, and some critics anticipate this tragedy may ultimately have the effect of binding these marginalized communities in significant forms.

To have progress, let us ponder and reimagine the futurity of queer Latinx spaces in the real world as well as more imaginary formations such as US cultural production for the sake of sustaining ourselves. What remains to be done for these groups to gather more intentionally and find ways of problem-solving so that the painful societal structures of racism and homophobia will be addressed? This line of questioning already has inspired artists to craft thoughtful responses in the forms of comics and song, which encourage us to reflect on larger queer Latinx histories and how these groups deal with spatial violence.⁹ Although many have believed there has been dramatic social progress with the obtaining of marriage equality, this "change" has felt like an illusion predicated on assimilation to the standards of white patriarchy and the heterosexual norms of the past. These structures of power continue to overlap, in which light-skinned people continue to indulge in a desire to rise above everyone else. Addressing these dynamics requires recognition of the intersectionality at work across US social and political landscapes. To address this intersection, we benefit by taking a more hybrid or mixed-method approach where we create (and illuminate) bridges between our multiple cultural contexts and knowledges. As Gloria Anzaldúa explains, "To bridge is to attempt community, and for that we must risk being open to personal, political, and spiritual intimacy."[10] In Anzaldúa's theory, the experience of "bridging" is not without challenges because of the risks involved, but there exists a belief that such bridging allows us to find way of problem-solving. To enact this critical endeavor, in the prior chapters I sought to illustrate how this book's archive of materials suggests that the development of queerly hybrid spatial strategies can (or has potential to) provide a means to examining our connectivities and thus address the intersecting experiences of ethnocentrism, purity ideals, and white supremacy that impede progress and harm vulnerable communities around us.

As Tara Yosso and others have suggested, there is evidence Latinx peoples are being disrespected, ignored, and underserved by putatively well-intentioned institutions such as universities and threatened by the immigration policies and practices of courts, which continue to deport thousands of children and young people annually.[11] In some of these cases, US citizens have been mistakenly misclassified by the system and expelled from the United States, thereby putting them and their families in abject peril. The US courts and immigration systems provide illusions of fairness, but it remains clear that alternatives must be imagined. In this way, much social justice work remains to be done across a diverse set of public and social spaces. Prioritizing the various kinds of spatial creativity is one of the areas that most needs addressing now both in the physical sense of spatiality as well as in the more imaginary sense of the concept. Although such initiatives are being carried out by activists and advocates, numerous artists and writers are working to improve the living conditions of people through publishing and lecturing about acts of violence. Myriad artists, researchers, and writers are attempting to foster resistance to apathetic corporate models that cite the need for numbers, money, and resources as the all-important logic and reasoning. As a result, changing the established structures of power feels impossible at times because of the forces entrenched within the processes of various companies, organizations, and institutions. For these reasons, the imaginary spaces of art, culture, and daily life enable queer Latinx people to disrupt some of the ingrained logics and reroute the ways in which power dynamics play out across a variety of public spaces. Illuminating our connections to one another in diverse forms is a means of chipping away at the extant problems that have continued to divide US cultures. To say it another way, the public recognition of locales and sites as hybrid (or mixed) spaces can become a key means of recognizing the need for change, but this extensive labor is not done without considerable resistance from the status quo.

As this book has brought to light the problems of the status quo and the feelings that have arisen in its shadow, the importance of intimate spaces both lived as well as imaginary have been highlighted to foster further belonging, community, healing, innovation, and self-development. Spaces such as the bedroom and the family home are the commonly imagined sites of intimate relationality, but as this book's archive of artists show, the closeness, desires, and sensibilities of intimacy such as queer domestic sentiments are present across a broader range of sites than many imagine at first blush. As Anzaldúa reminds us, the human world has produced a "sexual borderlands" where diverse desires and bodies come into contact, yet these borderlands "are not particular to the southwest" because these socio-spatial dynamics and experiences arise wherever "two or more cultures edge each other."[12] These points of intimate intersection often have been relegated to the margins, but as this book has aimed to show, previous assumptions and principles of spatial creation are being contested and reimagined as people of the United States and cultures beyond its borders are coming into contact through assorted kinds of displacement, migration, and movement. A case in point, the experience of home-making indeed takes many more forms than US popular culture would have us think. In research of transnational experiences of home life, David A. B. Murray elaborates on the intellectual thought of sociologist Ala Sirriyeh to elucidate that home is "better understood as a fluid process that is reconstructed through mobility and place, and can be conceived as a broad fusion between spatial, social, psychological, temporal and affective domains."[13] As these scholars tell us, the notion of home-spaces regularly involve more than simple concrete sites because home-spaces are generated through social forces of politics and powerful groups that inform our social trajectories.

Likewise, the research of queer Latinx intimacies in diverse spaces has required us to do what Lauren Berlant sees as being an ongoing rethinking of intimacy, in which we "appraise how we have been and how we live and how we might imagine lives that make more sense than the ones so many are living."[14] Berlant's idea of "making more sense" dovetails with Muñoz's concept of working toward the possibilities of queer futurity—an experience and space that seems to differ from the "toxic" present in which we find ourselves today.[15] This toxicity is made manifest in moments where queer Latinx people are forced to reckon with humiliation, marginalization, stress, and violence in their communities, workplaces, restaurants, and many more sites. The courageous work of early transgender activists such as Silvia Rivera has paved the way for today's activities to continue combatting such social toxicity, and as a part of this work, we must further advance our efforts.[16] To do so, let us continue investing in the people and praxis of imaginative worldviews like the queerly inventive artistry we see within the second half of this book and beyond. As manifestations of the queerly hybrid space concept, the notions of queer domesticity and the queerly inventive provide an adaptable and flexible framework for theorizing the personal experiences and community circumstances that take place in the spatial creativities and struggles that Latinx sexual minorities encounter in the world. This flexibility can be a boon for scholars and other critics who search for ways of making sense of the manner in which pieces of art and writing make manifest spaces where the imaginary and real intersect.

As my discussion of Rigoberto González's novel, *The Mariposa Club* suggests, self-identification plays a pivotal role for people who depart from naturalized and structured systems of gender and sexuality that tend to exclude people who understand themselves as transgender or genderqueer. As trans studies scholars have stated, there is a pressing need to (re)examine the underlying assumptions and processes that limit the sphere of possibility for trans youth and adults across a spectrum of social and political experience. Identification also plays key roles in the disciplinary convictions of scholars; for instance, Yolanda Martínez-San Miguel and Sarah Tobias posit, "Perhaps the most significant part of our own identification with Trans Studies comes from our conviction that all spaces, as imperfect as they are, should be open and accessible to all the forms of being in the world that each one of us constantly inhabits."[17] Changing such compromised spaces and creating more inclusive spaces have been a component of this book's focus; however, this subject certainly merits greater scrutiny because heterosexual normativity and cisgender privilege is reproduced again and again in the creation of imaginary and physical spaces such as bathrooms, homes, schools, and myriad public spaces. Coupled with the way English is normalized in an uncountable set of spaces, Latinx queer and trans people face significant barriers. Even imaginary spaces are by no means free from the touch of spatial normativities, although they tend to offer some agency and freedom. Consequently, it is necessary to reflect on what has been gathered over time and consider how these knowledges can be implemented in the creation of space. To continue this effort, we can learn much from the spatial strategies narrated in the recent news coverage of inventive Puerto Rican queers, who are building diverse spaces on the island of Puerto Rico following the hurricanes of 2017. As their creativity shows, "envisioning a better future starts with having somewhere to go," which signals to us that the *somewhere* can take multiple shapes.[18] In these cases, it is mostly a matter of opening dialogues and fostering a spatially informed network committed to an equitable social sphere.

BRIDGING AND REMEMBERING: CONNECTIVE MOMENTS AND REMAKING GEOGRAPHIES

In historical terms, the United States has witnessed how community organizing has proven effective in moving beyond oppressive and systemic US power structures. Looking back in time, we observe how abolition activists in the nineteenth century informed the public sphere and undermined systems of slavery, but this is not to say the sinister transatlantic slave trade is wholly comparable to the present struggles of contemporary Latinx queer peoples. Rather, these moments stand out as being points of inspiration and precedents to challenge ingrained social geographies as well as set the stage for communities to continue the fight for egalitarian spaces that can unify communities and create a socially hybridized dynamic. During the 1990s as well as before, researchers like Arjun Appadurai, May Joseph, Fernando Ortiz, and others put forward generative discussions concerning the national and transnational dimensions of hybridity as well as sites where hybrid lives play out on a daily basis.[19] In leading a discussion of these hybridities, *Imagining Latinx Intimacies* has aimed to illuminate the social and spatial dynamics of Latinx artwork, film, writing, and other forms of creativity where hybrid elements enabled productive alliances. Further, as this book has highlighted the value of being ethical, reflective, and more thoughtful of our impact, it is vital to highlight how this book owes much to (inter)disciplines such as feminist studies, geography, queer studies, and Latinx studies. These scholarly fields at times have looked at each other askance, yet their work complements one another in the discussion of hybrid experiences and ongoing problems such as colonization and displacement.

Much as the scholar May Joseph suggests, embracing culturally hybrid forms can challenge ingrained tendencies toward retrograde US monoculturalism and, therefore, helpfully "destabilizes authoritarian forms of control."[20] Such hybridities are also particularly of interest because prominent US figures such as community leaders and politicians enact forms of cultural essentialism and exhibit a "growing ethnocentric, anti-international tendency toward cultural consolidation and expansionism."[21] Despite national efforts like tightening border access, new forms of witch hunts, and the scapegoating of vulnerable social groups, ample opportunities of resistance are found in digital landscapes, youth scenes, and networks of cultural workers. These social collectivities enable a means to disseminate "counter-narratives" and foster what Tara J. Yosso and others have called "counterspaces" because of how they offer the tools for people who experience unbelonging at the national level.[22] Yet these tools are by no means simply "up for grabs." Spatial creativity, which is a well-defined form of artistic intelligence, is necessary for optimizing and realizing the spaces of the quotidian and the imaginary. Everyday and everynight spaces, which bridge the public and the private, provide a means to alternative geographies that are more hospitable, yet to foster such spaces, creative and critical thinkers are needed. Recent research concerning alternative geographies of queer Latinx peoples and related vulnerable groups demonstrates the benefits of bringing disparate discourses and spaces into conversation. In Radost Rangelova's study, the daily and social geographies of Puerto Rican women and "Other" social groups are examined, demonstrating how gender and cultural history influence the spatial existences of varied communities of women as well as their contacts and families.[23] Through a nuanced analysis, Rangelova explains how quotidian social practices and relationalities in beauty salons become sites "for the construction of subversive models of gender and sexuality that resist and critique those put forth by Puerto Rican cultural nationalism."[24] In a manner much like that of Rangelova's salon, the artwork, film, and writing explored in this book provide ways of thinking that can foster creative strategies for social and political interventions, which ultimately would make possible several ways of bettering lives in the here and now.

As US cultural contexts become more sexually open, our social and spatial relations continue to transform in manifold ways at both home and within the numerous quotidian spaces. Yet the question remains" Have these changes benefited most queer and transgender people in measurable and substantive ways? Likewise: Have perspectives on queer spaces changed substantively since the 1990s and early 2000s? In the fall 2016 issue of *XY Magazine*, a cultural impresario of queer events in California explains his perspective on queer spaces. Angel Bonilla writes, "Gay space is so fragile. You never think it will be there at all. And when you find it, you think it will be there forever. But it's not. It's precious and fleeting."[25] This viewpoint has much in common with the ideas articulated by queer critics in prior decades, yet there is a certain romanticizing of queer space. But this loving of queer space is not uncritical in its approach. On further reflection, Bonilla explains why this form of spatial experience matters so much to him and many more sexual minorities. In his poignant statement, he explains:

> These spaces still matter. It's still a safe space where you get to be yourself. But then I remember that there is NOTHING like going to a gay club where you don't have to wonder who is gay and you can flirt with anyone you want and you can make a network of friends. . . . a warm night in a gay space is a rare, special kind of magic. It always was, and it always is, and it always will be.[26]

For Bonilla, the opportunity of shedding one's self-consciousness and worry about being attacked for being queer is worth all the effort of coordinating and producing a set of events that remain markedly evanescent. This "magic" that "always will be" is the affect constituted by queer spaces where they live in memory in delightful ways, but as Bonilla goes on to explain, not everyone is on board with such perspectives. Many critics, including this author, contend such sites can still be exclusionary to particular groups such as people living with disabilities or HIV. Nevertheless, Bonilla concludes his commentary by saying, "We ought to value gay spaces more. The opportunity to enter an alternate reality, then go right up and say to someone, 'I think you're really sexy,' is a precious moment of thrill and dreams. That is ourselves. That is us."[27] Equating ourselves to the affect of queer spaces intricately ties ourselves to such sites, suggesting we are all one with the larger scope of collective feelings. Such a concept of *queers as feelings* calls attention to the ways in which alternative forms of cognitive, physical, and psychological elements of daily life play roles in constructing queer experiences.

Moreover, as this book has shown, there has been significant proliferation of queer hybrid spaces during between the 1990s and early 2000s. Scholars such as José Esteban Muñoz hypothesized the work of Richard Fung as queerly hybrid in the late 1990s, laying bare the manner in which non-normative forms of desire intersect with cultural identities.[28] Nevertheless Muñoz urges caution on the ways that ideas of hybridity are often collapsed into a singular or general sense of mixing. As Muñoz suggests, representing the idea of hybridity as singular and unified belies the multiplicity of hybridizing that exist in forms of creolization, mestizaje, and syncretism across the Americas and beyond. This dynamism of discussions of queer hybridity has been extended by paying heed to the expanding and infinite spatial elements of lived experience, but our work on these projects is by no means complete. There remain many queerer hybridities to be mined and theorized beyond what has been studied in the present book before you. In the broadening queer expanses of transfeminisms, global transgender studies, and pornography studies, there remains much to be considered through the lens of queer hybridity and spatialized forms of creativity. For that reason, charting the futures of queer spatialities now provides benefits both within the contexts of Latinx lives as well as beyond to new cultural contexts still undiscovered.

Although this project has brought several forms of Latinx experience into dialogue with one another, it is certainly evident that these diverse lived experiences are by no means easily generalizable, but there are benefits of considering their commonalities such as their similar vulnerabilities. To explore these perils, this project has taken the approach of comparative ethnic studies at times, which bridges the gaps as well as attempts to break down walls that continually go up around disciplines and forms of study within the rather regimented academy. Indeed, there are numerous phenomena that merit further spatial analysis in the hybrid contexts of Latinx culture and lived experience. For instance, trailblazing television programs like *Ugly Betty* and *Jane the Virgin* integrate queer elements alongside heteronormative culture, mixing Spanish with English akin to the creativities of Rane Arroyo, Frances Negrón-Muntaner, and Moisés Agosto-Rosario, among others. Activists, artists, and educators are but a few of the numerous people that are developing cultural practices that can both inspire people to think beyond complacency as well as challenge ingrained social injustices that are reproduced daily. In this manner, these artists, creators, and writers encourage us to look toward the future with the hopes of finding additional means of *queering* the mainstream and dominant cultures that have excluded diverse peoples repeatedly and unjustly. As I and others have begun to suggest, there is a significant need to foster new forms of allyship and spaces such as queer domesticities that attend to the sociopolitical problems of daily life. Ultimately, such efforts hold potentials to challenge the ingrained forms of bias, privilege, and power structures that are repeatedly reproduced in a large swath of sites. More queerly inventive sites are necessary so that people can gather in an uplifting and productive fashion akin to the community centers that scholars have identified as playing a key role in the development of queer Latinx relations during the past several decades.[29]

In a news article following the Orlando massacre, journalist Daniel D'Addario writes about the event's space and compares the nightclub to community centers as well as others such as religious spaces. The journalist describes the situation by referring to the way that LGBTQ+ people often feel as though they are on the outskirts of their social groups in more ways than one. D'Addario states, "There is, at first, no mother tongue to describe their experience of life, no tradition to bind them to the world. Gay bars are where gay people have historically found one another to learn that language and invent those traditions. Being gay is not a religion, but a space for people to come together to celebrate who they are in the face of life's obstacles could be compared to a church."[30] This writing suggests mainstream definitions of home and community should be broadened and transgressed to enable more alternative and radical ideas of belonging and ties of affinity. Activists, advocates, artists, community organizers, and writers (among the many others) have found success working in tandem, pushing on and breaking through those walls repeatedly to create the desired changes. Through such initiatives, we may continue the process of reworking the power dynamics built into the fabric of US cultural contexts.

To create a critical practice of Latinx queer space, we must mobilize a cognizance of cultural diversity and egalitarianism that contests the discourses and power structures that historically have kept down people. Similarly, the artists in this volume suggest we must be willing to take risks if we are to decolonize our surroundings. By blurring rigid boundaries in style, space, and identity, these artists and authors unfix us from some of the limitations that halt the development of bridges between diverse peoples. The aforesaid Latinx socialities of queer domesticity and invention make it possible to dream of alternative pathways and resistance to the claustrophobic circumstances of the heteronormative quotidian across US terrains. In these bridges of hybrid artwork and experience, the queer mixes of creativity, emotion, and space crisscross, creating opportunities. Tracing these patterns and phenomena may read as a fanciful act in the eyes of some critics, but understanding the creativities and feelings that drive the creation of social scenes and communities is unequivocally vital if we are to change the path of history for the betterment of humanity. Fostering a more sophisticated understanding of the aforesaid queer experiences and ideas provides a blueprint for creating such bridges, which hold the potential to unite communities and link diverse landscapes of the Americas to the world. To develop these blueprints further, let us continue supporting inventive projects, research, and intellectual work that carry forth these artistic acts of bridging. Melding ancient beliefs, diverse languages, and theory allows for generative methodologies that can help us to confront violence that threaten the realization of a more equitable set of trajectories throughout the world.

NOTES

1. Jacob Bernstein, John Koblin, Steven Kurutz, Katherine Rosman, et al., "'My First Gay Bar': Rachel Maddow, Andy Cohen and Others Share Their Coming Out Stories," *The New York Times*, June 22, 2016, D1.

2. Katie Acosta, "Pulse: A Space for Resilience, A Home for the Brave," *QED: A Journal of GLBTQ Worldmaking* (Fall 2016): 107–10; Micaela J. Díaz-Sánchez, "Bailando: We Would Have Been There," *QED: A Journal of GLBTQ Worldmaking* (Fall 2016): 154–56; Michael Hames-García, "When I Think of Pulse, I think of Shakti," *QED: A Journal of GLBTQ Worldmaking* 3, no. 3 (Fall 2016): 111–13; Larry La Fountain-Stokes, "Queer Puerto Ricans and the Burden of Violence," *QED: A Journal of GLBTQ Worldmaking* 3, no. 3 (Fall 2016): 99–102.

3. Dan Barry, "Realizing It's A Small Terrifying World After All," *The New York Times*, June 20, 2016, A13.

4. David R. Coon, "Sun, Sand, and Citizenship: The Marketing of Gay Tourism," *Journal of Homosexuality* 59, no. 4 (April 2012): 511–34.

5. Rosamond S. King, "Introduction: From the Foreign-Local to the Caribglobal," *Island Bodies: Transgressive Sexualities in the Caribbean Imagination* (Gainesville: University Pressvof Florida, 2014), 1–19.

6. Jasmine Aguilera and Madeline Fitzgerald, "Concerns, Controversy Surround the Planned Construction of a Memorial and Museum at Pulse Nightclub, Site of 2016 Mass Shooting," June 13, 2019, https://time.com/5605008/pulse-nightclub-onepulse-memorial-museum-audit/. Web.

7. Everett Maroon, "The Pulse Shooting was the direct consequences of racism and homophobia," *Global Comment*, 14 June 2016, Web.

8. Juana María Rodríguez, "Voices: LGBT Clubs Let Us Embrace Queer Latinidad, Let's Affirm This," NBC News, June 16, 2016, Web.

9. Marc Andreyko, ed., *Love Is Love* (San Diego: IDW Publishing, 2019). Melissa Etheridge, "Pulse," M. E. Records, 2016; Sisaundra Lewis, "Applause Applause," Grove 2 Glam Media, 2016.

10. Gloria E. Anzaldúa, "Preface: (Un)natural bridges, (Un)safe spaces," in *This Bridge We Call Home: Radical Visions for Transformation*, eds. Gloria E. Anzaldúa and AnaLouise Keating (New York: Routledge, 2002), 3.

11. Tara J. Yosso, William A. Smith, Miguel Ceja, and Daniel C. Solórzano, "Critical Race Theory, Racial Microaggressions, and Campus Racial Climate for Latina/o Undergraduates," *Harvard Educational Review* 79, no. 4 (2009): 659–60.

12. Gloria E. Anzaldúa, "Preface to the First Edition," in *Borderlands/La Frontera: The New Mestiza*, 4th ed., eds. Norma Cantú and Aída Hurtado (San Francisco: Aunt Lute Books, 2012) 19.

13. David A. B. Murray, *Real Queer? Sexual Orientation and Gender Identity Refugees in the Canadian Refugee Apparatus* (London: Rowman & Littlefield International, 2016), 137.

14. Lauren Berlant, "Intimacy: A Special Issue," in *Intimacy*, ed. Lauren Berlant (Chicago: University of Chicago Press, 2000), 6.

15. José Esteban Muñoz, *Cruising Utopia: The Then and There of Queer Futurity* (New York: New York University, 2009), 27.

16. Raquel Willis, "How Sylvia Rivera Created the Blueprint for Transgender Organizing," Out.com, May 21, 2019, Web.

17. Yolanda Martínez-San Miguel and Sarah Tobias, "Introduction: Thinking beyond Hetero/Homo Normativities," in *Trans Studies: The Challenge to the Hetero/Homo Normativities* (New Brunswick, NJ: Rutgers University Press, 2016), 240.

18. Alejandra Rosa and Patricia Mazzei, "'A Space Where You Could Be Free': Puerto Rico's L.G.B.T. Groups Rebuild After a Hurricane," *The New York Times*, A12.

19. Arjun Appadurai, *Modernity at Large, Cultural Dimensions of Globalization* (Minneapolis: University of Minnesota Press, 1996); May Joseph, "Introduction: New Hybrid Identities and Performance," in *Performing Hybridity*, eds. May Joseph and Jennifer Natalya Fink (Minneapolis: University of Minnesota Press, 1999), 1–24; Fernando Ortiz, *Cuban Counterpoint: Tobacco and Sugar*, trans. Harriet de Onís (Durham, NC: Duke University Press, 1995).

20. Joseph, *Performing Hybridity*, 9–10.

21. Joseph, *Performing Hybridity*, 18.

22. Tara J. Yosso, et al., "Critical Race Theory," 660.

23. Radost Rangelova, *Gendered Geographies in Puerto Rican Culture: Spaces, Sexualities, Solidarities* (Chapel Hill: University of North Carolina Press, 2015).

24. Rangelova, *Gendered Geographies in Puerto Rican Culture*, 123.

25. Angel Bonilla, "The Fragility of Gay Space," The Wonderland Issue, *XY Magazine* 50 (Fall 2016): 41.

26. Bonilla, "The Fragility of Gay Space," 43.

27. Bonilla, "The Fragility of Gay Space," 43.

28. José Esteban Muñoz, "The Autoethnographic Performance: Reading Richard Fung's Queer Hybridity," in *Performing Hybridity*, eds. May Joseph and Jennifer Natalya Fink (Minneapolis: University of Minnesota Press, 1999), 112–30.

29. Ramón H. Rivera-Servera, *Performing Queer Latinidad: Dance, Sexuality, Politics* (Ann Arbor: University of Michigan Press, 2012), 94–133.

30. Daniel D'Addario, "The Gay Bar as Safe Space Has Been Shattered," Time.com, June 15, 2016, Web.

Appendix

Three Brief Resource Lists for Latinx and LGBTQ+ Communities

At present, there exists a desire for more resources and information concerning Latinx LGBTQ+ lives around the world because of several factors. A high number of schools and universities for instance, have said they are supportive of LGBTQ+ communities, but often these groups have stopped short of supplying the information that would enable the same communities to grow and thrive. The following three short lists are meant to provide some guideposts, though more and more resources continue to come online as the years pass. As a caveat, it should be noted that these lists are by no means comprehensive; rather, this selection of information speaks to many of the subjects that are explored in this book's chapters.

I. INFORMATION FOR COMMUNITY, CIVIC ENGAGEMENT, AND CULTURE

- Audre Lorde Project of New York, USA: https://alp.org/
- allgo, an organization for QTPOC of Austin, USA: http://allgo.org
- Chicago Latino Film Fest: https://chicagolatinofilmfestival.org/
- El/La Para Translatinas organization, USA: http://ellaparatranslatinas.yolasite.com/
- Entre Hermanos: Tu Organización Latina LGBTQ, USA: https://entrehermanos.org/
- Familia: Trans Queer Liberation Movement, USA: https://familiatqlm.org/staff/
- Gender Spectrum organization: https://www.genderspectrum.org/
- Immigration Equality organization: https://www.immigrationequality.org/
- International Lesbian, Gay, Bisexual, Trans, and Intersex Association: https://ilga.org/
- Intersex Society of North America: http://www.isna.org/
- Lambda Legal Defense and Education, USA: https://www.lambdalegal.org/
- Latinx Spaces in media: https://www.latinxspaces.com/

- National Center for Transgender Equality, USA: https://transequality.org
- Outright Action International Organization: https://outrightinternational.org/
- Q Center of Portland, Oregon: https://www.pdxqcenter.org/
- Queer Puerto Rican Filmfest: http://www.puertoricoqueerfilmfest.com/
- Seattle Latino Film Fest: https://www.slatinoff.org/
- Translatina Network, USA: https://translatinxnetwork.org/
- *The Advocate* Magazine: https://www.advocate.com/
- Trevor Project Hotline concerning suicide, USA: https://www.thetrevorproject.org/
- Voto Latino organization: https://votolatino.org/

II. INFORMATION FOR FAMILIES, RELATIONSHIPS, AND YOUTHS

- *A Positive View of LGBTQ*, a book by Riggle and Rostosky
- Campus Pride organization: https://www.campuspride.org/
- CenterLink: The Community of LGBT Centers: https://www.lgbtcenters.org/
- Chicanos por La Causa: https://www.cplc.org/
- The Family Equality Council: https://www.familyequality.org/
- Gender and Sexuality Alliance (GSA) Network: https://gsanetwork.org/
- Gay, Lesbian & Straight Education Network (GLSEN): https://www.glsen.org/
- Hispanic Scholarship Fund: https://www.hsf.net/scholarship
- LGBT National Help Center, San Francisco USA: http://www.glbtnationalhelpcenter.org/
- *LGBTQ: The Survival Guide*, a book by Kelly Huegel Madrone
- Parents and Friends of Lesbians and Gays, USA: https://pflag.org/
- Safe Schools Coalition, USA: http://www.safeschoolscoalition.org/
- Somos Familia Organization, USA: https://www.somosfamiliabay.org
- Stop Bullying Resources: https://www.stopbullying.gov/
- Sex, Etc.: https://sexetc.org/
- *The Pride Guide*, a book by Jo Langford
- Trans Lifeline in USA and Canada: https://www.translifeline.org/
- *When We Love Someone We Sing to Them: Cuando Amamos Cantamos*, an illustrated book by Ernesto Javier Martínez, Maya Christina González, and Jorge Gabriel Martinez Feliciano

III. INFORMATION FOR INSTRUCTORS AND SCHOLARS

- ACT-UP Oral History Project of New York: http://www.actuporalhistory.org/
- Australian Lesbian and Gay Archives: https://alga.org.au/
- Canadian Lesbian and Gay Archives: https://arquives.ca/
- Center for LGBTQ Studies, USA: https://clags.org/
- *Encyclopedia of Sex and Gender*, edited resource by Fedwa Malti-Douglas et al.
- Gay and Lesbian Archive of Mid-America: http://library.umkc.edu/spec-col/glama/index.htm
- Gay and Lesbian Archives of the Pacific Northwest, USA: http://www.glapn.org/
- Gay and Lesbian Memory in Action, South Africa: https://gala.co.za/
- Gulf Coast Archive and Museum, USA: http://gcam.org/
- *Finding Out: An Introduction to LGBT Studies*, edited by Gibson, Alexander, and Meem
- GLBTQ Archives in San Francisco, USA: https://www.glbthistory.org/archives
- John J. Wilcox, Jr. LGBT Archives of Philadelphia: www.waygay.org/archives/
- *Keywords for Latina/o Studies*, edited collection by Vargas, Mirabal, and La Fountain-Stokes
- Kinsey Institute for Research in Sex, Gender & Reproduction, USA: www.kinseyinstitute.org
- Latin American Center on Sexuality and Human Rights, Brazil: http://www.clam.org.br/
- Leather Archives and Museum of Chicago, USA: https://leatherarchives.org/
- Lesbian and Gay Archives of New Zealand: http://www.laganz.org.nz/
- Lesbian and Gay Newsmedia Archive, UK: http://www.lagna.org.uk/
- Lesbian, Gay, Bisexual, and Transgender Community Center, USA: https://gaycenter.org/
- Lesbian Herstory Archives, USA: http://www.lesbianherstoryarchives.org/
- LGBT Archive UK: http://www.lgbtarchive.uk/
- LGBT Foundation in Manchester, UK: https://lgbt.foundation/
- *LGBTQ America Today: An Encyclopedia*, edited collection by John Charles Hartley
- National LGBT Health Education Center, USA: https://www.lgbthealtheducation.org/

- National Norwegian Archive for Queer History: https://skeivtarkiv.no/en
- Old Lesbian Oral Herstory Project, USA: www.olohp.org
- One National Lesbian and Gay Archives, USA: www.onearchives.org
- People with a History: LGBTQ Histories: https://sourcebooks.web.fordham.edu/pwh
- Quatrefoil Library of Minneapolis, USA: https://www.qlibrary.org/
- *Queer: A Graphic History*, a graphic novel book by Meg-John Barker
- Queer Archive at Archivos de Arte Latinoamericano, Colombia: www.fundacionarkhe.com
- Rainbow History Project of Washington DC, USA: https://www.rainbowhistory.org/
- *Space, Place, and Sex: Geographies of Sexualities*, research by Johnston and Longhurst
- Stonewall National Museum of Fort Lauderdale, USA: www.stonewallnationalmuseum.org
- Transgender Archives of Victoria, Canada: www.uvic.ca/transgenderarchives/

Bibliography

Abate, Michelle Ann, and Kenneth Kid. "Introduction." In *Over the Rainbow: Queer Children's and Youth Adult Literature*, eds. Michelle Ann Abate and Kenneth Kidd. Ann Arbor: University of Michigan Press, 2011.
Acevedo, David Caleb, and Luis Negrón. *Los otros cuerpos: Antología de temática gay, lésbica y 'queer' desde Puerto Rico y su diaspora.* San Juan: Editorial Tiempo Nuevo, 2007.
Acosta, Katie. *Amigas y Amantes: Sexually Nonconforming Latinas Negotiate Family.* New Brunswick, NJ: Rutgers University Press, 2013.
———. "Pulse: A Space for Resilience, A Home for the Brave." *QED: A Journal of GLBTQ Worldmaking* 3, no. 3 (Fall 2016): 107–10.
AIDS in the Barrio: Eso no me pasa a mi. Directed by Frances Negrón-Muntaner and Peter Biella. Cinema Guild. 1985.
Agosto-Rosario, Moisés. *Nocturno y otros desamparos.* San Juan: Terranova Editores, 2007.
Aguilera, Jasmine, and Madeline Fitzgerald. "Concerns, Controversy Surround the Planned Construction of a Memorial and Museum at Pulse Nightclub Site of 2016 Mass Shooting." June 13, 2019. https://time.com/5605008/pulse-nightclub-onepulse-memorial-museum-audit.
Alexander, M. Jacqui. *Pedagogies of Crossing: Meditations on Feminism, Sexual Politics, Memory, and the Sacred.* Durham, NC: Duke University Press, 2005.
Alonso, Andoni, and Pedro Oiarzabal. *Diasporas in the New Media Age: Identity, Politics and Community.* Reno: University of Nevada Press, 2010.
Alvarado, Leticia. *Abject Performances: Aesthetic Strategies in Latino Cultural Production.* Durham, NC: Duke University Press, 2018.
Andreyko, Marc. *Love Is Love.* San Diego: IDW Publishing, 2019.
Anzaldúa, Gloria E. *Borderlands/La Frontera: The New Mestiza.* Eds. Norma Cantú and Aida Hurtado. San Francisco: Aunt Lute Books, 2012.
———. *The Gloria Anzaldúa Reader.* Ed. AnaLouise Keating. Durham, NC: Duke University Press, 2009.
———. "Now Let Us Shift . . . Paths of Conocimiento . . . Inner Work, Public Acts." In *This Bridge We Call Home: Radical Visions for Transformation*, eds. Gloria E. Anzaldúa and AnaLouise Keating, 541. New York: Routledge, 2002.
———. "La Prieta." *This Bridge Called My Back: Writings by Radical Women of Color*, 4th ed. Eds. Cherríe Moraga and Gloria Anzaldúa, 209. Albany: State University of New York Press, 2014.
———. "Preface: (Un)natural bridges, (Un)safe spaces." In *This Bridge We Call Home: Radical Visions for Transformation*, eds. Gloria E. Anzaldúa and AnaLouise Keating, 1. New York: Routledge, 2002.
———. "Preface to the First Edition." In *Borderlands/La Frontera: The New Mestiza*, 4th ed. Eds. Norma Cantú and Aída Hurtado, 20. San Francisco: Aunt Lute Books, 2012.
Anzaldúa, Gloria E., and Linda Smuckler. "Spirituality, Sexuality and the Body: An Interview with Linda Smuckler." In *The Gloria Anzaldúa Reader*, ed. AnaLouise Keating, 94. Durham, NC: Duke University Press, 2009.
Aparicio, Frances R. "Latinidad/es." In *Keywords for Latina/o Studies*, eds. Deborah R. Vargas, Nancy Raquel Mirabal, and Lawrence La Fountain-Stokes, 116. New York: New York University Press, 2018.

———. *Listening to Salsa: Gender, Latin Popular Music and Puerto Rican Cultures*. Hanover, CT: Wesleyan University Press, 1998.

Appadurai, Arjun. *Modernity at Large, Cultural Dimensions of Globalization*. Minneapolis: University of Minnesota Press, 1996.

Arao, Brian, and Kristi Clemens. "From Safe Spaces to Brave Spaces: A New Way to Frame Dialogue Around Diversity and Social Justice." In *The Art of Effective Facilitation: Reflections of Social Justice Educators*, ed. Lisa M. Landremen, 140. Sterling, VA: Stylus Publishing, 2013.

Arroyo, Rane. *How to Name a Hurricane*. Tucson: University Press of Arizona, 2005.

———. *The Buried Sea: New and Collected Poems*. Tucson: University of Arizona Press, 2008.

———. *The Singing Shark*. Tempe, AZ: Bilingual Press, 1996.

Augenbraum, Harold, and Margarite Fernández Olmos. "Introduction: An American Literary Tradition." *The Latino Reader: Five Centuries of an American Literary Tradition from Cabeza de Vaca to Oscar Hijuelos*, eds. Harold Augenbraum and Margarite Fernández Olmos, xix. New York: Houghton Mifflin, 1997.

"Awards of Courage: Moisés Agosto-Rosario." *AMFAR: The Foundation for AIDS Research*. 2002. October 5, 2010. www.amfar.org/spotlight/article.aspx?id=4508.

Barker, Meg-John. *Queer: A Graphic History*. Lanham, MD: Icon Books, 2016.

Barrett, Sarah Hayley, and Juana María Rodríguez. "Latinx: The Ungendering of the Spanish Language." LatinoUSA.org. January 29, 2016. www.latinousa.org/2016/01/29/latinx-ungendering-spanish-language/.

Barry, Dan. "Realizing It's a Small Terrifying World After All." *The New York Times*, June 20, 2016, A13.

Berlant, Lauren. "Intimacy: A Special Issue." In *Intimacy*, ed. Lauren Berlant, 1–8. Chicago: University of Chicago Press, 2000.

Berlant, Lauren, and Michael Warner. "Sex in Public." *Critical Inquiry* 24, no. 2 (Winter 1998): 558.

Bernstein, Jacob with John Koblin, Steven Kurutz, Katherine Rosman, et al. "'My First Gay Bar': Rachel Maddow, Andy Cohen and Others Share Their Coming Out Stories." *The New York Times*, June 22, 2016, D1.

Blasini, Gilberto M. "Hybridizing Puerto Ricanness." *Caribbean Studies* 36, no. 1 (2008): 198.

Bonilla, Angel. "The Fragility of Gay Space." The Wonderland Issue, *XY Magazine* 50 (Fall 2016): 41.

Bonnefoy, Pascale. "Documenting U.S. Role in Democracy's Fall and Dictator's Rise in Chile." *The New York Times*, April 14, 2017, A7.

Boroughs, Michael S. with Ross Krawcsyk and J. Kevin Thompson. "Body Dysmorphic Disorder among Diverse Racial/Ethnic and Sexual Orientation Groups: Prevalence Estimates and Associated Factors." *Sex Roles* 63, nos. 9/10 (2010): 725–37.

Bourdieu, Pierre. *Outline of a Theory of Practice*. Translated by Richard Nice. Cambridge: Cambridge University Press, 1977.

Boys Beware. Directed by Sid Davis. Sid Davis Productions, 1961.

Brady, Mary Pat. *Extinct Lands, Temporal Geographies: Chicana Literature and the Urgency of Space*. Durham, NC: Duke University Press.

Brewer, Paul R. "The Shifting foundations of Public Opinion about Gay Rights." *The Journal of Politics* 65, no. 4 (Nov. 2003): 1208–20.

Brincando el charco: Portrait of a Puerto Rican. Directed by Frances Negrón-Muntaner. Philadelphia: National Latino Communication Center, 1994. VHS.

Brinkerhoff, Jennifer. *Digital Diasporas: Identity and Transnational Engagement*. New York: Cambridge University Press, 2009.

Brooks, Daphne A. *Bodies in Dissent: Spectacular Performances of Race and Freedom, 1850–1910* (Durham, NC: Duke University Press), 32.

Brown, Michael, and Larry Knopp. "Queer Diffusions." *Environment and Planning D: Society and Space* 21 (2003): 409–24.

Cahill, Sean. "Black and Latino Same-Sex Couple Households and the Racial Dynamics of Antigay Activism." In *Black Sexualities: Probing Powers, Passions, Practices and Policies*, eds. Juan Battle and Sandra L. Barnes, 244. New Brunswick, NJ: Rutgers University Press, 2010.

Calafell, Bernadette Marie. *Monstrosity, Performance, and Race in Contemporary Culture*. New York: Palgrave Macmillan, 2015.

Campo, Rafael. *What the Body Told*. Durham, NC: Duke University Press, 1996.

Capetillo-Ponce, Jorge. "Exploring Gloria Anzaldúa's Methodology in *Borderlands/La Frontera—The New Mestiza*." *Human Architecture: Journal of the Sociology of Self-Knowledge* 4, no. 3 (2006): 87–94.

Capó, Julio. "Pulse and the Long History of Violence against Queer Latinos." *Time Magazine*. June 17, 2016. https://time.com/4372479/queer-latino-violence-history/.

Castillo, Debra Ann. "http://www.LAlit.com." In *Latin American Literature and the Mass Media*, eds. Debra Ann Castillo and Edmundo Paz-Soldán, 232–48. New York: Routledge, 2000.

Cianciotto Jason, and Sean Cahill. *LGBT Youth in America's Schools*. Ann Arbor: University of Michigan Press, 2012.

Cisneros, Sandra. *The House on Mango Street*. Houston: Arte Público Press, 1984.

Chávez, Karma R. *Queer Migration Politics: Activist Rhetoric and Coalitional Possibilities*. Urbana: University of Illinois Press, 2013.

Chauvin, Elizabeth A., Heidi S. Kulkin, and Gretchen A. Percle. "Suicide among Gay and Lesbian Adolescents and Young Adults: A Review of the Literature." *Journal of Homosexuality* 40, no. 1 (2000): 2.

Chen, Mel Y. *Animacies: Biopolitics, Racial Mattering and Queer Affect*. Durham, NC: Duke University Press, 2012.

Civale, Cristina. *Perra Virtual*. Buenos Aires, Argentina: Planeta, 1998.

Clark, Timothy. *The Cambridge Introduction to Literature and the Environment*. New York: Cambridge University Press, 2011.

Collin, Ross. "Making Space: A Gay-Straight Alliance's Fight to Build Inclusive Environments." *Teachers College Record* 115, no. 8 (2013): 7.

Collins, Patricia Hill. "It's All in the Family: Intersections of Gender, Race and Nation." *Hypatia* 13, no. 3 (1998): 62–82.

Conde, Rosina. *La Genera*. Mexico City: Universidad Autónoma de la Ciudad de México, 2006.

Conway, Thomas R., and Ruthann Crawford-Fisher. "The Need for Continued Research on Gay-Straight Alliances." *Journal of Curriculum and Pedagogy* 4, no. 2 (2007): 125–29.

Cooke, Janet. "Gays Coming Out on Campus, First Black Group at Howard." *The Washington Post*. April 24, 1980. Web.

Cooke, Jennifer. "Making a Scene: Towards an Anatomy of Literary Intimacies." In *Scenes of Intimacy: Reading, Writing and Theorizing Contemporary Literature*, ed. Jennifer Cooke, 3–22. New York: Bloomsbury, 2013.

Coon, David R. "Sun, Sand, and Citizenship: The Marketing of Gay Tourism." *Journal of Homosexuality* 59, no. 4 (April 2012): 511–34.

Correa-Díaz, Luis. "Literatura latinoamericana, española, portuguesa en la era digital (nuevas tecnologías y lo literario)." *Arizona Journal of Hispanic Cultural Studies* 14 (2010): 149–55.

Cotten, Trystan. "Introduction: Migration and Morphing." In *Transgender Migrations: The Bodies, Borders, and Politics of Transition*, ed. Trystan Cotton, 1–8. New York: Routledge, 2012.

Crenshaw, Kimberlé. "Demarginalizing the Intersection of Race and Sex: A Black Feminist Critique of Antidiscrimination Doctrine, Feminist Theory and Antiracist Politics." *University of Chicago Legal Forum* 1 (1989): 140.

———. "Mapping the Margins: Intersectionality, Identity Politics and Violence Against Women of Color." *Stanford Law Review* 43 (1993): 1241–99.

Crimp, Douglass. "DISS-CO (A FRAGMENT): From *Before Pictures*, A Memoir of 1970s New York." *Criticism* 50, no. 1 (Winter 2008): 1–18.
Crisp, Thomas. "The Trouble with Rainbow Boys." In *Over the Rainbow: Queer Children's and Youth Adult Literature*, eds. Michelle Ann Abate and Kenneth Kidd. Ann Arbor: University of Michigan Press, 2011.
Cuevas, T. Jackie. *Post-Borderlandia: Chicana Literature and Gender Variant Critique*. New Brunswick, NJ: Rutgers University Press, 2018.
Cvetkovich, Ann. *An Archive of Feelings: Trauma, Sexuality and Lesbian Public Cultures*. Durham, NC: Duke University Press, 2003.
D'Addario, Daniel. "The Gay Bar as Safe Space Has Been Shattered." Time.com. June 15, 2016. https://time.com/4365403/orlando-shooting-gay-bar-pulse-nightclub/.
Danielson, Marivel. *Homecoming Queers: Desire and Difference in Chicana Latina Cultural Production*. New Brunswick, NJ: Rutgers University Press, 2009.
De Certeau, Michel. *The Practice of Everyday Life*. Translated by Steven Rendall. Los Angeles: University of California Press, 1984.
De Jesús Vega, Manuel. "Chicano, Gay and Doomed: AIDS in Arturo Islas's '*The Rain God*.'" *Confluencia* 11, no. 2 (Spring 1996): 112–18.
De la Tierra, Tatiana. "Porcupine Love." In *Ambientes: New Queer Latino Writing*, eds. Lázaro Lima and Felice Picano, 75–83. Madison: University of Wisconsin Press, 2011.
De Onís, Catalina M., and Roy Pérez. "What's in an 'x': An Exchange about the Politics of 'Latinx.'" *Chiricú Journal: Latina/o Literatures, Arts, and Cultures* 1, no. 2 (Spring 2017): 78–91.
De Souza e Silva, Adriana. "From Cyber to Hybrid: Mobile Technologies as Interfaces of Hybrid Spaces." *Culture and Space* 9, no. 3 (2006): 261–62.
Debord, Guy. *The Society of the Spectacle*. Detroit: Black & Red, 2000.
Decena, Carlos Ulises. *Tacit Subjects: Belonging and Same-Sex Desire among Dominican Immigrant Men*. Durham, NC: Duke University Press, 201.
DeFalco, Beth and Geoff Mulvihill. "N.J. Student Kills Self After Sex Broadcast." *Washington Post*, 30 September 2010, Section A, Page 3.
Diaz, Von. "How Latino Activists Fought for Transgender Rights in Massachusetts." Colorlines.com, November 15, 2013, Web.
Díaz-Sánchez, Micaela J. "Bailando: We Would Have Been There." *QED: A Journal of GLBTQ Worldmaking* (Fall 2016): 154–56.
Douglas, Mary. *Purity and Danger: Concepts of Pollution and Taboo*. New York: Routledge, 2002.
Douglass, Frederick. *Narrative of the Life of Frederick Douglass*. Eds. John W. Blassingame, John R. McKivigan, and Peter Hinks. New Haven, CT: Yale University Press, 2001.
Driskill, Qwo-Li with Chris Finley and Brian Joseph Gilley, eds. "Introduction." In *Queer Indigenous Studies: Critical Interventions in Theory, Politics and Literature*, eds. Qwo-Li Driskill with Chris Finley and Brian Joseph Gilley, 1–30. Tucson: University of Arizona Press, 2011.
Duany, Jorge. "Nation and Migration: Rethinking Puerto Rican Identity in a Transnational Context." In *None of the Above: Puerto Ricans in the Global Era*, ed. Frances Negrón-Muntaner, 51. New York: Palgrave Macmillan, 2007.
———. *Puerto Rican Nation on the Move*. Chapel Hill: University of North Carolina Press, 2001.
———. *Puerto Rico: What Everyone Needs to Know*. New York: Oxford University Press, 2017.
Dyer, Richard. "In Defense of Disco." In *Out in Culture: Gay, Lesbian, and Queer Essays on Popular Culture*, eds. Corey K. Creekmur and Alexander Doty, 408–10. Durham, NC: Duke University Press, 1995.
Edelman, Lee, Tim Dean, et al. "The Antisocial Thesis in Queer Theory." *PMLA* 121, no. 3 (2006): 819–28.

Edge, Sami. "SPD Sets National Example with LGBTQ-friendly Safe Haven Plan." *The Seattle Times*. Crime. August 10, 2015, Web.
Eng, David. *The Feeling of Kinship: Queer Liberalism and the Racialization of Intimacy*. Durham, NC: Duke University Press, 2010.
Etheridge, Melissa. "Pulse." M. E. Records. 2016.
Everett, Anna. *Digital Diaspora: A Race for Cyberspace*. Albany: State University of New York Press, 2009.
Fairchild, Amy L., and Eileen A. Tynan. "Policies of Containment: Immigration in the Era of AIDS." *American Journal of Public Health* 84, no. 12 (December 1994): 2011–22.
Ferré, Rosario. *Sweet Diamond Dust and Other Stories*. New York: Plume, 1996.
Flores, Dan. *Coyote America: A Natural and Supernatural History*. New York: Basic Books, 2016.
Flores, William V., and Rina Benmayor, "Introduction: Constructing Cultural Citizenship." *Latino Cultural Citizenship: Claiming Identity, Space and Rights*, 1. Boston: Beacon Press, 1997.
Frank, Gillian. "Discophobia: Antigay Prejudice and the 1979 Backlash against Disco." *Journal of the History of Sexuality* 15, no. 2 (May 2007): 276–306.
Frazier, Lessie Jo. *Salt in the Sand: Memory, Violence, and the Nation-State in Chile, 1890 to the Present*. Durham, NC: Duke University Press, 2007.
Freeman, Kimberly A. *Love American Style*. New York: Routledge, 2003.
Foucault, Michel. *The History of Sexuality—An Introduction Volume 1*. Translated by Robert Hurley. New York: Random House, 1978.
Galeano, John. "On Rivers." In *The Environmental Humanities*, eds. Serpil Oppermann and Serenella Iovino, 331–38. London: Rowman & Littlefield International, 2017.
Garcia, Lorena. *Respect Yourself, Protect Yourself: Latina Girls and Sexual Identity*. New York: New York University Press, 2012.
García Canclini, Néstor. *Hybrid Cultures: Strategies for Entering and Leaving Modernity*. Translated by Christopher Chiappari and Sylvia L. Lopez. Minneapolis: University of Minnesota Press, 2005.
Garza, Elisa. "Chicana Lesbianism and the Multigenre Text." In *Tortilleras: Hispanic and U.S. Latina Lesbian Expression*, eds. Lourdes Torres and Inmaculada Pertusa, 196–212. Philadelphia: Temple University Press, 2003.
Gere, David. *How to Make Dances in an Epidemic: Tracking Choreography in the Age of AIDS*. Madison: University of Wisconsin Press, 2004.
Giannetti, Louis. *Understanding Movies*, 9th ed. Upper Saddle Creek, NJ: Prentice Hall, 2002.
Glee. Directed by Bradley Buecker, Fox, April 17, 2012.
Goldman, Dara. *Out of Bounds: Islands and the Demarcation of Identity in the Hispanic Caribbean*. Lewisburg, PA: Bucknell University Press, 2008.
Goldman, Russell. "Here's a List of 58 Gender Options for Facebook Users." ABCNews.go.com. February 13, 2014. Web.
Gómez-Barris, Macarena. *Beyond the Pink Tide: Art and Political Undercurrents in the Americas*. Berkeley: University of California Press, 2018.
———. "Mestiza Cultural Memory: The Self-Ecologies of Laura Aguilar." In *Laura Aguilar: Show and Tell*, ed. Rebecca Epstein, 83. Los Angeles: University of California Press, 2017.
González, Rigoberto. *So Often the Pitcher Goes to Water until It Breaks*. Urbana: University of Illinois Press, 1999.
———. *The Mariposa Club*. Boston: Alyson Books, 2009.
———. *The Mariposa Gown*. Maple Shade, FL: Tincture Press, 2012.
Gonzalez-Barrera, Ana with Mark Hugo Lopez and Eileen Patten. "Closing the Digital Divide: Latinos and Technology Adoption." March 7, 2013. www.pewhispanic.org/2013/03/07/closing-the-digital-divide-latinos-and-technology-adoption.
Gosine, Andil. "Brown to Blonde at Gay.com: Passing White in Queer Cyberspace." In *Queer Online: Media Technology and Sexuality*, eds. Kate O'Riordan and David Phillips, 139–54. New York: Peter Lang, 2007.

Gourdine, Angeletta KM. *The Difference Place Makes: Gender, Sexuality, and Diaspora Identity*. Columbus: The Ohio State University Press, 2002.
Gray, Mary L. *Out in the Country: Youth, Media and Queer Visibility in Rural America*. New York: New York University Press, 2009.
Gray, Mary L., with Colin R. Johnson and Brian J. Gilley. "Introduction." In *Queering the Countryside: New Frontiers in Rural Queer Studies*, eds. Mary L. Gray, Colin R. Johnson, and Brian J. Gilley, 1–22. New York: New York University Press, 2016.
Greenfield, Beth. "Gay Getaways: The New Wave." *The New York Times*, 14 July 2006, Section F, Page 1 and 12.
Guidotti-Hernández, Nicole M. "Borderlands." In *Keywords for Latina/o Studies*, eds. Deborah Vargas, Nancy Raquel Mirabel, and Lawrence La Fountain Stokes, 21–24. New York: New York University Press, 2017.
Habell-Pallán, Michelle. *Loca Motion: The Travels of Chicana and Latina Popular Culture*. New York: New York University Press, 2005.
Halberstam, Jack. *Female Masculinity*. Durham, NC: Duke University Press, 1998.
———. *In a Queer Time and Place: Transgender Bodies, Subcultural Lives*. New York: New York University Press, 2005.
Hames-García, Michael. "When I Think of Pulse, I think of Shakti." *QED: A Journal of GLBTQ Worldmaking* 3, no. 3 (Fall 2016): 111–13.
Haraway, Donna J. *When Species Meet*. Minneapolis: University of Minnesota Press, 2007.
Harrington, Joseph. "Poetry and the Public: The Social Form of Modern U.S. Poetics." In *Poetry and Cultural Studies: A Reader*, eds. Maria Damon and Ira Livingston, 266. Chicago: University of Illinois Press, 2009.
Hartinger, Brent. *The Geography Club*. New York: HarperCollins, 2003.
Healy, Patrick. "Laramie Killing Epilogue a Decade Later." *New York Times*. September 16, 2008: Section A, Page 1.
Hendriks, Aart, with Rob Tielman and Evert can der Veen, eds. *The Third Pink Book: A Global View of Lesbian and Gay Liberation and Oppression*. Buffalo, NY: Prometheus Books, 1993.
Hennen, Peter. *Faeries, Bears, and Leathermen: Men in Community Queering the Masculine*. Chicago: University of Chicago Press, 2008.
Hennessy, Rosemary. "Queer Visibility in Commodity Culture." *Cultural Critique* 29 (Winter 1994–1995): 31–76.
Hernández, Daisy. *A Cup of Water Under My Bed: A Memoir*. Boston: Beacon Press, 2014.
Holmes, Christina. *Ecological Borderlands: Body, Nature and Spirit in Chicana Feminism*. Urbana: University of Illinois Press, 2016.
Holmes, Steven A. "Jesse Helms Dies at 86; Conservative Force in the Senate." *The New York Times*, July 8, 2008. https://www.nytimes.com/2008/07/05/us/politics/00helms.html.
hooks, bell. *Talking Back: Thinking Feminist, Thinking Black*. Cambridge: Between the Lines, 1989.
Human Rights Campaign. The League of United Latin American Citizens and the Human Rights Campaign. "Supporting and Caring for Our Latino LGBT Youth." 2012. https://www.hrc.org/youth-report/latino-youth.
Hunt, Lynn. *Inventing Human Rights*. New York: W. W. Norton and Company, 2007.
Hurtado, Albert T. *Intimate Frontiers: Sex, Gender, and Culture in Old California*. Albuquerque: University of New Mexico Press, 1999.
In the Life. "Orgullo Latino." Episode 2109. PBS network. June 1, 2012.
Indiana, Rita. *La estrategia de Chochueca*. San Juan: Editorial Isla Negra, 2003.
Jeffords, Susan. *Hard Bodies: Hollywood Masculinity in the Reagan Era*. New Brunswick, NJ: Rutgers University Press, 1993.
Jenainati, Cathia. *Feminism: A Graphic Guide*. Lanham, MD: Icon Books, 2010.
Jenkins, Candace M. *Private Lives, Proper Relations: Regulating Black Intimacy*. Minneapolis: University of Minnesota Press, 2007.

Jennings, Kevin. *One Teacher in 10: Gay and Lesbian Educators Tell their Stories*. Boston: Alyson Press, 2005.

Johnston, Lynda, and Robyn Longhurst. *Space, Place, and Sex: Geographies of Sexualities*. London: Rowman & Littlefield International, 2009.

Joseph, May. "Introduction: New Hybrid Identities and Performance." In *Performing Hybridity*, eds. May Joseph and Jennifer Natalya Fink, 1–24. Minneapolis: University of Minnesota Press, 1999.

Kafka, Franz. *The Metamorphosis and Other Stories*. Translated by Michael Hofmann. New York: Penguin Books, 2007.

Kaplan, Carla. "Identity." In *Keywords for American Cultural Studies*, eds. Bruce Burgett and Glenn Hendler, 126. New York: New York University Press, 2007.

Kaufman, Linda S. *Discourses of Desire: Gender, Genre, and Epistolary Fictions*. Ithaca, NY: Cornell University Press, 1986.

Keating, AnaLouise. "Introduction." In *The Gloria Anzaldúa Reader*, ed. AnaLouise Keating, 5. Durham, NC: Duke University Press, 2009.

King, Rosamond S. "Introduction: From the Foreign-Local to the Caribglobal." *Island Bodies: Transgressive Sexualities in the Caribbean Imagination*. Gainesville: University Press of Florida, 2014.

Kline, Anna, Emma Kline, and Emily Oken. "Minority Women and Sexual Choice in the Age of AIDS." *Social Science and Medicine* 34, no. 4 (1992): 447–57.

La Fountain-Stokes, Lawrence. "Autobiographical Writing and Shifting Migrant Experience." In *Queer Ricans: Cultures and Sexualities in the Diaspora*, 19–22. Minneapolis: University of Minnesota Press, 2009.

———. "Queer Diasporas, Boricua Lives: A Meditation on Sexile." *Review: Literature and Arts of the Americas* 41, no. 2 (2008): 294–301.

———. "Queer Puerto Ricans and the Burden of Violence." *QED: A Journal in GLBTQ Worldmaking* 3, no. 3 (2016): 99–102.

———. *Queer Ricans: Cultures and Sexualities in the Diaspora*. Minneapolis: University of Minnesota Press, 2009.

———. "Translatinas/os." *Transgender Studies Quarterly* 1–2 (2014): 237.

Langford, Jo. *The Pride Guide: A Guide to Sexual and Social Health for LGBTQ Youth*. London: Rowman & Littlefield, 2018.

Lara, Ana M. "Uncovering Mirrors: Afro-Latina Lesbian Subjects." In *The Afro-Latin@ Reader: History and Culture in the United States*, eds. Miriam Jiménez Román and Juan Flores, 307. Durham, NC: Duke University Press, 2010.

Latino Outdoors. "Mission Statement." February 27, 2016. http://latinooutdoors.org/about-us/. Web.

Lefebvre, Henri. *The Production of Space*. Translated by Donald Nicholson-Smith. Malden, MA: Blackwell, 1974.

Leff, Lisa. "Effort to Repeal Gay History Law Prompts Complaint." *San Diego Union Tribune*. October 3. March 19, 2014. www.utsandiego.com/news/2011/Oct/03/effort-to-repeal-gay-history-law-prompts-complaint.

Lewis, Sisaundra. "Applause." Grove 2 Glam Media, 2016.

Lombardo, Keith. "Encuentra Tu Parque: Cabrillo National Monument." NPS.gov, August 8, 2016. https://www.nps.gov/media/video/view.htm?id=6C9B8D80-FA90-B6A9-5C1333B6294DFAC2.

López-Calvo, Ignacio. *Latino Los Angeles in Film and Fiction: The Cultural Production of Social Anxiety*. Tucson: University of Arizona Press, 2014.

Lozada, Ángel. *No quiero quedarme sola y vacía*. San Juan: Isla Negra Editores, 2006.

Lumpkin, Bernard. "Rigoberto González: Populating Bookshelves." *Lambda Literary*. May 4, 2013. https://www.lambdaliterary.org/interviews/05/04/rigoberto-gonzalez-populating-the-bookshelves/.

Lytle, Mark Hamilton. *America's Uncivil Wars: The Sixties Era from Elvis to the Fall of Richard Nixon*. Oxford: Oxford University Press, 2006.

Madigan, Nick, Benjamin Mueller, and Sheryl Stolberg. "49 Lives Lost to Horror in Orlando: Mostly Young, Gay and Latino." *The New York Times*. June 13, 2016.

Madrone, Kelly Huegel. *LGBTQ: The Survival Guide for Lesbian, Gay, Bisexual, Transgender, and Questioning Teens*. Minneapolis, MN: Free Spirit Publishing, 2018.

Malek, Alia. "Moving Beyond the Label of 'War Refugee.'" *The New York Times Magazine*. May 17, 2019. Web.

Malti-Douglas, Fedwa, ed. *Encyclopedia of Sex & Gender*. New York: Macmillan Reference, 2007.

Maroon, Everett. "The Pulse Shooting was the direct consequences of racism and homophobia." *Global Comment*. June 14, 2016. Web.

Martínez, Ernesto Javier. *On Making Sense: Queer Race Narratives of Intelligibility*. Stanford, CA: Stanford University Press, 2013.

Martínez-San Miguel, Yolanda. *Caribe Two Ways: Cultura de la migración en el Caribe insular hispánico*. San Juan: Ediciones Callejón, 2003.

———. "Female Sexiles: Toward an Archeology of Displacement of Sexual Minorities in the Caribbean." *Signs* 36, no. 4 (June 2011): 813.

Martínez-San Miguel Yolanda, and Sarah Tobias. "Introduction: Thinking beyond Hetero/Homo Normativities." In *Trans Studies: The Challenge to the Hetero/Homo Normativities*, eds. Yolanda Martínez-San Miguel, and Sarah Tobias, 14. New Brunswick, NJ: Rutgers University Press, 2016.

Marwick, Alice E. *Status Update: Celebrity, Publicity, & Branding in the Social Media Age*. New Haven, CT: Yale University Press, 2013.

Mata, Irene. *Domestic Disturbances: Re-Imagining Narratives of Gender, Labor, and Immigration*. Austin: University of Texas Press, 2014.

Matthews, Glenna. *Just a Housewife: The Rise and Fall of Domesticity in America*. New York: Cambridge University Press, 1989.

Matthews, Kristin L. *Reading America: Citizenship, Democracy, and Cold War Literature*. Amherst: University of Massachusetts Press, 2016.

Mayo, Jr., J. B. "Critical Pedagogy Enacted in the Gay-Straight Alliance: New Possibilities for a Third Space in Teacher Development." *Educational Researcher* 42, no. 5 (June/July 2013): 267.

McCready, Lance Trevor. "Some Challenges Facing Queer Youth Programs in Urban High Schools: Racial Segregation and Denormalizing Whiteness." In *Gay, Lesbian, and Transgender Issues in Education: Programs, Policies and Practices*, ed. James T. Sears, 190–92. New York: Routledge, 2005.

McGlotten, Shaka. *Virtual Intimacies: Media, Affect, and Queer Sociality*. Albany: State University of New York Press, 2013.

Mckiernan-González, John. "Health." In *Keywords for Latina/o Studies*, eds. Deborah R. Vargas, Nancy Raquel Mirabel, and Lawrence La Fountain-Stokes, 79. New York: New York University, 2017.

McMahon, Marci R. "Self-Fashioning through Glamour and Punk in East Los Angeles: Patssi Valdez in Asco's Instant Mural and A La Mode." In *The Chicano Studies Reader: An Anthology of Aztlán, 1970–2015*, eds. Chon A. Noriega, Erica Avila, Karen Mary Davalos, Chela Sandoval, et al., 295. Los Angeles: UCLA Chicano Studies Research Center Press, 2016.

Milk, Harvey. "The Hope Speech." In *The Mayor of Castro Street: The Life and Times of Harvey Milk*, ed. Randy Shilts, 362. New York: St. Martin's Press, 1982.

Mohanram, Radhika. *Black Body: Women, Colonialism, and Space*. Minneapolis: University of Minnesota Press, 1999.

Moreno, Marisel C. *Family Matters: Puerto Rican Women Authors on the Island and Mainland*. Richmond: University of Virginia Press, 2012.

———. "Revisiting la Gran Familia Puertorriqueña in the Works of Rosario Ferré and Judith Ortíz Cofer." *CENTRO Journal* 22, no. 2 (Fall 2010): 76.

Morgensen, Scott. "Radical Faeries." In *LGBTQ America Today: An Encyclopedia*, ed. John Hawley, 1012. Westport, CT: Greenwood Press, 2009.

Mortimer-Sandilands, Catriona, and Bruce Erickson, eds. *Queer Ecologies: Sex, Nature, Politics, Desire*. Bloomington: Indiana University Press, 2010.

Muñoz, José Esteban. "The Autoethnographic Performance: Reading Richard Fung's Queer Hybridity." In *Performing Hybridity*, eds. May Joseph and Jennifer Natalya Fink, 112–30. Minneapolis: University of Minnesota Press, 1999.

———. *Cruising Utopia: The Then and There of Queer Futurity*. New York: New York University Press, 2009.

———. "Feeling Brown: Ethnicity and Affect in Ricardo Bracho's The Sweetest Hangover (and Other STDs)." *Theater Journal* 52, no. 1 (March 2000): 67–79.

Muñoz, Manuel. *The Faith Healer of Olive Avenue*. Chapel Hill, NC: Algonquin Books, 2007.

Murray, David A. B. *Real Queer? Sexual Orientation and Gender Identity Refugees in the Canadian Refugee Apparatus*. London: Rowman & Littlefield International, 2016.

Nakamura, Lisa. *Cybertypes: Race, Ethnicity, and Identity on the Internet*. New York: Routledge, 2002.

Negrón-Muntaner, Frances. "Comment: Dance with Me." In *Gay Latino Studies: A Critical Reader*, eds. Michael Hames-García and Ernesto Javier Martínez, 313. Durham, NC: Duke University Press, 2011.

———. "Frances Negrón-Muntaner." In *Women of Vision: Histories in Feminist Film and Video*, ed. Alexandra Juhasz, 286. Minneapolis: University of Minnesota Press, 2001.

Nelson, Michael. "An Interview: Rane Arroyo, Author of The Portable Famine." https://www.newletters.org/bkmk-books/portable-famine. BKMK Press, 2007. Web.

Newton. Esther. *Cherry Grove, Fire Island: Sixty Years in America's First Gay and Lesbian Town*. Boston: Beacon Press, 1993.

Nieuwenhuis, Marijn, and David Crouch. *The Question of Space: Interrogating the Spatial Turn between Disciplines*. London: Rowman & Littlefield International, 2017.

Ocampo, Anthony C. "The Gay Second Generation: Sexual Identity and Family Relations of Filipino and Latino Gay Men." *Journal of Ethnic and Migration Studies* 40, no. 1 (2013): 155–73.

Olivares, Julian. "Sandra Cisneros: *The House on Mango Street* and the Poetics of Space." In *Charting New Frontiers in American Literature: Chicana Creativity and Criticism*, eds. María Herrera-Sobek and Helena Viramontes. Albuquerque: University of New Mexico Press, 1996.

Ortiz, Fernando. *Cuban Counterpoint: Tobacco and Sugar*. Translated by Harriet de Onís. Durham, NC: Duke University Press, 1995.

Ortíz, Ricardo L. "Diaspora." In *Keywords for Latina/o Studies*, eds. Deborah R. Vargas, Nancy Raquel Mirabal, and Lawrence La Fountain-Stokes. New York: New York University Press, 2017.

Palmer, Paulina. *The Queer Uncanny: New Perspectives on the Gothic*. Cardiff: University of Wales Press, 2012.

Parkin, David. *Kinship: An Introduction to Basic Concepts*. Malden, MA: Wiley-Blackwell, 1997.

Parkin, Robert, and Linda Stone, eds. *Kinship and Family: An Anthropological Reader*. Malden, MA: Wiley-Blackwell, 2004.

Pascoe, C. J. *Dude, You're A Fag: Masculinity and Sexuality in High School*. Berkeley: University of California Press, 2007.

Pascoe, Peggy. "Race, Gender, and The Privileges of Property." In *American Studies: An Anthology*, eds. Janice A. Radway, Kevin K. Gaines, et al., 89–98. Malden, MA: Wiley Blackwell, 2009.

Peeples, Jase. "RuPaul Further Responds to Transphobic Accusations." The Advocate.com. May 26, 2014. https://www.advocate.com/%5Bprimary-topic-path-raw%5D/2014/05/26/rupaul-further-responds-transphobic-accusations-ive-been-tranny.

Pérez, Daniel Enrique. "Toward a Mariposa Consciousness: Reimagining Queer Chicano and Latino Identities." In *The Chicano Studies Reader: Anthology of Aztlán, 1970–2015*, eds. Chon A. Noriega, Eric Avila, Karen Mary Davalos, Chela Sandoval and Rafael Pérez-Torres, 570. Los Angeles: UCLA Chicano Studies Research Center, 2016.

Pérez, Hiram. *A Taste for Brown Bodies: Gay Modernity and Cosmopolitan Desire*. New York: New York University Press, 2015.

Pérez-Torres, Rafael. "Refiguring Aztlán." In *The Chicano Studies Reader, an Anthology of Aztlán, 1970–2015*, eds. Chon A. Noriega, Eric Avila, Karen Mary Davalos, Chela Sandoval, Rafael Pérez-Torres, 185. 3rd ed. Los Angeles: University of California Los Angeles Press, 2016.

Philo, Chris with Chris Wilbert. "Animal Spaces, Beastly Places: Introduction." In *Animal Spaces, Beastly Places: New Geographies of Human-Animal Relations*, eds. Chris Philo with Chris Wilbert, 4. New York: Routledge, 2000.

Pose. Directed by Ryan Murphy. Produced by Steven Canals and Brad Falchuk, FX network, 2018.

Pulido, Laura. *Environmentalism and Economic Justice*. Tucson: University of Arizona Press, 1996.

Rangelova, Radost. *Gendered Geographies in Puerto Rican Cultures: Spaces, Sexualities, Solidarities*. Chapel Hill: University of North Carolina Press, 2015.

Rees-Turyn, Ann. "Coming Out and Being Out as Activism: Challenges and Opportunities for Mental Health Professionals in Red and Blue States." *Journal of Gay and Lesbian Psychotherapy* 11, nos. 3/4 (2007): 155–72.

Reisen, Carol, Miguel A. Iracheta, Maria Cecilia Zea, Fernanda T. Bianchi, and Paul J. Poppen. "Sex in public and private settings among Latino MSM." *AIDS Care* 22, no. 6 (May 2010): 697–704.

Reyes, Guillermo. *Madre and I: A Memoir of Our Immigrant Lives*. Madison: University of Wisconsin Press, 2010.

Rich, Adrienne. *Blood, Bread, and Poetry*. New York: W. W. Norton, 1994.

Richardson, Samuel. *Pamela or Virtue Rewarded*. New York: Penguin, 1981.

Riggle, Ellen D. B., and Sharon S. Rostosky. *A Positive View of LGBTQ*. Lanham, MD: Rowman & Littlefield, 2012.

Rivera-Servera, Ramón H. *Performing Queer Latinidad: Dance, Sexuality, Politics*. Ann Arbor: University of Michigan Press, 2012.

Rodríguez de Ruíz, Alexandra, and Marcia Ochoa. "Translatina Is About the Journey: A Dialogue on Social Justice for Transgender Latinas in San Francisco." In *Trans Studies: The Challenge to Hetero/Homo Normativities*, eds. Yolanda Martínez-San Miguel and Sarah Tobias, 154–55. New Brunswick, NJ: Rutgers University Press, 2016.

Rodríguez, Juana María. *Queer Latinidad: Identity Practices and Discursive Spaces*. New York: New York University Press, 2003.

———. *Sexual Futures: Queer Gestures and Other Latina Longings*. New York: New York University Press, 2014.

———. "Sexuality." In *Keywords for Latina/o Studies*, eds. Deborah R. Vargas, Nancy Raquel Mirabal, and Lawrence La Fountain Stokes, 199. New York: New York University Press, 2017.

———. "Voices: LGBT Clubs Let Us Embrace Queer Latinidad, Let's Affirm This." NBC News. June 16, 2016. https://www.nbcnews.com/storyline/orlando-nightclub-massacre/voices-lgbt-clubs-let-us-embrace-queer-latinidad-let-s-n593191.

Rodriguez, Ralph E. *Latinx Literature Unbound: Undoing Ethnic Expectation*. New York: Fordham University Press, 2018.

Rodríguez, Richard T. "Architectures of Latino Sexuality." *Social Text* 33, no. 2 (June 2015): 83–84.

———. "Family." In *Keywords for Latina/o Studies*, eds. Deborah R. Vargas, Nancy Raquel Mirabal, and Lawrence La Fountain-Stokes, 62. New York: New York University Press, 2017.

———. *Next of Kin: The Family in Chicano/a Cultural Politics*. Durham, NC: Duke University Press, 2009.

Román Garcia, Luis H. "In Search of My Queer Aztlán." In *Queer Aztlán: Chicano Male Recollections of Consciousness and Coming Out*, eds. Adelaida Del Castillo and Gibran Guido, 317–18. San Diego: Cognella Academic Publishing, 2015.

Roof, Judith. *Come as You Are: Sexuality and Narrative*. New York: Columbia University Press, 1996.
Roque Ramírez, Horacio N. "'That's My Place!': Negotiating Racial, Sexual and Gender Politics in San Francisco's Gay Latino Alliance." *Journal of the History of Sexuality* 12, no. 2 (Spring 2003): 224–58.
Rosa, Alejandra and Patricia Mazzei. "'A Space Where You Could Be Free': Puerto Rico's L.G.B.T. Groups Rebuild After a Hurricane." *The New York Times*, A12.
Ross, Kristen. "Rimbaud and the Transformation of Social Space." *Yale French Studies* 73 (1987): 104–10.
Rueda Esquibel, Catrióna. *With Her Machete in Her Hand: Reading Chicana Lesbians*. Austin: University of Texas Press, 2006.
Saavedra, Yvette, and Deena J. González. "Latino/Latina Americans and LGBTQ Issues." In *LGBTQ America Today: An Encyclopedia Vol. 2*, ed. John C. Hawley. Westport, CT: Greenwood Press, 2009.
Sánchez, Alex. *Getting It*. New York: Simon & Schuster, 2006.
———. *Rainbow Boys*. New York: Simon & Schuster, 2001.
Sandilands, Catriona. "Queer Ecology." In *Keywords for Environmental Studies*, eds. Joni Adamson, William A. Gleason, and David N. Pellow, 169–71. New York: New York University Press, 2016.
Sandoval-Sánchez, Alberto. "Imagining Puerto Rican Queer Citizenship: Frances Negrón-Muntaner's *Brincando el charco: Portrait of a Puerto Rican*." In *None of the Above: Puerto Ricans in the Global Era*, ed. Frances Negrón-Muntaner, 153. New York: Palgrave Macmillan, 2007.
Santos-Febres, Mayra. *Sirena Selena Vestida de Pena*. Doral, FL: Stockcero, 2008.
Savage, Dan, and Terry Miller. "Timeline." It Gets Better Project. October 2011. March 2014. http://www.itgetsbetter.org/timeline.
Saxey, Esther. *Homoplot*. New York: Peter Lang Publishing, 2008.
Schneider, Cathy Lisa. "Racism, Drug Policy and AIDS." *Political Science Quarterly* 113, no. 3 (Autumn 1998): 427–46.
Sedgwick, Eve Kosofsky. *The Epistemology of the Closet*. Berkeley: University of California Press, 1990.
Seymour, Nicole. *Strange Natures: Futurity, Empathy and the Queer Ecological Imagination*. Chicago: University of Illinois Press, 2013.
Shah, Nayan. *Contagious Divides: Epidemics and Race in San Francisco's Chinatown*. Berkeley: University of California Press, 2001.
Snediker, Michael. *Queer Optimism: Lyric Personhood and Other Felicitous Persuasions*. Minneapolis: University of Minnesota Press, 2009.
Solis Ybarra, Priscilla. "Borderlands as Bioregion: Jovita González, Gloria Anzaldúa and the Twentieth Century Ecological Revolution in the Rio Grande Valley." *MELUS: Multi-Ethnic Literature of the U.S.* 34, no. 2 (2009): 175–89.
Somerville, Siobhan B. "Queer." In *Keywords for American Cultural Studies*, eds. Bruce Burgett and Glenn Hendler, 187. New York: New York University Press, 2007.
Soto, Sandra K. *Reading Chican@ Like a Queer: The De-Mastery of Desire*. Austin: University of Texas Press, 2010.
Stack, Liam. "Before Orlando Shooting, an Anti-Gay Massacre in New Orleans Was Largely Forgotten." *The New York Times*. June 14, 2016. www.nytimes.com/2016/06/15/us/upstairs-lounge-new-orleans-fire-orlando-gay-bar.html.
Stanley, Penelope, and Susan Wolfe. *The Coming Out Stories*. Watertown, MA: Persephone Press, 1980.
Stryker, Susan. "(De)Subjugated Knowledges: An Introduction to Transgender Studies." In *The Transgender Studies Reader*, 1–17. New York: Routledge, 2006.
Thomson, Rosemarie Garland. "Introduction: From Wonder to Error—A Genealogy of Freak Discourse in Modernity." In *Freakery: Cultural Spectacles of the Extraordinary Body*, ed. Rosemarie Garland Thomson. New York: New York University Press, 1996.

Tinsley, Omise'Eke Natasha. *Ezili's Mirrors: Imagining Black Queer Genders*. Durham, NC: Duke University Press, 2018.
Tongson, Karen. *Relocations: Queer Suburban Imaginaries*. New York: New York University Press.
Toomey, Russell B. "High School Gay-Straight Alliances (GSAs) and Young Adult Well-Being: An Examination of GSA Presence, Participation, and Perceived Effectiveness." *Applied Developmental Science* 15, no. 4 (October 2011): 176.
Travers, Ann. *Writing the Public in Cyberspace: Redefining Inclusion on the Net*. New York: Garland Publishing, 2000.
Trebay, Guy. "A Kiss Too Far?" *The New York Times*. February 18, 2007. ST1.
Urbanik, Julie. *Placing Animals: An Introduction to the Geography of Human-Animal Relations*. Lanham, MD: Rowman & Littlefield Publishers, 2012.
US Census Bureau. "Census Brief: Hispanic Owned Businesses." October 2001. Web.
Valenti, Jessica. *The Purity Myth: How America's Obsession with Virginity Is Hurting Young Women*. Berkeley: Seal Press, 2010.
Valenzuela, Angela. "Education." In *Keywords for Latina/o Studies*, eds. Deborah R. Vargas, Nancy Raquel Mirabal, and Lawrence La Fountain-Stokes, 52. New York: New York University Press, 2017.
Vargas, Deborah R., Nancy Raquel Mirabal, and Lawrence La Fountain-Stokes. "Introduction." In *Keywords for Latina/o Studies*, eds. Deborah R. Vargas, Nancy Raquel Mirabal, and Lawrence La Fountain-Stokes, 2. New York: New York University Press, 2017.
Vargas, Deborah R. *Dissonant Divas: The Limits of La Onda in Chicana Music*. Minneapolis: University of Minnesota Press, 2012.
———. "Ruminations on Lo Sucio as a Latino Queer Analytic." *American Quarterly* 66, no. 3 (2014): 723.
Vorobjovas-Pinta, Oskaras, and Brady Robards. "The Shared Oasis: An Insider Ethnographic Account of a Gay Resort." *Tourist Studies* 17, no. 4 (2017): 383.
"Vote to Repeal 'Don't Ask, Don't Tell' a Win for All." *Arizona Daily Star*, 21 December 2010. http://azstarnet.com/news/opinion/editorial/article_7fde0fa5-9d7d-5350-a122-88f7f81c16ca.html.
Walters, Suzanna Danuta. *All the Rage: The Story of Gay Visibility in America*. Chicago: University of Chicago Press, 2001.
Wells, H. G. *The Island of Dr. Moreau*. New York: Bantam Classics, 1994.
Whatmore, Sarah. *Hybrid Geographies: Natures Cultures Spaces*. Thousand Oaks, CA: Sage Publications, 2002.
White, Edmund. *Loss within Loss: Artists in the Age of AIDS*. Madison: University of Wisconsin Press, 2002.
Whiting, Jason B., Douglas B. Smith, Megan Oka, and Gunnur Karakurt. "Safety in Intimate Partnerships: The Role of Appraisals and Threats." *Journal of Family Violence* (April 2012): 314.
Willis, Raquel. "How Sylvia Rivera Created the Blueprint for Transgender Organizing." Out.com. May 21, 2019. https://www.out.com/pride/2019/5/21/how-sylvia-rivera-created-blueprint-transgender-organizing.
Yountae, An with Peter Anthony Mena. "Anzaldúa's Animal Abyss: Mestizaje and the Late Ancient Imagination." In *Divinanimality: Animal Theory, Creaturely Theology*, eds. Stephen Moore and Laurel Kearns, 161–81. New York: Fordham University Press, 2014.
Yosso, Tara J., with William A. Smith, Miguel Ceja, and Daniel C. Solórzano. "Critical Race Theory, Racial Microaggressions, and Campus Racial Climate for Latina/o Undergraduates." *Harvard Educational Review* 79, no. 4 (2009): 659–60.

Index

Activism, xxvi, 20, 30, 50, 133
Afro-Latinx, 46, 50
Age of AIDS, xiv, xv, 22
Acquired Immunodeficiency Syndrome (AIDS/HIV), xiv, 92, 98
AIDS Coalition to Unleash Power (ACT-UP), xxv
Agency, 108, 116, 151
Aguilar, Laura, 100, 111
Allies, 59, 76
Alterity, 130
Alternative narratives, 56
American Civil Liberties Union, 59
American Dream, xi, xxxiii, 40, 54, 102, 106, 139
Animals, 97, 104
Anxiety, 58, 137
Anzaldúa, Gloria, xi, xiii, xv, 36, 71, 97, 106, 126–127, 149; Anzaldúa's theory of sexual borderlands, 150; Anzaldúa's portrayal of animals, 107; Anzaldúa's poetry, 110–111
Aztecs, 101, 103, 104
Aztlán, 101

Beauty, 56, 117, 125, 131
Belonging, 102, 103, 124; Unbelonging, 54, 152
Bias, xiv, 98
Bisexuality, 51, 139
Bodies, 21, 56, 72, 99, 111, 116, 125, 141; Body Dysmorphic Disorder (BDD), 131, 137
Border Studies, xxvii
Borderlands, xvi, xxi, 99, 150
Borderlands / La Frontera: The New Mestiza, 101
Borders, xv, 98
Bowers v. Hardwick, 99

Bridges, xx, 70, 98, 108; Anzaldúa's theory of bridge-building, xxvii, 119, 127, 149
Brincando el charco: Portrait of a Puerto Rican, 3–8, 51
Buddhism, 103
Bullying, xxiii, 20, 36

Capitalism, xvii, xxii, xxx, 4, 19, 74, 108, 134
Chatrooms, 87
Chicana feminism, xxviii, xxix
Chicana/o and Chicanx, xii, xv, xxiii, xxviii, xxix, xxxii, 102, 105; Chicana lesbian writing, 110; Chicana music, 22; Chicana/o movement, xxv; Chicana representation, xiv; Chicano identities, 105
Chilean Americans, 123–124
Cisneros, Sandra, xxix
Citizenship, xxvii, 8
City, xvi, xviii, 11, 20, 23
Class, xiv, 10, 76, 108, 126
Coalitions, xxii, xxvi
Code-switching, 113
Cold War, xx
Colonialism, 9, 16
Colonization, 4, 90
Coming out, xv, 133, 134; Coming out as an ally, 54
Community, 54, 70, 155
Compton Cafeteria, 133
Compulsory heterosexuality, xvi, 108
Conformity, 55
Consumerism, 57
Counterculture, xxi, 81, 108
Cuba, xxix, 127
Cuir, 134
Cultural scripts, 77
Cyberspaces, 70

175

Cybertexts, 79

Dance spaces, 6, 9, 17, 23, 148
Decolonizing, 42, 45, 62, 69, 75, 155
Detention, 116–117
DiaspoRicans, 10
Difference, 52, 57, 109, 117, 127, 134, 141, 142
Disability, 98, 116
Displacement, xii, xvi, 3, 35, 42, 61, 98, 124, 150
Dispossession, 117
Domestic sphere, xxii, xxiv, xxix
Domestic ideals, 40–41; Domestic sensibility, 5

Eco-criticism, 109
Education, 36–38, 40, 42, 46, 54, 55, 57
Egalitarianism, 127, 155
Emotions, xiii, 9, 22, 72, 133, 145, 148, 154, 156; Emotional development, xxxi; Emotional difficulty, 136; Emotional refreshment, xxvi; Emotional support, 14; Emotional well-being, xx, xxiii; Feeling of closeness, 30, 38; Experience of turmoil, 15, 30, 146; Happiness, 24, 28, 55, 138; Loneliness, 25, 27, 79, 118; Shame, 125
Environment, 103
Equal Access Act, 39, 59
Ethics, 132
Ethnic Studies, 103, 154
Ethnicity, xxiii, 16, 76, 114, 126, 128, 140–142; Ethnicity and space, 45–46; Intersections of ethnicity, 29; Performance of ethnicity, 80
Ethnocentrism, 126
Exceptionalism, 104
Excess, 28, 44, 47, 89, 130, 137
Ezili, 45

Familia, xiv
Family, xv, xxiv, xxix, 3–4, 27–30, 35; Blended families 5.42; Dancing family, 18, 27; Extended family, 41; Family-making, 29; Family of friends, 6; Kinship, 29; Latinx families, 52; Queer family, 6

Femininity, xxiii, xxvii, 35, 45, 50, 74, 84
Feminism, xxviii; Feminist Studies, xxviii, xxix, 152; Women's lives, 152
Ferré, Rosario, xxix
Film, xiii, xvi, xxix, 3–8, 11–24, 59, 99
Fire Island, New York, 27–28
First Amendment, 39
Foucault, Michel, 61
Futurity, xxii, 53, 63, 136, 148, 150

Gay and Straight Alliances (GSAs), 35–39
Gay liberation, 133
Gay men, 52, 57, 99, 124, 133
Gay Union of Trenton State (GUTS), xxi
González, Elián, 127–128
Gender, xxiii, 74, 101; Gender-fluid, 80; Gender performance, 50. *See also* transgender
Genderqueer, xxxiiin2, 44, 52, 57, 101, 151
Genders and Sexualities Alliance, 41
Geography, xxi, 102, 109
Getting It , xxxi, 36–38, 41–42
Glee, 46
The Gloria Anzaldúa Reader , 106
Government, 9, 39, 105, 106, 124
Gran Familia Puertorriqueña, 10

Hart-Cellar Act, 124
Health, 62, 89, 92
Heterosexuality, 8, 38, 39, 54
Hiding oneself, 54, 75, 130, 136, 139
History, xv, 30, 42, 61, 98, 105, 106, 107, 124, 153, 156; Colonial history, xii, 90; History of Chile, 124–125; History of disco, 19; Personal History, 124; Puerto Rican history, 12–14
HIV/AIDS, xiv, 92, 98
Hollywood, 47, 59
Home, xxi, xxvi, 3, 15, 19, 30, 35, 38, 41, 45, 51, 69, 102, 138–139, 150; Alternative domesticity, 16; Dance spaces as home, 6, 9, 17; Domesticity, 12–14, 25; Home away from home, 36; Queer domesticity, 8

Homophobia, xv, xvii, xviii, 4, 58, 83, 100; Homophobic policy, 74; Homophobic spaces, xxxi, 103, 109, 139
How to Name a Hurricane, 71
Hybrid space, xx, xxvii, 5, 30, 40, 42, 71, 74, 87, 101, 110, 125, 150
Humor, 48, 77, 99, 115

Identity, 76, 141
Ideology, xxvi, 4, 81, 133, 134, 142
Imagination, 53
Immigration, xv, 124, 149; Migration, xiii, xv, xxxi, 3, 6, 9, 12, 24, 124–126, 128, 149–150
Immigration and Nationality Act of 1965, 124
Indigenous culture, xxviii, 79, 97–98, 103; Queer Indigenous Studies, 114
Interdisciplinarity, xxix
Intimacy, xi–xii, 50, 98, 111, 150; Creative intimacy, 109; Familial intimacy, 140; Intellectual intimacy, 108; Latinx intimacy, xxx; Queer intimacy, 99; Sexual intimacy, 108, 137; Social intimacy, 5, 38, 59, 103; Virtual intimacy, 75
The Internet, xxv, 62, 71, 72, 74, 77, 79, 82, 85, 93; Cyberspaces, 70; Technology, 88; Websites, 56
Intersectionality, xiv, 11, 44, 46, 50, 81, 126, 141, 149; Theory of intersectionality, xxiii, 128
Isolation, 9, 62, 79

Jane the Virgin, 154
Jones-Shafroth Act, 9
Judicial System, 149

Kahlo, Frida, 110

Latina/o, xxiii
Latinidad, xxiv, 50, 123–124
Latinx, xii, xxxiiin2
Latinx Studies, 123; Latina/o Studies B03.18
Law and policy, xii, xv, 40, 58, 74
Lawrence v. Texas, 99
Lesbian sexuality, 14–16

LGBTQ, ix, 155
Liberace, 50
Liminal, xxi, xxviii, 47, 102
Literature, xxiv, xxvi, 23, 84; Latinx literature, 41
LLEGÓ (National Latina/o Lesbian and Gay Organization), xviii

Madre and I: A Memoir of Our Immigrant Lives, xxxii, 124, 126, 130, 140, 142–143
Marginality, 106
Mariposas, 36
The Mariposa Club, xxiii, 36
Marriage equality, 148
Masculinity, 108; Machismo, 44, 51, 88
Media, xiv, 6, 44, 56, 71, 74, 82, 84, 116, 117, 127; LGBTQ media, xii; Multimedia, 70; New media, 85; Social media, 56, 76, 103; Visual media, xxviii
Memoir, xxxiii, 123–124, 125, 126, 131; Memoir as coming out story, 134
Mestiza, xv, 101; Mestizaje, 101, 154
Metronormativity, 103
Mexican Americans, xii, xviii, xxxi, xxxii, 35, 36, 46, 110, 139; Mexican American cultural contexts, 104–105
Michael, George, 128
Monoculturalism, 152
Montreal, Canada, 25, 29
Monsters, 98, 111, 130
Moraga, Cherríe, xxix
Multiculturalism, xxviii, 80, 139
Muñoz, José Esteban, xvi, xxii–xxiii, 8
Muñoz, Manuel, 49
Music, 21–22, 26–27, 28–29, 32n47, 46, 56, 70, 72, 76; Latin music, 148; Music and community, 23; Music in film, 11, 131; Music in the disco, 17; Musical film, 99

Nation, xvi, 106, 124, 136
National identity, xii
National imaginary, 146
Nationalism, xx
Nature, xvii, 98, 107, 111, 118
New York, New York, xvi
No quiero quedarme sola y vacía, 71

Nocturno y otros desamparos, 4, 9, 21–22
Nuyorico, xx, 114

Obama, Barack, 146
Operation Bootstrap, 6
Oppression, xxviii, 127, 145
Othering, 116, 127
Outdoors, 91
Outing, 128, 141
Otherness, 142

Philadelphia, Pennsylvania, 12
Paradigms, 51, 82, 108
Paratexts, 84
Patriarchy, 3, 7, 12
Performance, 74–78, 86
Pinkwashing, 148
Pinochet, Augusto, 124
Place, xxi, 3, 11, 22–23, 27, 35, 44, 48, 51, 87, 98, 116–118, 139–140; Home as place, 150; Intersections of place, 102, 103; Place of learning, 131; Place of origin, 123; Place-making, 73; Social place, 146
Poetry, 105, 110–111, 113, 118–119
Polysemy, 129
Popular culture, xxviii, 45, 46, 71, 102, 115, 150
Pose, 45
Power, xx, 60, 78, 104, 127, 149
Pride parades, 19–21
Privacy, xviii, xxiii, 88, 99; Private spaces, xii, xviii, 102, 129, 142, 152
Privilege, xiii, 16, 69, 103, 115, 128, 131, 155
Pronouns, 35, 74
Propriety, 72–73, 83
Psychology, 131, 132, 137, 154
Public life, xiv, 53, 131, 142
Puerto Rican Young Lords, xxv
Puerto Rico, 3, 5, 9, 10, 19, 73, 88, 114
Puerto Rican lives, 6, 69, 71
Pulse Nightclub, xxxiii, 6, 145–148, 155
Purity, 75, 85, 101

Queer, xxv, 21, 42, 76, 127, 129. *See also* LGBTQ and Sexuality
Queer domesticity, xxiv, 8, 10, 150; Domestic reimagining, 35

Queer Eye for the Straight Guy, 48
Queerly inventive, xxiv, 69, 73, 74, 100, 124, 151, 155
Queer people of color, 127
Queer visibility, 81
Queer world-making, 3, 5, 103

Race, xi, 11, 16, 45, 50, 140–141; Race and sexuality, 76; Race and online spaces, 80
Racism, xv, 98, 100
Reform, xxv, 6
Relationality, 21, 73, 109, 150
Remembrance, 28, 49, 118, 125, 135, 145, 146, 152, 153; Honoring the past, xiii, 8, 38, 53, 103, 108
Resistance, xxvi, 6, 7, 48, 69, 71, 75, 86, 129, 150, 152, 155; Corporeal resistance, 72; Creative resistance, xxix, 101–102
Respectability, 76
Rivera, Sylvia, 150
Rodríguez, Tino, xxxii, 100, 110
Rupaul's Drag Race, 44

Safe zone, xviii; Safe spaces, 53, 138
San Francisco, California, xvi
San Juan, Puerto Rico, 20
Seattle, Washington, xviii, 24
Self-fashioning, 43, 57, 62, 109
Sexile, 4, 11, 42, 45
Sexual others, 14, 128
Sexuality, xv, 74, 128, 140, 151; Heterosexuality, 8, 38, 39, 54; Lesbian sexuality, 14; Sexual diversity, 57; Sexuality and ethnicity, 76, 81, 128, 141; Sexuality and identity, 100, 125–126, 134; Sexuality Studies, xxii. *See also* Queer
Silence, xv, xviii, 102, 129, 134, 142, 152; Silencing, xxxii, 53, 91
Social acceptance, 138
Social justice, xxix, 43, 118, 146, 149
Social transformation, 62–63, 119
Shepard, Matthew, 20
The Singing Shark by Rane Arroyo, 102, 114, 116
Small towns, xviii, 47

Space, xiii–xiv, xviii, 47; Alternative spaces, xvi, 62, 69, 70; Bodily space, 111; Counterspaces, 152; Educational space, 36, 40, 42, 46, 62; Everyday space, 152; Everynight space, 153; Family space, 5; In-process space, 10; Irregular space, 55; National space, xiv; Social spaces, 58; Spatial creation, xvi, xx, 151; Spatial normativity, 151; Spatial otherness, 139
Stereotypes, 57
Stonewall Riots, 133
Stress, 56, 131
Student unions and clubs, xxi; Gay Straight Alliances (GSAs), 35–39
Syncretism, 154

Television, xxix, 15, 44, 48, 113, 154
Therianthropy, xxxii
Theory, xviii, 62, 73, 103, 116, 134, 149, 156; Cultural theory, 73; Queer theory, xxvi
Translation, xxviii, 55, 74, 80, 88
Transgender, xviii, 11, 44–45, 51, 151; Translatina, 44; Transgender Studies, 44, 151
Transgender Equal Rights Bill of Massachusetts, 11
Transphobia, 50
Transnational experience, xiii, xv; Transnational research, 150, 152
Trauma, 38, 129, 130, 133, 137, 145
Truth, 76, 85

Twitter, 71, 91

Ugly Betty, 154
UndocuQueer Movement, xxv
Upstairs Lounge, 6
Utopia, xviii, 17, 43, 77

Violence, 51, 52, 124; Anti-queer violence, 7, 11, 14, 23, 26; Community violence, xvi, xxvii; Racist violence, 40; Spatial violence, xxi, xxxi, 148; Violence in schools, 36, 43
Visual Art, 27; Paintings, 100, 110; Photography, 111

Walt Disney World, 145
Washington Heights, New York, 87
West Side Story, 99, 114
White supremacists, xv, 10, 97, 98, 149
Women's experiences, 6, 12–15, 17, 134, 153; Women of color, 50, 111, 128

Xenophobia, xx

Young adult fiction, xxxi, 35, 41
Youths, xxvii, 35–42, 44, 47, 50–51, 53, 57–62; Latinx LGBTQ youths, xviii, xxiii, xxxi, xxxiii

Zamora, Pedro, xxix
Zamudio, Daniel, 136

About the Author

Dr. **Edward Chamberlain** is a faculty member in the Division of Culture, Arts, and Communication at the University of Washington Tacoma. He studies the creative work and cultural experiences of diverse groups including lesbian, gay, bisexual, transgender, and queer peoples from the Caribbean, Chile, Mexico, and the United States. This research has been published in such journals as *CLCWeb*, *The CEA Critic*, *Lateral*, and *Writing from Below*. He also regularly teaches courses that examine a variety of cultural artefacts, popular culture, and storytelling that explore the intersections of gender, ethnicity, sexuality, and space. Along with being a teacher and researcher, he is an advocate for the arts, equity, and building bridges across communities. He began this work by earning his PhD in American studies and comparative literature at Indiana University Bloomington.

Milton Keynes UK
Ingram Content Group UK Ltd.
UKHW041443150823
426909UK00017B/190